JUDGEMENT DAY

JUDGEMENT DAY

The Trial of Slobodan Milošević

Chris Stephen

Atlantic Books
London

First Published in Great Britain in 2004
by Atlantic Books, an imprint of Grove Atlantic Ltd

1 3 5 7 9 8 6 4 2

A CIP catalogue record for this book is available from the British Library.

1 84354 154 8

Designed by Richard Carr
Printed in Great Britain by CPD, Ebbw Vale, Wales

Atlantic Books
An imprint of Grove Atlantic Ltd
Ormond House
26–27 Boswell Street
London WC1N 3JZ

AUTHOR'S NOTE
The peoples of former Yugoslavia speak different languages and many
places have alternative names, particularly in Kosovo where most towns
have a Serb and an Albanian title. This account uses the place names as they
appear on international maps, but no political bias is either implied or intended.

List of contents

Acknowledgements

It may sound odd to say that writing a book on the subject of war crimes could be inspiring, but that is how it was. Throughout my research on *Judgement Day* I was lucky enough to meet people who, in many different ways, believed enough in the court to make it happen.

My thanks go firstly to Nusreta Sivac in Prijedor for agreeing to give so much of her time for what must have been a painful recollection of her wartime experiences: also to Anel Alisic for meticulously translating her experiences and to Muharem Murselovic for his many perceptive insights.

I am much indebted to some of the key figures of war crimes justice for giving so much of their time to me, and my thanks go to former prosecutors Louise Arbour and Richard Goldstone, and especially former court president Professor Antonio Cassese for giving me the inside picture of those early, frantic, years.

For insights into the creation of the court, I am grateful to Larry Johnson and David Talbot, the latter for giving up an entire weekend to answer what must have seemed patently elemental questions.

In the United States Jim O'Brien at the Albright Foundation was key to my understanding of the leading role played by the United States, and America's ambassador for war crimes at the State Department, Pierre-Richard Prosper, and the first man to hold the post, David Scheffer, gave invaluable insights into America's crucial role in the war crimes process.

Special thanks to Ed Vulliamy of The *Observer* for explaining that astonishing trip into the heart of darkness in Bosnia in 1992, and for reminding us all about the possibilities of the often-derided craft of journalism.

For their expertise and wartime recollections I am indebted to journalists Ardijan Arifaj, Yigal Chazan, Victoria Clark, Phillipe Deprez, Misha Glenny, Peter Green, Goca Igric, Belma Kartal, Amra Kebo, Adam Lebor, Milanka Saponja-Hadzic, Sanja Mahac, Alec Russell,

Marcus Tanner, Ian Traynor, Tom Walker and Jeta Xharra. Special thanks are due to Tim Judah for his Balkans' expertise, for reviewing the manuscript and for giving advice on the fine art of taxi-sharing from Belgrade to Badakhshan sub-province. Nerma Jelaćić in Sarajevo was invaluable in explaining the post-war complexities of Bosnia and provided a dash of encouragement when most needed.

Insights into the Hague Tribunal's sometimes bumpy relationship with the outside world came from Duncan Bullivant of Henderson Risk, Dominic Raab of the British embassy, The Hague and David Slinn, formerly of the British embassy, Belgrade.

In The Hague I was lucky enough to find a remarkable group of permanent correspondents whose help and advice were priceless; Judith Armatta of *Coalition for International Justice*, Geraldine Coughlan of the BBC, Valentina Cosmati of *Radio Radical*, Ljubica Gojgic of *B92*, Mirko Klarin of *Sense News Agency*, Augustin Palokaj of *Koha Ditore*, Sonja Robla of the *Spanish Press Agency*, Emir Suljagic of *Dani*, Stefanie Maupas of *Le Monde*, Marlise Simons of *The New York Times*, Thomas Verfuss of *ANP Dutch News Agency*, Isabelle Wesselingh of *Agence France Press*, and Othon Zimmermann of *Algemeen Dagblad*. Much expertise and advice was also provided by ICTY press officers Jim Landale and Liam McDowall.

At the International Criminal Court, officers Brigitte Benoit, Cecelia Baltanu and Sam Muller explained the complexities of The Hague's other war crimes court, and for explaining the battle to create the ICC I am indebted to Jennifer Schense and Cecilia Nielsen of the Coalition for the International Court, whose patience and supply of chocolate biscuits were inexhaustible. For guiding me through the labyrinth of human rights issues, my thanks go to Richard Dicker of Human Rights Watch, Guy Lesser of *Harper's Magazine*, Professor Andrei Ruskin of Moscow State University Journalism Faculty and Nina Bang-Jensen and Stefanie Frease of *Coalition for International Justice*. Invaluable support was also provided by Ilana Ozernoy. For help with research, and also for reminding me of the part played in the war crimes courts by hundreds of brave witnesses, my thanks to Amira Saric and Azra Alijagic.

For helping me understand at least the basics of war crimes law I am grateful to lawyers John Ackerman, Fiona Campbell, Karim Khan and Steven Powles, and especially to Rod Dixon for insights into the Tribunal from his unique platform working with both prosecution and defence. My great thanks to barrister John Jones, for advising on the book from its first inception, for putting me in touch with key figures in the court's history, and for spending long hours advising on drafts of the book, and above all for finding ingenious ways to explain complicated laws to a simpleton such as myself.

At Atlantic Books, I am grateful to publisher Toby Mundy for sticking with the project through an alarming number of twists and turns, and to my editor Louisa Joyner for extreme forbearance in picking through draft after draft. Thanks also to the staff of the Atlantic office for giving me the welcome fizz I needed in the final hectic weeks of producing this book. To everyone mentioned, *Judgement Day* could not have been written without you.

This book is dedicated to my mother and the memory of my father.

Chris Stephen, London 2004.

The publishers and author gratefully acknowledge the right to reproduce material from:

The Firm, by John Grisham, published by Century. Reprinted by permission of the Random House Group Ltd.

Marko the Prince: Serbo-Croat Heroic Songs, by Anne Pennington and Peter Levi, published by Duckworth.

Timeline

	1389	Battle of Kosovo
1690, 1737		Serb rebellions fail, mass migrations
20 August	1941	Slobodan Milošević born, Požarevac, Serbia, Yugoslavia
	1974	New Yugoslav constitution creates autonomous Serbian provinces in Kosovo and Vojvodina
	1978	Milošević appointed president of Beogradska Banka
4 May	1980	Tito dies
	1982	Milošević appointed head of Belgrade Stari Grad – Old Town – Communist party
	1984	Milošević leaves Beogradska Banka, appointed head of Belgrade Communist party
	1986	Milošević appointed head of Serbian Communist party *Memorandum* published by Serbian Academy of Arts and Sciences
April	1987	Milošević travels to Kosovo Polje
September	1987	Eighth Session of Serbian Communist party
October	1988	'Yogurt Revolution' Vojvodina
October	1988	Montenegro demonstrations
November	1988	Kosovo assembly suspended, demonstration Belgrade
March	1989	Autonomy of Kosovo revoked
May	1989	Milošević appointed Serbian president
June	1989	Milošević addresses nationalist rally, Gazimestan, Kosovo
November	1989	Fall of Berlin Wall
December	1989	Romanian revolution
January	1990	14th and last congress of Yugoslav Communist party
August	1990	Log Rebellion Knin, Croatia
December	1990	Serbian Socialist Party, formerly Communist Party, wins first multi-party elections in Serbia. Milošević elected Serbian president
March	1991	Anti–Milošević demonstrations, Belgrade
March	1991	Milošević and Croatian president Franjo Tudjman agree to divide Bosnia
May	1991	12 Croatian police killed, Borovo Selo
June	1991	Croatia and Slovenia declare independence
August	1991	Vukovar siege begins
November	1991	Fall of Vukovar. Massacre of 200 Croats, Ovcara

February	1992	Bosnia-Hercegovina referendum on independence
April	1992	EC and USA recognise Bosnia as independent country
		Siege of Sarajevo begins
April	1992	Serb prison camps set up at Omarska, Keraterm, Trnopolje
June	1992	Federal Yugoslavia formed, consisting of Serbia and Montenegro
August	1992	Serb prison camps revealed by British journalists
October	1992	UN Resolution 780 proposes creation of war crimes tribunal
February	1993	UN Resolution 808 orders creation of war crimes tribunal
May	1993	UN Resolution 827 creates war crimes tribunal
December	1993	Milošević elected second term, Serbian president
February	1994	Washington Agreement ends Croat-Bosnian government war
April	1994	Rwanda: Hutu genocide kills 800,000 Tutsis
July	1995	Fall of Srebrenica, 7,000 Muslims killed
August	1995	Operation Storm clears Serb forces from Croatian Krajina
		Ten day NATO air campaign against Bosnians Serbs
5 October	1995	Bosnia Ceasefire signed
November	1995	Dayton Peace Agreement signed
July	1997	Milošević elected president Yugoslavia
Winter	1996–97	Anti Milošević demonstrations, Belgrade
November	1997	First appearance of Kosovo Liberation Army
March	1998	Prekaz, 51 Kosovo Albanians killed
January	1999	Račak, 45 Kosovo Albanians killed
March	1999	NATO begins 78-day air war against Yugoslavia
27 May	1999	Milošević charged with war crimes in Kosovo
June	1999	NATO signs ceasefire with Yugoslavia
September	2000	Milošević loses Yugoslavia presidential election
5 October	2000	Anti-Milošević demonstrations depose Milošević
March	2001	Milošević arrested by Serb police accused of corruption
June	2001	Milošević transferred to The Hague
July	2001	Milošević first appearance at The Hague, refuses to plead
September	2001	Milošević charged with war crimes in Croatia
November	2001	Milošević charged with war crimes, including genocide, in Bosnia
February	2002	Milošević trial opens, The Hague
March	2003	Serbian prime minister Zoran Djindjić assassinated, Serbia
February	2004	Prosecution ends case, The Hague
		Chief trial judge Richard May announces retirement from case

The Balkans, c. 1992

Maximum extent of Serb
held territory December 1992

0   50 miles

0   100 kilometres

N
W   E

HUNGARY

ROMANIA

R. Danube

Vukovar   Novi Sad

Brčko

Bijeljina

Tuzla

Zvornik

Belgrade   R. Danube

Srebrenica

R. Drina

SERBIA-
MONTENEGRO

Sarajevo

Visegrad

Foča

Niš

Mitrovica

Prekaz   Priština

KOSOVO

Podgorica

Račak

Suva Reka

Meja

Morina

ALBANIA

Skopje

MACEDONIA

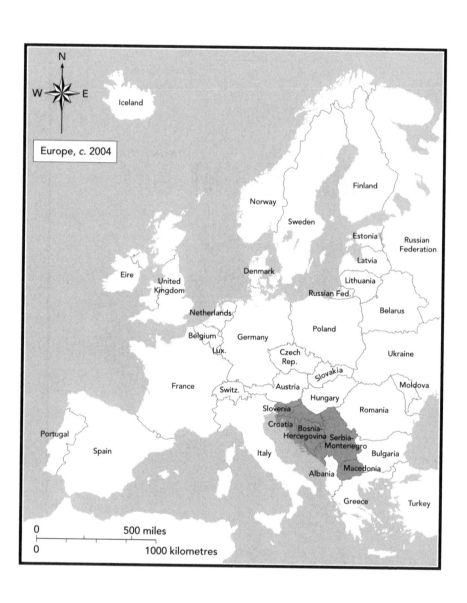

Europe, *c.* 2004

Iceland

Finland

Norway

Sweden

Estonia

Russian Federation

Latvia

Denmark

Lithuania

Russian Fed.

Eire

United Kingdom

Netherlands

Belarus

Belgium

Poland

Lux.

Germany

Czech Rep.

Ukraine

Slovakia

France

Switz.

Austria

Hungary

Moldova

Slovenia

Romania

Portugal

Croatia

Bosnia-Hercegovina

Serbia-Montenegro

Spain

Italy

Bulgaria

Albania

Macedonia

Greece

Turkey

0   500 miles
0   1000 kilometres

JUDGEMENT DAY

Kosovo Field

The border post at Morina on the Albanian frontier with Serbia was an island of light in a dark mountain landscape. A few yellow lamps illuminated a box-like office building by the side of the road and, over the road itself, a flat roof held up by four pillars. Mosquitoes buzzed around the lamps and two border guards, tired after a long day, sauntered along the highway. Two hundred metres away was the Serbian border post, more brightly lit. It was nearly midnight on 27 April 1999. For more than a month, NATO planes had been bombing Serbia and the detonations of that night's raid could be heard far away across the mountains.

Since the bombing started, the Serbs had been expelling ethnic Albanians from Kosovo, and each day this border post was packed with refugees arriving on tractors and trailers, in cars or on foot. It was impossible for journalists to get free access to Kosovo, so each day many waited at Morina, keen to hear the stories from the newly-arrived refugees. From these stories, the outside world had built up a picture of what appeared to be a vast campaign to empty the province of its ethnic Albanian population. Refugees described villages being shelled and Serb police giving orders for people to leave their homes and head towards the Albanian border. The roads on the Kosovo side of the border were reportedly crammed with civilians fleeing in long convoys, all of them heading for the half-dozen border crossings into Albania or Macedonia. There were stories, too, of Serb police, and even civilians, lining the road leading to Morina and demanding money in return for letting refugees pass in their cars.

Late at night the traffic slowed. The little groups allowed through had become irregular and most of the journalists had returned to rented rooms in the nearby town of Kukës, where the Red Cross was building a giant camp to house the refugees. I would have left myself, but my newspaper wanted something fresh for its 7 a.m. deadline the next day. A new group of refugees began moving towards us from the Serb side of the border. They arrived on the back of trailers towed by a group of rusty red tractors. As they drove onto the Albanian side of the border, the guards walked among them, not to ask for papers but to signal that they should keep moving onwards, towards the waiting refugee camp outside Kukës.

A handful of aid workers began moving from trailer to trailer, offering blankets and bottles of water. We journalists trailed after them, each one with a translator. Immediately we noticed something unusual. The trailers were loaded with women, children and the elderly, but there were no young or middle-aged men. The tractors were driven by either old men or teenagers.

One woman told my translator that the little group had left the town of Djakovica, not far from the border, that afternoon. They had been stopped by a Serbian armed unit at a small hamlet, named Meja, and the menfolk had been ordered off the tractors. A total of 37 men had got off the tractors, and they had been ordered into a nearby field and lined up. Then the tractors had been told to drive on, leaving the men behind. The woman was nervous, but she said this procedure was not so unusual. For more than a year, a guerrilla war between ethnic Albanian fighters and Serb forces had raged in Kosovo, much of it centred on Djakovica, and a familiar Serb tactic was to round up groups of men for questioning. None of her menfolk had fought with the guerrillas, she told me, so she hoped her husband would soon be free to join her.

Then the convoy was on its way again, the line of tractors rumbling away along the highway west towards Kukës, hidden behind a fold in the hills. The tail lights were still visible when a second group of refugees began to cross the border. This new convoy was much like the last, a group of tractors towing trailers piled high with people and their possessions. Many of these refugees were asleep. Again the journalists moved among them, all asking the same question. Had any of these people seen the men in the field at Meja?

The first people I asked stared blankly back at me. They were not from the border region and did not know this village, which was one of many they had passed through that day. Then a boy on the back of one of the trailers looked up. Yes, he told me, he had seen the men in the field at Meja. The men were all lying in the field 'like logs'. They were dead.

More tractors were arriving, and the Albanian border guards continued to signal the drivers to keep moving. We journalists had to run beside the trailers as they moved, shouting our questions. A woman on the back of one trailer began to wail. 'They killed them, they killed them!' she shouted. 'More than one hundred.'

Other refugees confirmed her story. One old man, his body covered in a blanket, walked across the border and sat on a suitcase he had been carrying. He said he had been with a group of tractors and had seen men being marched into a field, with their womenfolk running after them shouting for the soldiers to let them go. He had seen the soldiers shooting into the air, but then the trailer he had been on had rattled away up the road and he knew no more.

Several more tractors and trailers rattled past, and the occupants confirmed that there were indeed piles of dead men lying in the field at Meja. It seemed that between one convoy of refugees leaving Meja and another arriving, the soldiers in the field had executed their prisoners. I took a last look westwards. It was still possible to make out the red tail lights of that first convoy, full of women and children who were hours away from being told the news they dreaded.

In June 1999 the Serbs signed a peace agreement with NATO whereby Serb forces would pull out of the province and NATO forces would come in, together with eight hundred and sixty thousand ethnic Albanians who had been expelled in the previous two and a half months. The 78-day war, which NATO had waged solely from the air, was over. Together with the troops and refugees, journalists also flooded into Kosovo, and I went off in search of Meja.

The little hamlet was not easy to find. In those first days after the end of the war the border regions were mostly deserted. Meja is tiny, just a few houses, and is not listed on large-scale maps. There were no signposts indicating that the cluster of houses on the right of the dirt road constituted Meja, but a look at the field to the left confirmed that I had found it. A human leg, wrapped in a pinstriped trouser material, lay in the long grass. Nearby were remains of little bonfires where someone, presumably the Serbs, had burned bundles of identity cards.

On the far side of the field was a brook, overhung by trees. And there, in the shade, their bodies forming little dams against the babbling water, were the bodies of two men. One was dressed in the clothes of a young man, blue jeans and black leather jacket. He lay on his front and his head was missing. A second body, that of an older man with grey hair, lay also on his front, and this man's legs were missing.

A narrow path led through the trees to a higher field, invisible now from the road because of the mass of leaves. The track leading to this field had deep ruts and a wooden fence running along one side had been torn down, as if a vehicle, too wide to pass, had driven along it. There were a series of flat, yellow patches of grass in the higher field, spaced at regular intervals – a total of 33 patches altogether. Most of them were irregular in shape, but some seemed to form the outline of human figures. In the middle of these yellow patches were areas of dark earth which, on closer inspection, appeared to be formed by congealed blood. Looking more closely still, I could see chips of bone and teeth, white in the sunshine. There was the top half of a pair of dentures lying nearby. One of the yellow shapes traced the outline that a man would make if he were kneeling down, and were then tipped sideways and left to lie on his side long enough for the grass to become flattened and lose its colour. He would need to lie very still for at least a day.

No one has ever said publicly how many men were killed at Meja on that spring day in 1999. The bodies lay in the field for some time and were then recovered by heavy machinery. In subsequent investigations, seven of the partially burned identity cards found in the field were matched to bodies buried in mass graves constructed by Serbian security forces in other parts of the country.

Three years after standing in that dusty meadow, I was sitting in an air-conditioned courtroom in The Hague, looking through a thick glass wall at the man accused of responsibility for this crime. There, in the dock of the International Criminal Tribunal for the Former Yugoslavia, was the former president of Yugoslavia, Slobodan Milošević, instantly recognisable with his broad forehead, heavy jowls and trademark swept-back white hair.

Flicking through the copy of his indictment for war crimes I found the reference to Meja. Halfway down page 30 it says: 'a large and as yet undetermined number of Kosovo Albanian civilian males were separated from the mass of fleeing villagers and abducted. Many of these men were summarily executed and approximately 300 persons are still missing.'

In an ordinary courthouse anywhere else in the world, the killing of 300 men in a field would be a sensational charge. But the trial of Slobodan Milošević is no ordinary trial. The section dealing with Meja is only one of 12 sub-sections of two counts of murder in an indictment that runs to 66 counts. Altogether, the charge sheet is 125 pages long, so thick that it is bound in book form between blue covers, and relates to crimes in three separate wars spread over nearly nine years.

The trial is unusual for another reason. It is the first time in recorded history that a world leader has been brought before a court that has a valid claim to represent all the other nations of the world. What follows is the story of this epic achievement, and also of the struggle to bring Milošević himself to justice. To put Milošević on trial for these crimes meant creating a whole new level of justice, never previously attempted. Making this justice system work as it was intended involved a galaxy of pioneers, including lawyers, judges, soldiers, politicians, human rights workers, bureaucrats, journalists, and several courageous victims.

The short history of the International Criminal Tribunal for the Former Yugoslavia, first inaugurated in May 1993, has been dominated at every stage by the United States. It was America, more than any other nation, that set the war crimes court in motion, and it was American leaders who made it work in its early years. But with the success of the Tribunal in bringing about the trials of Milošević and many other Balkan warlords, America has moved from being the key supporter of the process to become its most formidable opponent. The US government is presently in the vanguard of efforts to prevent a truly worldwide system of war crimes justice from taking root. Almost by accident, the war crimes process has challenged the most fundamental building-block of international relations, which is the principle that every nation has the right to do as it likes within its own borders.

The Camps   2

Never Again.

Reaction to discovery of German concentration camps, 1945

The first sign Nusreta Sivac had that something was wrong was when she left her home in the small north-eastern town of Prijedor in Bosnia-Hercegovina one morning in early April 1992. She was a judge at the local law courts and, as usual, was about to take a twenty-minute walk to the city courthouse. Outside her apartment building, two men she recognised as Serb neighbours were standing close to the entrance. One of the men held a clipboard. They watched Nusreta with stern expressions and offered no greeting. One of them made a tick on the clipboard. Coming nearer, Nusreta saw that on the board was a list of names, and that hers was included. She decided not to ask them about it because she knew these were difficult times for Bosnia.

The problems had begun in February when Bosnians had voted on whether to become independent from Yugoslavia. There were three communities in the province – Croats, Muslims, and Serbs. The Croats and Muslims had wanted independence but the Serbs, who made up about one third of the population, had mostly wanted to stay inside Yugoslavia, which was dominated by Serbs. When the referendum was held, the Croats and Muslims voted for independence and the Serbs abstained. The result had, predictably, been a landslide in favour of independence. On 6 April the European Community and America had both acknowledged the result, and Bosnia-Hercegovina, for the first time in its history, was recognised as an independent state and given a place at the United Nations in New York. There were no celebrations in Prijedor, however. The town was almost equally divided between Serbs and Muslims, with a small Croat community, and the Serbs were known to be unhappy at the prospect of living as a minority in Bosnia.

The year before, Croatia had broken away from Yugoslavia and there had been war between Croats and the country's ethnic Serb minority. Croatia was only twenty miles from Prijedor and it had been possible to hear the gunfire from the fighting there the previous winter. Now Bosnia's Croats and Muslims were nervous about what their Serb neighbours might do. In particular, there was a fear that the fighting in Croatia would be replicated in Bosnia.

Nusreta was an optimist and hoped for the best. During the Second World War, many of Yugoslavia's ethnic communities had gone to war with each other but Prijedor had stayed united, with Muslims hiding Serbs and then Serbs hiding Muslims as first the Germans and then Serb guerrillas had entered the town. She hoped that, even if fighting broke out elsewhere in Bosnia, good sense would prevail in Prijedor.

That morning she told herself not to worry about her Serb neighbours. They were probably overreacting, possibly believing Serb propaganda from TV Belgrade which spoke of Islamic militants preparing an uprising in Bosnia. Nusreta had contacts in the police from her work as a judge and felt sure there was to be no Islamic rising. Bosnia's Muslims were laid-back about their religion, enjoying drinking and smoking, and many had married into the Serb and Croat communities. They wanted independence not because they were Islamic radicals but because Yugoslavia was now dominated by a hardline Serb nationalist, Slobodan Milošević, who was president of Serbia.

Nusreta walked along her usual route to work which took her down one of the main streets of Prijedor, and there she had her next surprise. Soldiers from the Yugoslav army had erected a checkpoint at a traffic junction. When she approached the soldiers, who were Serbs, she was asked for her papers. When they saw that she was a Muslim, they told her to go back. She asked what was going on and they said that they did not know, but they had their orders.

Nusreta protested that she was a judge and must go to work, and when she produced her papers she was let through. A few streets further on there was another roadblock, where soldiers again tried to stop her. Talking her way past them, she headed for the courthouse, a handsome stone building next to the Prijedor police headquarters in the centre of the town, thinking that she must talk to one of the police superintendents about this bizarre situation.

At the courthouse, she saw yet more soldiers, and once more they asked for her identification papers. These soldiers had a list of names and she noticed that it was a list of the staff of the courthouse, from judges to cleaners. From her quick glance it seemed that the staff had been divided into two categories, Serbs and non-Serbs. As a Muslim, she was told that she could not go in and must instead go home. She asked the soldiers the reason and they simply said they had orders.

Finally, she managed to persuade them at least to let her into her office so that she could take some things home with her. A soldier escorted her into the building and she saw more soldiers talking with Serb staff from the canteen. The staff knew her – she had worked as a judge for more than ten years – but they did not say hello and avoided eye contact.

Nusreta, aged 41, was divorced and lived alone. She went back home and phoned the president of the court, who was also a Muslim. He, too, had been sent home, and he said he had tried, and failed, to phone someone in higher authority who could explain what was going on. He said that army units had taken control of major points around the town.

Not knowing what else to do, Nusreta made some coffee and turned on the radio. This gave her alarming news of fighting going on in Bosnia. *Radio Sarajevo,* broadcasting from the capital, announced that the city was being shelled and talked of unconfirmed reports of violence in towns in eastern Bosnia. Sarajevo television spoke of the same things. She tuned to a Serb station, where a news announcer spoke of violence in several Bosnian towns but said that it was perpetrated by Muslims against Serbs.

The next day, the local television transmitter was shut down. Nusreta tried phoning friends in Sarajevo, to find that the long-distance phone lines had been cut. She then called her cousins and Muslim friends in the town, only to discover that everyone else was as confused as she was. Muslim friends she knew from work told her that a group of Serb officials, calling themselves the Crisis Staff, had taken over the town and the police, and that the army was there to enforce a state of emergency. They also said that roadblocks were stopping Muslims entering or leaving Prijedor.

On the third day a Serb neighbour invited her in for coffee and explained that the Crisis Staff, an all-Serb local government, had taken control of the town. He told her that the reason was not ethnic but economic, insisting that the previous Communist town council had been poor business managers.

She did not believe the man but, like other Muslims in Prijedor, had little choice but to go home and await developments. The days that followed brought more bad news from *Radio Sarajevo* which reported battles in the eastern Bosnian towns of Bijeljina, Foča and Zvornik. Serb radio was dominated by extraordinary claims that Islamic fundamentalist units were murdering Serbs across Bosnia. Prijedor remained calm.

Nusreta told me that, in retrospect, she thought the Serb Crisis Staff were unsure what the Muslim reaction would be to their bloodless takeover of the town. 'In my opinion they were waiting to see if Muslims had weapons, if there would be any resistance. They were scared.'[1]

One of Nusreta's cousins, whose husband was working in Germany, moved into her apartment. A few days later, though Nusreta cannot remember the date, she heard that Muslims could no longer take money out of the town banks. Going to her bank, she was told that the maximum she could withdraw was the equivalent of 100 German marks in Yugoslav currency, the dinar. She protested that she needed to buy food, but the bank staff, all of whom were Serbs, told her they had instructions.

Local travel agents started selling flights to Muslims at hugely inflated prices. A flight from the local airport at Banja Luka to the Yugoslav capital Belgrade normally cost about 50 German marks. Now the same flight cost 3000 German marks. Several rich Muslim families were paying these prices, which included an official permit from the police allowing the purchaser to pass the checkpoints on the edge of town.

More than two weeks after the Prijedor roadblocks had first gone up, *Radio Sarajevo* reported that the city was under heavy shellfire and was also giving reports of what appeared to be massive attacks on Muslim communities across a great swathe of Bosnia. On the streets of Prijedor, Nusreta saw a new kind of soldier. Unlike the men at the checkpoints, these soldiers were in small groups and were badly dressed, long-haired, bearded and undisciplined. Word went around the Prijedor Muslims that these men were paramilitaries, members of Serbian militias which in Croatia the previous year had terrorised and killed Croat civilians. The paramilitaries gathered on street corners and in cafés. Passing one group she heard them complaining to each other that they had no orders. 'They were complaining that nothing was happening. They were asking each other, when will this "thing" start?'

What this 'thing' was, Nusreta did not know. In late April 1992,[2] the electricity was cut. Shops began to close or run out of food. In her apartment building, one of Nusreta's Serb neighbours began covering the hallway lights with newspaper to dim them, telling her he feared an attack by roving bands of Islamic warriors. Nusreta thought the idea absurd but said nothing.

The next morning she went out to try and find a food shop, and saw the bodies of seven men she recognised as market traders who were ethnic Albanians from the southern province of Kosovo. All of them had been shot. The Serb soldiers were ignoring them. 'I was afraid. The radio was reporting bad things, terrible things, happening around Bosnia. I thought maybe we are going to be killed.'

Another cousin came to live with her, bringing her teenaged daughter. On 21 May 1992, more than a month after the Serbs had imposed the state of emergency, fighting broke out in a village called Harambrine on the outskirts of Prijedor. Rumours went around the Muslim community in Prijedor that Muslims in Harambrine had opened fire on a Serb checkpoint. The same day, Serb army units set up artillery positions outside Prijedor and started to bombard Harambrine, with the detonations reverberating all around Prijedor. On 23 May there was shooting from a different direction, and Nusreta heard from friends that this time the Serbian artillery was shooting at Kozarac, a large village which ran almost ten kilometres along the main highway leading eastwards. 'I was shocked. I could not believe this was happening. I just lay on the floor of the apartment; I did not know what to do.'

On 26 May fighting exploded inside Prijedor itself, when a group of Muslims and Croats, armed with machine guns, attacked the centre of the town. The group of around a hundred men, local villagers, stormed several government buildings. The occupation lasted only a few hours. Serb forces with heavier armaments counter-attacked and took back the buildings. Nusreta stayed inside her house, but in the afternoon she saw smoke billowing over the rooftops from the direction of the home of one of her male cousins. She phoned the man and found him in despair. He told her some Serb paramilitaries had attacked a block of houses, including his own, burning them down for no reason. He said he was now sitting on the front step of his burned home holding his phone in his hand. After a few minutes of talking the line went dead. She never saw her cousin again.

The next day, Nusreta's sister-in-law phoned in hysterics to say that Nusreta's brother, Nesret, had been arrested. Nusreta left her cousins in her apartment and hurried around to the house. By the time she arrived, Nesret had been released and had returned home. He told his sister that he had some bad news. The police had let him go, he explained, because it was a case of mistaken identity. The person they had actually wanted to arrest was Nusreta but they had got the names muddled up, so they had told him that he must find his sister and order her to report to the police headquarters as soon as possible.

Nusreta could not understand this because she had done nothing wrong. The two of them discussed it, wondering if she was wanted because the Serbs were rounding up influential Muslims. She discussed her options with her brother that evening. She could try to hide, but if she were found then perhaps it would be worse for her, with the Serbs more likely to think she had something to hide. She could also try to escape, but it seemed likely that she would be caught at one of the roadblocks around the town. They decided it was best for her to go to the police station and find out what they wanted. After all, she had done nothing wrong.

She went back to her apartment and after a mostly sleepless night she awoke the next day to find the weather unseasonably cold and rainy. She put on extra clothing and a raincoat, said goodbye to her cousins and left alone, saying it was better for the rest of the family that they did not come with her to the police headquarters. 'I gave my cousin most of my money. She wanted to come with me but I told her to stay. There was no use in that,' she said.

Nusreta then headed off towards the police headquarters. She arrived to see soldiers once more outside the building. As she arrived, a Serb official she recognised came out of the courthouse next door and she called out to him to help her. He turned away and refused to speak to her. The soldiers at the police headquarters seemed bored, and when she explained that she had been summoned one of them took her identity card and disappeared inside. He came out again a few minutes later to say that a senior officer would come out to talk to her and she must wait.

Not knowing what else to do she waited at the checkpoint. It began to rain. Nobody came out to see her, and the soldiers ignored her. So she waited, huddled in her coat, worrying. The hours passed and it was late afternoon when a bus pulled up outside. A group of police investigators sat inside, and a few seats away was a man in civilian clothing. Then the senior police officer, a man named Ranko, came out of the headquarters and brusquely ordered her aboard the bus, without giving a reason.

After she had boarded it, the bus pulled away, and was soon on the highway heading out of town. Nusreta recognised two of the police inspectors from having seen them presenting cases in court, but decided not to try to talk to them. Instead, she sat near the man in civilian clothes, who said he was a Muslim. Neither of them had any idea why they had been summoned by the police.

The bus drove quickly out of town. There were few vehicles on the roads. Outside of Prijedor, Nusreta was shocked to discover that much of the once-prosperous village of Kozarac was in ruins. Houses with whitewashed walls and red roofs had huge holes ripped in their sides by artillery shells. Some were burned, with tattered curtains flapping from smashed windows, and all were empty. At one house, a red, white and blue Serb flag hung from a balcony, below which stood Serb troops on guard. She saw some Serb farmers loading washing machines and televisions from these houses into their cars.

The bus turned right, heading for a small Serbian village called Omarska. When it arrived, a few minutes later, Nusreta saw that some kind of prison camp had been made in a factory across the road from the village. The bus drove in through the factory gate, where Serb soldiers stood guard. In a large compound she saw several hundred Muslim men in civilian dress milling around, being watched by soldiers. On the far side of the compound were enormous sheds with metal doors. In the middle stood a small white building, and to one side was a two-storey administration block. Some of the prisoners she saw looked healthy, but most were emaciated with sunken eyes and worn clothing.

The bus stopped and Nusreta and the male passenger were ordered out. He was sent in one direction and Nusreta was taken, with the police inspectors, into the office block. She was escorted upstairs to an office and told to sit down. Two police inspectors seated themselves on chairs facing her and said they had some questions to ask her. Only a few weeks before, she would have met these inspectors on equal terms inside the courtroom. Now she found it extraordinary that they wanted to interrogate her, a senior judge, who knew that she had done nothing wrong.

What followed was unlike any interrogation she had witnessed as a judge because the policemen appeared not to know what they wanted to find out. The inspectors asked her about Bosnia's independence referendum and how she had voted. Then they asked her if she realised that the result of this vote had been faked. She said that she had not heard this and thought it unlikely, because the Croats and Muslims had voted for independence and most Serbs had publicly boycotted the poll. Next, the inspectors asked her if she knew about plans for a Muslim takeover in Bosnia. She said she had never heard of this. They asked her why one of her cousins had recently repainted a café he owned in the centre of town. Nusreta was baffled by this question, saying she had no idea and suggesting that maybe the old paintwork was getting tatty. 'I thought this question was leading to something else, but it wasn't. The inspectors were nervous; they seemed to have no idea what they wanted to know.'

The police inspectors then said that they had finished their questions and that she would have to stay in the camp to face more questioning the next day. One told her, 'You go to the canteen. When you can recall these details let us know.' She asked what details he meant, but he refused to answer.

Downstairs she came across a group of twenty-five Muslim women who were cleaning a canteen that was located on the ground floor. They explained that they were prisoners and that their job was to serve food to the male prisoners. They told her she should not expect to be released any time soon. Most of these women were the wives of prominent Muslims who were themselves either outside of Prijedor or else prisoners in the camp.

In the evening, the women went upstairs and explained to Nusreta that they slept on the floor of two offices. There was no bedding, and Nusreta was grateful that she had brought with her extra clothing on which she could sleep. She used two books from the office bookshelf as a pillow.

The next morning she awoke, looked out of the window, and saw a man's body at the door of the white building, which was known in the camp as the White House. One of the women told her that the man had probably been killed in the night by Serb guards, that this was normal, and that she should get used to it.

There was no breakfast, and mid-morning the police inspectors arrived again and Nusreta was once more taken to an upstairs office to be questioned. The inspectors still seemed confused about what questions to put to her, and when she asked them why she had been arrested they refused to tell her. The session ended and the inspectors told her to go back downstairs and help the other women serve lunch.

Lunch was the only meal given to the prisoners, and was served at midday. It consisted of a watery bean soup, made elsewhere and delivered by truck to the back door of the canteen. The women's job was to dole out the soup, together with a small piece of stale bread, to the male prisoners. These men were escorted in files by Serb guards into the canteen from the sheds where they spent most of their days. Nusreta saw that some of the men were very thin, with hollow eyes. Some had torn clothing and untreated bloody wounds on their heads and bodies. They looked frightened, and refused to talk to the women who poured the soup into metal bowls. The prisoners took the bowls to a row of tables, ate quickly, then filed out again and were escorted back inside the big sheds.

Afterwards the women cleaned up, and Nusreta, looking out of the windows, watched as guards beat men at random. The beatings went on all day and seemed to have no pattern to them. Serb guards simply picked on someone and began punching him.

At night, men were selected from the sheds and she watched, by the light of the moon, as they were marched in twos and threes across the yard and into the White House. What happened once they were inside she could not tell, but their screams would punctuate the silence long into the night. In the morning she saw the bodies of dead men, and others beaten, bloody but still alive, lying in the dirt by the White House entrance. Other prisoners would be summoned by the guards to take away the living and the dead.

The guards often stank of alcohol and went about their beatings with great fury. 'I was reminded of those films I had seen of World War Two and the concentration camps; I thought, I am living in the Auschwitz film. These guards, they were so angry, they were so much indoctrinated with propaganda, they were saying we are terrorists, that they were doing it to us so we could not do it to them.'

Nusreta made special friends with one young woman named Edna Duatović, a fresh-faced 22-year-old from Prijedor. Edna was detained because her brother had been one of the men who had briefly taken over the town centre in May. She was accused of being a nurse and helping in the attack, although in fact she was a teaching student and had played no part in the violence. Her brother was kept prisoner in one of the sheds in Omarska and was often beaten.

When her brother came to get his food, Edna would give him her own bread ration as well as his. Sometimes he would not arrive for food for several days and she would grow worried and tense, and when he finally did show up he would be covered in bruises and open wounds. Despite all this, Edna remained an optimist. 'She was always saying it will be alright, we will get out of here,' said Nusreta. At night, the women were introduced to another feature of camp life. Guards, usually the duty commanders, would come into their room and take away one of the young women to rape her.

In late June 1992, when Nusreta had been in the camp for three weeks, a Serb husband and wife arrived as prisoners. One of the Muslim women told Nusreta that the Serb man was accused of giving weapons to Muslim fighters near Prijedor. He was consigned to one of the sheds, and his wife sent to join the women in the canteen. The Muslim women shunned her, not trusting the story they had heard and worried that she might be some sort of spy sent to stay among them.

A few days later, the suspicion that this was an elaborate ruse by the Serbs dissolved when the man was taken out of one of the sheds, dragged to the middle of the courtyard, and coolly beaten to death using fists, boots and rifle butts. By the end of the beating his clothes were torn and his face disfigured, the blood flowing freely and mixing with the dust of the compound. The body was left where it lay.

Later that day, the dead man's uncle drove into the camp in a VW Golf and stopped by the body. He got out and started to shout at the guards, then sat next to the body in the dust, crying. 'He was out there shouting at the guards, "Why did you do this?" The uncle took his nephew's body away, leaving the man's wife in the canteen. She had watched the killing of her husband and afterwards withdrew into herself. The Muslim women tried to make friends with her, but she refused to speak to them. Later, the dead man's uncle came back to the camp and brought her a suitcase with her clothes. From then on, throughout the summer, the Serb woman wore black. 'We nicknamed her the black widow. She didn't do any duties, she just wandered around the camp each day. Everyone left her alone,' said Nusreta.

Nusreta found it hard to keep track of the days as the long hot summer wore on. There was no news of what was happening in the world outside, although she heard that war had broken out across Bosnia and she guessed it was going badly for the Muslims. Then one July day Edna's brother vanished for another interrogation. The days passed and Edna grew worried, saving her pieces of bread for his return. He never came back, and word reached her a few days later that his last beating had been particularly vicious and he was dead.

One morning soon afterwards, Nusreta was ordered by one of the guards to go to the White House with one of the Muslim women who was a trained nurse. This woman was often told to go to there to administer to the survivors of the nightly beatings. That morning she was summoned to join the Muslim doctor, Esad Sadiković, and Nusreta was told to go too, to help move bodies. She followed the nurse into the building, noticing that inside it was divided into two sections. Each had a small window and no furniture. In the morning light Nusreta saw that one room was a mass of tangled bodies and limbs lying in a huge pool of blood. Between twenty and thirty prisoners were there, some dead, some dying, after an all-night beating. The air was thick with the smell of urine, faeces and putrefying flesh. As she looked, she saw smashed heads, limbs twisted at bizarre angles, and great gaping wounds. Some of the men were naked, some had clothing that was torn. 'Esad was saying it is impossible how these people are still alive,' she said. 'I was begging to leave.' Without medical equipment there was not much the doctor could do to help the men. Serb guards came in and ordered the two women out. Prisoners were then detailed to go in and bring out the bodies. The Serbs who had administered the beatings stood outside, smoking cigarettes.

Late July was the worst period of her captivity. Like the other women, she had lost weight and when she walked she had to hold up her skirt to stop it falling round her ankles. One day she awoke and felt chest pains. She remained lying on the floor of the office block, fearing she had a heart problem. She decided that she did not care if she was to die now, because death would be a relief. 'I thought this is it, I am going to die. And I wanted to die. I did not want to live any more. I lay down on the floor and that was it. But Edna came and said, "Come on, you must not give up."' Edna was always optimistic. 'She said, "Come on, we will all get out of here eventually."' Encouraged, or perhaps bullied is a better word, by Edna, Nusreta willed herself to get better and gradually returned to health, or at least to the state of anxiety and half-starvation that was the norm for Omarska.

A few days later, late at night while the women were lying down in the offices trying to sleep, a bus pulled into the compound. Nusreta looked out and saw, in the glare of the camp floodlights, that the bus had written on it 'Private Auto School Šešelj'. This was presumably some sort of joke, but it also indicated that the bus belonged to one of the most notorious of the Serb paramilitary units, that was controlled by Vojislav Šešelj, who had made a name for himself in 1991 with brutalities against Croatian civilians. Some soldiers with rough uniforms and long beards left the bus, reminding her of the paramilitaries she had seen in Prijedor two months previously.

One of the camp guards came upstairs to the offices where the women had been sleeping and said that two of the women must get up and go out to the bus. He told them that this was part of a prisoner exchange being organised with the Bosnian government. One of the names he read out was Sadeta Medunjanin, who was in Omarska because her husband had been a member of the Muslim SDA party and had been killed, with their 20-year-old son, in the bombardment of Kozarac in May. The second name called out was that of Edna. 'They told them, "Gather your things and come outside," but they had nothing to gather, so they just went out. We told them they were so lucky, they will now go free, unlike us, and we gave them all that we had, which was a few cigarettes.'

The women were taken outside, and Nusreta watched from the window as Edna and Sadeta boarded the bus. A group of male prisoners was also ordered aboard the bus, which then drove noisily out of the camp and away into the night. This was the last time Nusreta saw Edna alive. Early in 2000, a farmer exploring caves in northern Bosnia came across a large group of human remains. Some of these were sent to Sarajevo, where a DNA registration centre held samples from more than seventeen thousand missing Bosnians. Preliminary tests indicated that one of the bodies matched a sample of Edna's DNA which had been provided by her mother. Edna's mother was contacted. She had spent the years since 1992 in a gradually more hopeless search for her daughter, never knowing whether to give up hope or to keep on looking. Nusreta agreed to identify the body. 'I recognised her because of her clothing, and because of her long dark hair,' Nusreta told me.[3]

Two weeks after Edna was taken away on the bus, Nusreta awoke one morning to be given unusual orders. The women were told to go downstairs and clean the windows of the canteen. Outside in the yard, Nusreta saw male prisoners sweeping the yard. After serving the prisoners their midday meal, the women were assembled in the canteen by one of the guard commanders. He announced that he would read out a list of names and those women must board a bus which was leaving the camp. Nusreta's name was called out, along with all but five of the Muslim women.

Half-nervous and half-hopeful, Nusreta gathered the only belongings she had, the extra clothes she had come with, and boarded the bus. It drove out of the camp and headed through a maze of back roads until, after about half an hour, it arrived at the village of Trnopolje. Here she saw another camp. There was a long barbed-wire fence and behind it several thousand male prisoners, watched by Serb guards. Some of the men looked well fed, but others seemed starved like the Omarska prisoners.

The women were ordered off the bus, but as they stood in the sunshine a Serb officer came out of the main gate and started arguing with the soldiers who had been on the bus, telling them that the women must be taken back to Omarska. As the argument intensified, Nusreta took a look around. She could see guards wandering around, but no beatings. The camp appeared better than Omarska and she began hoping that they would not be sent back.

The soldiers from the bus ended the argument by getting back on board, shutting the door in the face of the Trnopolje commander, and driving away, leaving him standing facing the women. In an angry voice he told them to go inside a building that had been a café, and not to leave. A guard opened the glass door and they went inside. The café had long since been emptied of food and drink, but the stools, bar and even a few cheerful posters were still there, so they sat around not knowing what to expect.

They were still inside the building two days later. They had been fed and allowed out to go to the toilet, and from what they had seen Trnopolje was an improvement on Omarksa. There were few beatings and most of the men in the camp seemed to be comparatively well treated. Some of their womenfolk lived in nearby villages and were allowed to come to the camp gates with clothing and food. Nusreta greedily watched one woman pass a bag of fresh tomatoes to a man she guessed must be her husband.

On the morning of the second day at Trnopolje there was a commotion by the camp fence, and when Nusreta looked out she could see a group of people in civilian dress standing by the wire, including a man with what looked like a television camera. A few Serb guards were standing around them, and these people were talking with prisoners behind the wire. Then the strangers, whom she assumed to be journalists, walked in through the main gate and the guards made no attempt to stop the prisoners swarming round them. After about an hour, the strangers walked back out of the camp gates, boarded a small bus, and drove away with a Serb army escort. 'Honestly, I did not think anything about this incident. I did not know who they were. I thought that if this was a TV crew then it must be a Serb official TV crew. It was not likely that they would have wanted some outside TV crew to see inside one of these camps.'4

For Ed Vulliamy, the Rome correspondent of the *Guardian* newspaper, the Bosnian war was the biggest story of his life. After a long and distinguished career covering foreign assignments and working for a time in Washington, Vulliamy had been introduced to the Balkans in 1990 when he covered the Romanian revolution. In

1991 he witnessed the fighting that broke out in Croatia when it declared independence from Yugoslavia. Then, in April 1992, he chronicled the war in Bosnia and the campaign, dubbed 'ethnic cleansing', which saw Serb forces drive hundreds of thousands of Croats and Muslims from their homes.

In the middle of the summer Vulliamy was in London preparing to return to Bosnia. Also in London at that time was Radovan Karadžić, a former psychiatrist and self-proclaimed poet who was now president of the Bosnian Serbs. He was a stout man, recognisable by a grey bouffant hairstyle, and he was in London to try to fend off growing Western anger at the atrocities being carried out by his forces. More than half a million Bosnian refugees had now fled to Western Europe, and their stories of terror, rape and brutality were filling Western newspapers. Meanwhile, the TV screens showed each night the indiscriminate shelling his forces were inflicting on the civilians of Sarajevo, a bombardment he refused to stop even when confronted with pictures of dead and seriously injured Muslim children.

After meeting with British and other Western officials at the beginning of August to assure them that he was committed to working for peace in Bosnia, he gave a press conference. The journalists' questions were dominated by a single subject: reports of Serb prison camps operating in northern Bosnia. An American journalist, Roy Gutman, had published a story about a visit to one of these camps, Manjaca, in late July. Gutman had visited with the Red Cross and reported that civilians were being kept behind wire and badly fed. More intriguingly, he had met prisoners who spoke of other camps, deeper inside Bosnia, where conditions were even more severe. One name in particular kept coming up: Omarska, a camp outside the town of Prijedor, where, he was told, killings were commonplace.

Unlike Manjaca, the Red Cross had not been given permission to visit these other camps. Faced with this barrage of questions, Karadžić replied that it was true that these camps existed, but they had been built not to hurt the Muslims and Croats but to protect them from the fighting taking place in the local countryside. He denied stories of mistreatment and, as the press conference began to wind down, casually invited any journalists who did not believe him to visit the camps for themselves.

Most of the journalists assumed this was not a serious offer, because Karadžić had a reputation for being unreliable. His forces hardly ever allowed Western journalists to visit their zones in Bosnia. At the *Guardian*, foreign editor Paul Webster was curious. He found out that Karadžić had a car phone and managed to track down the number, calling him directly and asking straight out whether a *Guardian* journalist could visit the Prijedor camps. Taken by surprise, Karadžić said of course, and told Webster to send a correspondent to Belgrade, the Yugoslav capital, where a visa for Bosnian Serb territory would be arranged. Britain's Independent Television News also contacted Karadžić and was given the same information. Webster phoned Vulliamy and gave him new instructions: instead of going to Sarajevo as he had planned, he should fly to Budapest, where ITN had a crew, and together they would drive down to Belgrade for their visas.

From Belgrade a helicopter flew them across the border to the Bosnian Serb capital, Pale, where they had meetings with Karadžić and other leaders while waiting for their white minibus to be driven in from Belgrade. Their host in Pale was Nikola Koljević, one of Karadžić's deputies and an unlikely figure to be found in a hardline administration. Before the war he had been a Sarajevo university professor and was known as Yugoslavia's foremost Shakesperean scholar.

The journalists were dispatched, not to Prijedor, but on a tour that took them through a series of Serb-held towns in northern Bosnia. 'We got messed around,' said Vulliamy. 'I now know that they needed to buy time, they had begun the clear-out of Omarska.'[5]

On 3 August 1992 they drove to Bijeljina, in north-eastern Bosnia, where they stayed the night and were again met by Koljević. 'Koljević kept bobbing up. He wanted to show how many Shakesperean quotes he could work into each paragraph. I was getting so pissed off I was not concentrating on what the silly man was saying.' said Vulliamy.

Next, the group drove west to the largest Serb-held town, Banja Luka, still 50 miles from their destination. They were met by local army officials and given briefings about the security situation. On the following day they drove west to Prijedor, passing abandoned villages shattered and burned by Serb attacks. Other Muslim villages were still inhabited, the occupants having been told that they would be deported but that they must wait. The Serbs had found it impossible to deport so many hundreds of thousands of people in a few weeks, so many communities were bypassed and told to remain in their homes, flying white flags to keep them safe from attack. Now Vulliamy drove past mile after mile of houses with every kind of white material draped from the windows by the terrified Muslims living inside. 'They had hung white flags, sheets, pillowcases, anything white. Part of me was thinking, oh my God, this is horrible, but part of me was terribly detached. I wanted to get to Prijedor.'

In Prijedor, a town that was half empty with most of the shops shut, the military escort took the journalists to the town hall, headquarters of the Serbian Crisis Staff. Inside they were met by its chief, Milomir Stakić, later to achieve fame as the first man ever to be jailed for life by The Hague Tribunal. Stakić took the journalists to an office where they were told to sit on one side of a table, while Serb officials and military officers sat facing them. The lead was taken not by Stakić but by a big, heavy-set man who introduced himself as Milan Kovačević, director of the local hospital. He wore a T-shirt with the logo US Marines emblazoned on it, and told them that he was the architect of the chain of prison camps set up south of the town. As Karadžić had done in London, Kovačević denied that there was mistreatment in the camps, insisting that in many cases the Muslims had chosen to go there voluntarily in order to be protected from roving bands of Islamic warriors.

Kovačević reminded the journalists that the Croatians had run a concentration camp during the Second World War at nearby Jasenovac, where at least seventy thousand Serbs had died, and he said that he himself had been born in that camp. 'Kovačević was a big bear of a man, overweight, but with delusions of his own fitness. He seemed to think he was in his own movie. He talked about a fundamentalist jihad going on in this area. Then he got into a history lesson. He got out these maps and started showing how the Serbian lands in Bosnia have been shrunk.'

Kovačević told them that the land around the camps was not secure and it was suggested that they go instead to another camp at Manjaca in northern Bosnia. The journalists insisted on seeing Omarska. Kovačević's mood soured, and they were ordered to leave the room and wait outside the town hall.

Out in the street the journalists saw a group of Muslim women standing by the side of the building. Using the ITN translator, Misha, a Serb from Belgrade, they asked what they were doing. Frightened to talk, the women nevertheless said that they were waiting for the chance to find out what had happened to their husbands, who had been arrested.

The conversation was stopped by one of the Serb officials, Simo Drljača, appearing at the door and telling the journalists to get into their minibus immediately and follow him. He boarded an army jeep and led them out of Prijedor, back on the road to Banja Luka. When they passed a signpost indicating the turn-off for Omarska, they feared their mission had failed and they were being ordered out.

A few minutes later, Drljača's jeep suddenly swung right onto a dirt track. Soon there came the sound of shooting from woodland to the left of the road. Drljača's jeep and another one behind the minibus stopped and soldiers, guns at the ready, jumped out and took up positions ready to fire back. The shooting continued, but Vulliamy suspected there was something wrong. The soldiers seemed too enthusiastic and too careless of enemy bullets – not the way he had seen soldiers act in real combat. 'I had been doing this job for a while so I knew what a real shoot-out looked like and this was just play action. I just remember saying to them, "Sorry, no, bollocks, we're going on." They did not want us to get to those camps.'

The journalists waited for the shooting to stop, then told Drljača that they were not afraid and wanted to go on to Omarska. A few minutes later they were driven up to the main gate of the camp. There were Serb guards but no sign of any prisoners. Ahead of Vulliamy was a line of big sheds with closed metal doors. The journalists were led into the compound and towards a two-storey office block. Then one of the doors of the sheds opened and a group of prisoners came walking out. 'The sight that greeted our eyes was twenty to thirty men emerging from a huge, rust-coloured hangar blinking into the light. My first thought was, "It's dark in there." Their condition varied. Some had shaven heads, very gaunt, skeletal. Others were in better condition, even hefty. They went walking past in a column. There was a machine gunner in some sort of turret on a building above us who was watching them, keeping his gun on them.'

The group of journalists followed the men into the office building and saw that downstairs was a canteen. 'These men looked absolutely terrified. There were some women behind the counter, serving, and the men lined up, nobody saying anything, to get some sort of ration. The food was a watery bean stew and when they sat down they started to devour the stuff. The thing was, they were only given five minutes to eat. Then they all got up again to leave. I saw some of them had got a piece of bread, held in their hand down by their side so the guard would not see.'

The journalists asked each of the prisoners in turn if he would talk, but most refused. Finally one of them stopped and told Vulliamy that he would speak. 'I do not want to tell any lies but I cannot tell the truth,' he said. Lowering his eyes he walked out after the other prisoners. Another walked by, with a bloody gash on the side of his face. Misha asked how he had got it. The man said, 'I fell over,' and kept walking. 'People's eyes when they are too scared to talk tell you a lot. Their eyes are extremely articulate. These men were absolutely terrified of the guards who were shuffling around the canteen.'

When the prisoners had gone, Drljača led the journalists upstairs, where the commander of the camp Željko Meakić was waiting to meet them, sitting at his desk. 'He was scary. This man looked like the worst of our soccer boys on a bad day with a machine gun. He wasn't big and tough, he just looked nasty. He was very tense.' Vulliamy felt that the

commander, like the officials he had met in Prijedor, was furious that Karadžić had allowed journalists to visit the camps. 'They were all amazed that Karadžić had put them in this position.'

The briefing wound on, a detailed description of different kinds of prisoner, while Vulliamy worried about when he would get the chance to look around the camp. 'It was long and tedious, telling us about category A prisoners, category B prisoners, category C prisoners.' Then a single male prisoner was brought into the office. The commander told the journalists that the man had been a leader of the Muslim SDA party in Prijedor and would speak with them. They objected. 'We said we don't want anyone you have chosen. Ian Williams of ITN started arguing. He said, "Dr Karadžić has given us his word; we've seen nothing."'

With tempers rising, they were led back outside into the hot, empty yard. Guards were milling around, and the sheds on the far side had their metal doors closed. Williams and Vulliamy walked towards the sheds. Drljača and the commander ran forwards to block their path. When they kept walking, Drljača and the commander brandished machine guns at the journalists. There was now no doubt that the visit was over, and the journalists had not had a single interview with a prisoner. 'We felt bad; we felt we had half a story. We felt like there was this horrific secret, beyond the door of the hangar, and that we needed to open that door.' Vulliamy told me.

Drljača, angry, ordered the party back into their minibus, and they drove out through the camp gates. Instead of turning to take them to the main Banja Luka–Prijedor road, however, Drljača led them through a maze of back roads. The reason for this remains a mystery, though possibly it was in order to avoid passing once more through the remains of Kozarac, the village bombarded by Serb forces in May. Whatever the reason for his decision, it was to have momentous consequences. The route taken by Drljača led straight past the back gate of another camp, at Trnopolje. The journalists were not to know it at the time, but Trnopolje was a less brutal camp than Omarska. Trnopolje was a transit camp, used to hold the thousands of Muslim and Croat civilians being shunted around the countryside in the ethnic cleansing operations. That day the Serbs had tried to hide some of the prisoners from Omarska by busing them to Trnopolje. Some had arrived only a few hours before and now stood by the wire fence.

The Serb police escort jeep kept moving, but the journalists following in their minibus saw the fence and the prisoners and decided to stop. Grabbing their camera, the ITN crew leapt out and began filming on the spot. 'We were lucky because these guys were inept as well as brutish. We stopped right across from this extraordinary sight. That was the moment when I pinched myself, I thought, am I really seeing this?'

Vulliamy reached the fence to be confronted by a man, his body skin and bone. The man smiled at him. Vulliamy, not knowing what else to do, simply put out his hand. The man reached through the wire and shook it, and introduced himself as Fikret Alić, a Bosnian Muslim transferred that morning from a camp named Keraterm. 'We all shook hands. God knows who was the more amazed to see who. In that moment very oddly the guards melted away. I don't think they knew what to do.'

Alić told Vulliamy his story. Some days before, he had been in one of the sheds at Keraterm, near Prijedor, his home for many weeks. Then the guards had pulled open the door, set up a machine gun, and with no warning simply opened fire. Men fell to the ground, the living and the dead, and Alić threw himself down also. In a matter of seconds the firing stopped and there was silence broken by the groans of the wounded. Alić was untouched but lying among the bodies of the dead. A Serb voice ordered the survivors to get up. Then they were told to load the dead onto a waiting truck. 'He said two hundred had been killed and he had been forced to load the bodies. He said he had broken down in tears and an older man had come forward to take his place.'

A Serb officer from inside the camp came over and introduced himself, then led the journalists inside the compound, passing a small building that had been used as a café and moving towards the former schoolhouse. Inside there was a small medical centre which the Serbs proudly showed off, insisting that the prisoners in Trnopolje got prompt medical treatment. Vulliamy was introduced to a Muslim doctor, also a prisoner, working there, Dr Idris. They asked the doctor about any mistreatment and he said nothing, but found another way to communicate. 'He rolled his eyes.' As they were talking, the doctor produced a roll of film he had kept in his pocket and, unseen by the guards, slipped it to one of the ITN crew. When the film was developed it showed the torsos, beaten black and blue, of people he had been trying to treat. Back in the yard the crew began to interview prisoners, who confirmed the existence of a third camp, Keraterm. Then Serb officials broke in and demanded that the journalists leave. The trip was over.

Vulliamy and the ITN crew decided to drive straight back across northern Bosnia to Belgrade. On the journey, to break the nervous tension, they spent their time trying to recite the complete *Sergeant Pepper* Beatles album. Their concern was, just how much of a story did they have? They had some footage from Trnopolje and had spoken with some prisoners. Although the film that the camp doctor had given them might be interesting, Vulliamy feared that they had failed in their most important task which was to get inside the sheds at Omarska.

Arriving in Belgrade, the ITN crew took Vulliamy to the best hotel, the Hyatt, then drove away, heading north to Budapest where they had editing facilities. Vulliamy got up early then phoned his newspaper. Deputy foreign editor Peter Murtagh was on duty and Vulliamy told him what he had seen and asked nervously what sort of story it would make. Murtagh told him to write five thousand words, an extraordinary length for a paper where even the longest feature articles were rarely more than three thousand words. Still unsure of how newsworthy his experience had been, Vulliamy asked if the story would be the splash, the lead story. 'Peter just said, "Is the Pope a Catholic?"'

That evening, 6 August 1992, ITN broke the story to the world. The editors decided on a single image to lead their news broadcast, a short of the half-starved men behind the wire. Next morning, the *Guardian* was the only newspaper with an eyewitness report from the camps. Other newspapers in Britain and around the world ran a brief story gleaned from the ITN broadcast, together with a still taken from the ITN footage showing the men behind the barbed wire. The *Daily Mirror* ran the picture across the whole of its front page with a black border and a simple headline reading 'BELSEN 1992'.[6] Nusreta and Vulliamy[7] could not know it at the time, but the visit to the camps that day would have far-reaching consequences, setting in motion events that would see the United Nations invent a new system of justice which would one day claim the scalp of a president.

The Great Dictator 3

Contemporary experience shows that princes who have achieved great things have been those who have given their word lightly, who have known how to trick men with their cunning, and who, in the end, have overcome those abiding by honest principles.

Niccolò Machiavelli, The Prince

S lobodan Milošević rose to power through a single act of betrayal against the man who was both his best friend and mentor. With this move, he transformed himself from a successful but anonymous Yugoslavian bureaucrat into the most powerful man in the Balkans, setting a course that would end in the worst crisis to hit Europe since the Second World War.

In April 1987, Milošević was the 46-year-old chief of the Communist party of Serbia, the largest of the six republics that together made up the state of Yugoslavia. The position was a powerful one. Yugoslavia was a Communist dictatorship and political parties, and democracy, were banned. Political power was held in just two institutions, the government and the Communist party. The only check on individual power was that government and party were split, with some powers being held by the state and some by the six republics.

Milošević owed his job to the largesse of just one man, Ivan Stambolić, who considered Milošević to be his best friend. The pair had met at Belgrade University in 1960. Milošević had been a brilliant but reserved student, awkward in social situations and making few friends. He had only one other close friend, his girlfriend Mira, whom he had met while at school in the small town of Požarevac where he was born.

Stambolić, in contrast, was outgoing, charismatic and well connected. He had an uncle, Petar, who was president of Serbia and who would ease his path in politics. Official positions in Yugoslavia depended not on elections but on party committees. At university, Stambolić got Milošević his first political post, as secretary of the Communist party branch attached to the law faculty. Milošević did well, showing himself willing to do the back-room filing and organisational work. In 1964 he graduated with a law degree, and in March 1965 he married Mira and asked Stambolić to be his best man.

After university, Milošević had gone to work at Belgrade city hall, while Stambolić's connections saw him given a top post at Tehnogas, the state gas company. In 1970 Stambolić became chief of the company and offered Milošević a place in its management. When Stambolić moved into full-time politics in 1974, he arranged for Milošević to replace him as Tehnogas manager. Milošević did well, showing a flair for administration. In 1978 his own merits, plus support from Stambolić, got him the job of president at Beobank, a state merchant bank.

As a banker, Milošević thrived, showing the same flair for organisation that had distinguished him at Tehnogas. His job meant being sent on frequent trips to America to meet with the IMF and World Bank. There he delighted in shopping for his young family, and was careful also to bring presents back for Stambolić's family. Stambolić was regarded as his 'kum', a Serb word that means something between best friend and blood-brother.

Milošević might have remained a successful financier, but in 1982 Stambolić was appointed head of the Belgrade branch of the Communist party. This was a key step on the political ladder and Stambolić wanted an ally, someone to watch his back as he climbed to the top. He asked Milošević if he would become a party official. Milošević – ironically, considering his later career – was reluctant to take the job, because he was enjoying life as a banker. In the Yugoslavia of the early 1980s, the president of a bank was in a good position. He had a nice apartment and a chauffeur-driven car plus access to scarce goods such as hand-made suits, imported whisky and American cigarettes. However, Milošević agreed to give politics a try if he could do the job part-time. Stambolić arranged for him to become head of the Old Town committee of the Belgrade Communist party, allowing him to keep his post at the bank.

Two years later, Stambolić was promoted again, to become chief of the Serbian Communist party, and now he asked Milošević to take on his old job. Milošević agreed and left the bank to replace Stambolić as head of the Belgrade Communist party. In 1986, Stambolić moved a third time, crossing from party to government to become Serbian president. Again he asked Milošević to follow him up the ladder and again Milošević agreed, but this move came with a slight sting in the tail. Milošević had assumed that he could nominate his replacement as Belgrade party boss, but Stambolić overruled him and appointed one of his protégés, Dragisa Pavlović. If Milošević felt any bitterness at this slight, he was careful not to show it, though the following year he had a spectacular chance to take revenge.

Milošević's successful career contrasted with a troubled personal life. He was born in August 1941 in the small Serbian town of Požarevac four months after the German invasion of Yugoslavia. His father, Svetozar, was deeply religious. His mother, Stanislava, was a committed Communist. When Slobodan was four, Svetozar abruptly left home, moving back to his native province of Montenegro and leaving Stanislava to raise him and his elder brother Borislav alone. Then, when he was seven, a favourite uncle shot himself in a fit of depression. In 1962, when Slobodan was 21, news reached him that his father, depressed and alone in Montenegro, had also killed himself with a gun. He chose not go to his father's funeral, for reasons that were not made public.

Milošević's mother never remarried and was left alone when both her boys went to work in Belgrade. In 1974 she was passed over for promotion in the school where she worked, and, lonely and depressed, she hanged herself. Milošević's feelings about these deaths are not recorded. He is a secretive man, with few friends outside his family, and he has yet to give any interviews on the subject. Certainly his personal problems did not impair his career, and as head of the Serbian Communist party he showed, as he had in banking, a flair for administration.

By 1986, Milošević was in a strong political position. He enjoyed a life of privilege and a good salary. Since 1978 he had lived amid the country's elite. His party connections helped his wife in her career as a professor of Marxism at Belgrade University, and his position also meant an entrée for his children, Marija and Marko, into the nightclubbing and parties enjoyed by the sons and daughters of the elite. Now teenagers, they could expect to choose their place at university with none of the tiresome need to compete in entrance exams. Afterwards they could have their choice of jobs in an economy that was 90 per cent state controlled. Milošević also had great prestige. In fact, unlike many privileged senior officials, he spurned the life of restaurants and nightclubs, preferring that of a family man. According to his biographer, Adam LeBor,[1] Milošević would come home from work promptly, change from his suit into comfortable clothes and a jumper, sit in an easy chair with his favourite drink, Scotch whisky, and listen to the news from his wife and children.

Yet even at this time of domestic tranquillity there were clouds gathering on the horizon. The Communist system which had been so good to him was by the 1980s in serious trouble. In 1980, Tito, the man who had created Communist Yugoslavia, died without nominating a successor. He had ruled the country with a firm hand, but had also taken care to ensure that none of the nationalities that made up Yugoslavia – Serbs, Croats, Macedonians, Albanians, Bosnian Muslims and Slovenes – was in a position of dominance. Tito's legacy was the division of power within the country between the national republics and the federal government. The mix of party and government in the republics, and the division between the republics and the federal state, were designed to prevent any one person or nation dominating the process of government. As an added precaution, Tito had arranged for the economy to be run not by capitalists, as in the West, nor by the state, as in the Soviet Union, but through workers' councils. In theory, the workers controlled their own factories. In practice, this device, together with all the other layers of government and control, meant that Yugoslavia was a country run by committee. It began to sink under the weight of red tape. The economy fell into recession and by 1986 Yugoslavia owed foreign banks the equivalent of US$21 billion, an amount almost impossible to repay. It also suffered because during the Cold War it had received aid from both the capitalist West and the communist East, each anxious to curry favour with Tito, who had declared himself neutral in the superpower stand-off of the late twentieth century.

The loss of Western aid as the Cold War drew to a close, plus the confusion of government, saw the recession deepen, with the republics and central government unable to agree on strong action. Some Communists wanted reform, giving more freedom to the people and democracy, while others blamed the recession on the lack of firm central control. This crisis was not unique to Yugoslavia. Across the Communist world, and in particular in the Soviet Union, there were demonstrations by people who felt that their system could not match the West for either prosperity or political freedom. Milošević found himself in the position of a middle-aged man who had spent his career climbing to the top of an organisation only to find that it was crumbling beneath his feet.

Yugoslavia was a composite of different national and ethnic groups, and protest against the Communist authorities was expressed through nationalism. However, nationalists took aim not just at the authorities but also at each other. The richest of the republics, Slovenia and Croatia, complained that they were being held back by having to send large subsidies to poorer regions such as Macedonia and Bosnia. The poorer regions responded that their cheap labour, used to manufacture components, allowed the Slovenes and Croats to export economically competitive products; while everyone blamed the Serbs for having a disproportionate number of jobs in the bureaucracy, police and army. The Serbs muttered that this showed ingratitude for their having taken the lead in defending Yugoslavia during the Second World War and having run the country's bureaucracy ever since.

In April 1987, Serbs in the southern province of Kosovo held protest rallies accusing the ethnic Albanian majority of discriminating against them, and complaining that the government was doing nothing to help. Kosovo was the country's poorest province and home to Albanians and

Serbs with a long history of rancour. Since the end of the war, censuses had been showing Kosovan Serbs migrating to richer parts of the country while Albanians stayed in the province, so that by the late 1980s they outnumbered the Serbs by six to one.[2] The Serbs complained that the Albanians were giving jobs in local government and the police to people connected to their extended family networks. The Albanians said that the Serbs were simply upset at no longer being the bosses of a province they had once dominated.

Stambolić asked Milošević if he would go down to Kosovo to speak with the conflicting sides. It was not really Milošević's job. The head of the Communist party was the keeper of the ideological flame, not a day-to-day problem solver. Any concessions or arrangements would need to be made by the government, not the party. Nevertheless, Milošević owed his past three promotions to Stambolić, so he may have felt obliged to accept the order.

On 20 April Milošević journeyed to Kosovo to meet local leaders in a meeting hall in Kosovo Polje, a small Serb village on the edge of the capital, Priština. He must have known it was a hopeless mission. Whatever the truth of the discrimination claim, Milošević would have understood that the root problem for Kosovo was money. Kosovo was Yugoslavia's poorest province, but the government was too mired in its own economic problems to be in a position to offer any new subsidies. Milošević would have to stick to the official line, which was to urge Serbs and Albanians to remember the key tenets of the Communist regime – brotherhood and unity. He must ask them simply to find a way of getting along.

Milošević was greeted at the Dom Kulture, or Culture House, of Kosovo Polje by a crowd of ten thousand angry Serb farmers and workers. A line of police held them back so that he and the local leaders could get through the front door of the meeting house. Inside, each side dutifully gave their version of events, but attention turned to the crowd outside whose roars reverberated through the building. Milošević decided to venture outside to address the crowd. He was no public speaker, being more used to operating in committee rooms where key decisions were made. As expected, he gave a short speech calling for brotherhood and unity. 'Exclusive nationalism based on national hatred can never be progressive,' he told them.[3] The crowd was unimpressed. His next remark gave them pause. He promised to return in four days' time. This was a surprise. The Serbs had expected Milošević, having done his duty, to scuttle back to Belgrade and stay there. Instead, here was a man who seemed, at least, to be taking their complaints seriously.

The four days Milošević then spent in Belgrade saw him make a major decision. He was a lifelong Communist, but he was also a Serb, and he knew the power of Serb nationalism. The Serbs had spent most of the past six hundred years living under a succession of tyrannies. Folk history was based around the memories of injustices committed against them and the need to stick together simply to survive. When Communist Yugoslavia had prospered after the Second World War, the insecurities and anxieties had faded. Now Yugoslavia was in trouble and Serb writers and academics were again asking whether it was not better to band together in a Serb-only state. Increasing numbers of the Serb population were voicing their support.

Milošević's decision to return to Kosovo was, he said, designed to show his concern about the problem. As a Serb, he knew the powerful position Kosovo held in the Serb imagination. It was on Kosovo Polje, which translates as Blackbird Field, that in legend, if not quite in fact, the Serbs had fought, and lost, their most important battle. In 1389 they had been defeated on this great rolling plain by an Ottoman army, and the Serb empire which once stretched from the River Danube to the Adriatic Sea fell under Ottoman rule for five hundred years. In fact, historical evidence indicates that the battle ended in stalemate with the Serbian leader, Prince Lazar, slain along with the Ottoman sultan, Murad. Both armies withdrew from the field. The Ottomans then had to repel an attack by Tamerlane in the east of their empire before they were free to concentrate on the Serbs, and it was seventy years after the battle that the last free Serb territory fell under Turkish rule.

Ottoman rule was often cruel. A favoured method used by the Turks to execute disloyal subjects was to impale them on wooden stakes.

These were inserted so that they did not pierce major blood vessels, thus ensuring that the victim's death was slow. The Ottomans also kidnapped thousands of children from the Balkan peoples, they subjugated and took them away to be raised as janissaries, elite soldiers who, having no clear idea of their origin, would be loyal only to the sultan.

In 1690, encouraged by Austria, the Serbs rebelled. But the rebellion was defeated and, to escape Ottoman retribution, the Serb Orthodox patriarch, Arsenije Čarnojević, led the army, the people, the priests and the bones of St Lazar (the leader of the Serb army at the Battle of Kosovo Polje) in a great migration north into exile. His successor as patriarch, Jovanović-Sakabenta, led another uprising in 1737, with the same result and ending in a second great migration. In 1788 the Serbs rebelled again and, with Austrian help, were granted an autonomous province. Four more rebellions followed, from 1804 to 1815, with the Serbs under the command of a ruthless general, Karadjordje, or Black George. He managed to extend their territory, after a series of bloody reverses, one of which saw the Ottomans sell eighteen hundred women into slavery. Karadjordje's reward was to be assassinated in 1817 by a rival for the position of Serb leader, Miloš Obrenović, who sent his head, skinned and stuffed, to the Sultan. The Serbs, upset about high taxes, rebelled three times against Obrenović.

In 1877 the Serbs rebelled in support of peasants in the neighbouring province of Bosnia. The following year, the Congress of Berlin recognised Serbia as an independent state for the first time. The late nineteenth century saw Serb nationalism romanticised by the liberal currents swirling around Western Europe. The Serb yearning for a free national homeland, and the return of their southern province of Kosovo, was encapsulated by poets and writers. The greatest poem of all was an old one, *The Downfall of the Serbian Empire,* which had been told and retold around family hearths for generations and assumed a totemic quality when it was finally put into written form by the chronicler Vuk Karadžić. This poem tells the mythical version of the Battle of Kosovo Polje. On the eve of the battle, it says, God sent a winged messenger to meet Prince Lazar, the Serbian commander, with a difficult choice. He could have an empire on earth, or an empire in heaven, and he must choose which:

> Which is the empire of your choice?
> Is it the empire of heaven?
> Is it the empire of the earth?
> If it is the empire of the earth,
> Saddle horses and tighten girth straps,
> And, fighting men, buckle on swords,
> Attack the Turks,
> And all the Turkish army shall die,
> But if the empire of heaven,
> Weave a church on Kosovo,
> Build its foundation not with marble stones,
> Build it with pure silk. And crimson cloth.[4]

Lazar, with an eye to the future, chose the second option, declaring, 'The empire of earth is brief, heaven is everlasting.' The poem became a rallying cry for the nineteenth-century Serbs who wanted a new state, Greater Serbia, which would include not just their existing territory but also Serb lands held by the Turks and Austrians.

This vision was put into writing in the Načertanije, or 'Draft Plan', which was literally a blueprint for Greater Serbia.[5] This document was kept secret for nearly thirty years until it was made public in 1906, and it called for the Serbs to control not just Serb territory but also that of other Balkan nations. The rationale was that the Serbs were the only group strong enough to keep the Balkans free of the influence of the competing Ottoman, Russian and Austrian empires.

In 1882 the Serb leader, Milan Obrenović, upgraded his status by declaring himself king of the Serbs. In 1903 descendants of Karadjordje took their revenge when they threw Milan Obrenović's son, Aleksandar, from the third-floor bedroom of the royal palace in Belgrade. Legend says that Aleksandar clung to the ledge by his fingers, but the Karadjordje men gleefully stamped on them until he lost his grip. After Milan Obrenović's death, the throne was taken by Petar Karadjordjević.

Serbia finally reconquered Kosovo in 1912 when its army, along with Balkan allies, drove the Ottomans back almost to Istanbul. Serb soldiers stood in tears when they realised that they stood once more on Kosovo Polje. The Kosovo Albanians had fought on the side of the sultan, and the Serbs burned their villages in revenge, an event recorded by a young Russian war correspondent travelling in the region, named Leon Trotsky.[6]

Then in June 1914 a Serb named Gavrilo Princip assassinated Austria's crown prince Franz Ferdinand during a visit to the Bosnian capital, Sarajevo. An escalation of tensions between the Great Powers ensued, culminating in August 1914 with the start of the First World War, and a new catastrophe befell the Serbs. In the winter of 1915 an Austro-German army smashed Serb defences around Belgrade, and the king, the remnants of his army and tens of thousands of his population fled in a great migration on the scale of the moves of 1690 and 1737. This time they migrated south, over the frozen Kosovo battlefield and on to the coast of modern-day Albania to be picked up by British and French ships. The losses on this march, resulting from starvation, disease and attacks by vengeful Albanians, added up to Serbia suffering the worst losses, proportionately, of any nation in the First World War, with approximately one quarter of its population dead.

To try to end the squabbling of the Balkan nations, at the end of the First World War the Great Powers created a new state of the Southern Slavs, which is the literal translation of Yugoslavia. The capital was Belgrade and the king was a Serb – and the other Balkan nations, including the Croats, Slovenes and Albanians, were angry at this Serb domination. When the Germans invaded in 1941 the army collapsed. What followed was a multi-sided war of great ferocity. The Serbs split into two armies. One was the Communist partisans of Josip Broz Tito,[7] and the other comprised the royalists. These two armies fought both the Germans and each other. Other Yugoslav nations fought both on the side of the partisans and against them. Tito was the most ruthless, fighting on even when the Germans began executing one hundred Serb civilians for every German soldier killed. Croat fascists, with Nazi blessing, set up a concentration camp at Jasenovac where seventy thousand Serbs perished.

Tito seized Belgrade before the end of the war and proclaimed Yugoslavia a Communist state. He executed thirty thousand men who had fought against the partisans, but once his iron rule was established he began to relax his grip. Under Tito, the Serbs enjoyed the most prosperous period of their long and troubled history.

Yet even as the country prospered, the Serbs kept alive memories of their past sufferings as a warning to a new generation. In the early years of the twentieth century a passing Ottoman army had gouged the eyes from the paintings of saints on the walls of the monastery at Gracanica in Kosovo. Serb bishops chose not to restore the paintings, preferring to leave the site as a warning to the Serbs of what their enemies might do. To the north, in the town of Niš, a museum was created to preserve the remains of the Skull Tower, built by one Ottoman commander in 1809 from the skulls of 973 dead Serb soldiers.

During Tito's years, the desire for a Greater Serbia was still expressed by dissident writers, but it was only when the wheels began to come off the Yugoslav economy in the 1980s that they gained a substantial audience. In September 1986 the Serbian Academy of Sciences and Arts leaked a report called the *Memorandum* which conjured up the ideals of a Greater Serbia. This document accurately summed up the failings of Communist Yugoslavia, then argued that the state would collapse and that Serbs must either stick together, in their own state, or face peril at the hands of their former enemies. In emotive and rather unscientific language, the *Memorandum* complained that Albanian discrimination against the Serbs in Kosovo amounted to 'genocide' because the effect was to cause Serbs to leave the province.[8]

The Communist authorities complained about the incendiary nature of the *Memorandum* but, crucially, did not move against the authors. Tito would have imprisoned, and possibly executed, such dissidents. The fact that the Communists chose no such action only confirmed to the nationalists that they were weak.

Eight months after the *Memorandum* was published, in April 1987, Milošević found himself in Kosovo. Now that he had seen for himself the power of Serb nationalism he decided, for reasons he has yet to explain, to turn his back on his lifetime creed of Communism and its tenet that all men are equal. It was to be a huge betrayal, not just of the system and his former beliefs but also of Stambolić, his mentor. Possibly he felt that he needed to do this just in order to survive. If the Communist system were to collapse, he would be worried, as were other top officials, what would become of him. If democracy took the place of dictatorship, would they maintain their privileged positions? Would men like Milošević, skilled at manipulating a closed system, have the skills, late in life, to rise to the top of a new kind of hierarchy? The alternative was to jump from Communism to nationalism, particularly at this juncture, when the nationalists lacked direction and leadership.

To turn himself overnight into a nationalist was also a huge risk. The Serb nationalists were not yet strong and would not be in a position to help him. Meanwhile, such a change would infuriate his Communist party colleagues. During his four days in Belgrade, Milošević consulted the one person he trusted above all others, his wife Mira. Should he go back to Kosovo to criticise the Serb nationalists or to praise them? 'He consulted me, should he speak?' Mira later confided. 'How far should he go? I said the time had come to back the Kosovo Serbs.'[9]

In Kosovo, meanwhile, the Serb nationalists were organising a major protest to greet Milošević's return. A chubby Serb rabble-rouser, Miroslav Šolević, arranged for a gang of young men to whip the crowd into a frenzy, and parked two trucks loaded with stones in a nearby side street to make sure that the crowd would have plenty of ammunition to throw at the police.

On 24 April 1987, four days after his first trip, Milošević arrived back in Kosovo Polje to find a crowd of fifteen thousand Serbs waiting to meet him. As before, he entered the building with a line of straining police officers holding back the crowd. Inside, he began talks with Albanian and Serb leaders.

The meeting was dominated by the booming roar generated by the crowd outside. Milošević left the meeting and walked out. Television footage shows him standing in a grey suit, looking awkward as, feet away, Serbs roar and shout. An old man, very close to him, shouted that the Serbs were being beaten by the Albanians. Milošević, almost absent-mindedly, called back: 'No one should dare beat you again.'[10]

Then Milošević invited a delegation from the mob to come inside and join the scheduled meeting with community leaders. He gave them a short speech: 'This is your land, your fields, your gardens; your memories are here,' he told them. 'Surely you will not leave your land because it is difficult here? You should also stay here because of your ancestors and because of your descendants. Otherwise you would disgrace your ancestors and disappoint your descendants. I do not propose, comrades, that in staying you should suffer and tolerate a situation in which you are not satisfied. On the contrary, you should change it.'[11]

The audience was shocked. The Serbs, who had expected hostility, were ecstatic. Milošević's remark, 'No one should dare beat you again,' became a catchphrase. The Albanian Communist leaders were perplexed.

On his return to Belgrade at the end of April, Milošević met an instant firestorm from Stambolić. 'I told him, if you go on like this, what will become of our country?' Stambolić said later.[12] But he no longer recognised his old friend. 'Milošević was transformed,' Stambolić recalled.[13]

Milošević tried to keep both sides happy. He met with Communist party grandees to reassure them his support for the Serbs did not mean he was turning his back on them. The nationalists meanwhile were delighted. A Serb cultural magazine wrote in stirring tones of his visit to the most sacred of Serb provinces:

'But a handsome young speaker arrived.
The setting sun falling on his brushed hair.
I will speak with my people in open spaces,'
he says, 'in schoolyards and in fields.'[14]

The nationalists thought that they had found a man from the top echelons of the state whom they could use. In the end, as it turned out, it was Milošević who used them.

That summer, Milošević executed his great betrayal. He had set his sights on taking control of Serbia and that meant controlling not just the party but also the government, and the head of the government was Ivan Stambolić. He would need to destroy the career of his best friend.

The battleground for this betrayal was the Eighth Session of the Serbian Communist party, which took place in September 1987. Milošević needed a majority of the party to vote out Stambolić and to vote in a man who would be loyal to Milošević. It was a tall order, and he realised that he could not hope to get these votes on the grounds of nationalism. The weapon he would use to beat Stambolić was not Serb nationalism but reform.

Stambolić was only five years older than Milošević but he was identified with the older generation of leaders still ruling the Communist party, known as the partisan generation because many had been guerrillas alongside Tito in the Second World War. Many middle-aged party leaders of Milošević's generation were frustrated that they could not aspire to jobs at the very top of the government because the partisan generation hung on long after retirement. To this frustration was added a second concern, which was that without major reforms the Communist system might not survive the economic woes dragging it down. Milošević lobbied party men throughout the summer, suggesting that reform was not possible with Stambolić who owed too much to the partisan generation. By contrast, Milošević portrayed himself as belonging to a younger, more dynamic group of Communists, who could bring about reform, which was easy to credit because of his banking experience.

By September 1987, a large group of party chiefs believed that Milošević might be able to save the economy. He controlled several newspapers through his party post, and shortly before the Eighth Session opened he used one of them to attack Dragisa Pavlović, the man whom Stambolić had insisted take Milošević's old job as Belgrade party chief, in an article bluntly accusing Pavlović of opposing reform. Pavlović hit back, telling local party members that he did not oppose reform and that he had the support of Stambolić. This was a mistake because officials in the party and government were not expected to interfere in each other's business. The idea that Stambolić would use his influence as head of the government to interfere with party matters was frowned upon.

When the Eighth Session of the party began, Milošević launched a blistering attack on both Pavlović and, by implication, Stambolić. 'We expected trouble from the Kosovo separatists. But we didn't expect it from party members here.'[15] Stambolić was bewildered, unable to understand why his friend was acting in this way. He first offered to mediate, suggesting that Milošević and Pavlović could work out their problems 'over a lemonade'. But Milošević did not want to resolve the issue. He wanted to take power. He refused offers of compromise and called for Pavlović to be sacked and other 'dictators' to be disciplined. A Milošević ally accused Stambolić of being a dictator. 'I don't understand, why do you accuse me of being a dictator?' cried Stambolić. 'It's not my problem. I'm not the dictator.'[16]

Possibly many of the party faithful understood that Stambolić was not really a dictator, but they also feared for their futures and the future of their state. Milošević, the party leader, told them they must either back him, a young reformer, or else back Pavlović, and through him Stambolić, and by extension the partisan generation. So, biting their lips, the party grandees made their choice, and voted to expel Pavlović.

Stambolić, stunned, realised too late that Milošević wanted his job. Knowing he would be next, he met with Milošević a few days later and agreed that he would step down as president on 14 December. Milošević installed one of his allies, a Serb general, Petar Grácanin to take Stambolić's place. This was a gesture designed to attract support from the military.

In January 1988 Milošević completed the process of taking control of Serbia by starting a root-and-branch purge of the state system. He set up a commission, the Milošević Commission, which was officially tasked with removing inefficient managers in government and state industry. In fact, the hundreds of sackings of key people in the two years that followed were used not to make the system more efficient but to ensure that managers in politics, government, the police, media and industry were loyal to Milošević. With his base secure, and his best friend sidelined, he planned his next move, an assault on the government of Yugoslavia.

Supreme power in Yugoslavia was vested in the presidency. As part of Tito's legacy of ensuring that no one person held too much power, the presidency was composed of eight members, one from each of the six republics, plus representatives from two autonomous provinces in Serbia, Vojvodina and Kosovo. On paper, this meant that no group could dominate the country because key decisions, such as going to war, needed five of the eight votes. Milošević, however, saw a loophole in the system. His control of Serbia meant that he could nominate the Serbian presidency member – but another three votes were also within his grasp. One was the member for Montenegro, a republic with many Serbs which traditionally allied itself to Serbia. Then there were the presidency members nominated by the governments of the autonomous provinces of Vojvodina and Kosovo. These provinces had been created by Tito in order to make sure that Serbia did not become too strong. Now Milošević planned to seize control of them. Altogether, he could hope to control four of the eight representatives to the national presidency.

His first step was to use the media to support Serbian nationalism. He appointed a university acquaintance, Dušan Mitević, as head of Serbian Television, and Mitević began screening programmes reminding Serbs of how they had suffered in the Second World War and beforehand, and how they might suffer again if Yugoslavia were to collapse. The message was simple: if Yugoslavia is dying, then the Serbs must stick together.

Milošević contacted Miroslav Šolević, the man who had led the Kosovo Serb protests in April 1987, and had him organise a travelling protest which moved from town to town, holding rallies against the local Communist authorities. These so-called 'Meetings of Truth', which came complete with Serbian flags and banners, attracted large crowds and were covered by Mitević as if they were spontaneous eruptions of national opposition throughout Serbia. Careful observers would note, however, that the same faces – those of Šolević's men – were present at each one.

A second series of roadshows got going in 1988 when Serbia, with the support of the Orthodox Church, organised the disinterment of the remains of St Lazar, leader of the Serbs at the 1389 Battle of Kosovo Polje. His bones were taken on a year-long tour around the country.

Throughout 1988 and 1989 the two roadshows criss-crossed Serbia, all part of a campaign, given blanket coverage on Serbian television, to see a nationalist revival take shape. At its centre Mitević weaved a personality cult around Milošević. 'Milošević, contrary to the declared official views of the political party he belonged to, systematically built and cherished his personality cult,' Serbia's former Yugoslav presidency member, Borisav Jović, would later tell Milošević's war crimes trial. 'People carried photographs of Milošević and myself as well as other distinguished officials, which provoked my reaction and I asked Milošević to make it stop. We had had enough of the personality cults of Stalin and Tito. His reaction was meek, as if it had been a trivial issue, but what was done was that all other photographs were removed except his.'[17]

In October 1988 Šolević and his nationalist mob went to demonstrate outside the Vojvodina parliament. They staged a noisy rally, demanding that the provincial government resign. Allegations of incompetence had frequently been levelled at the local Communist leaders, and local Serbs joined the demonstration. Inside the parliament building Milošević loyalists demanded that they be given power. Milošević was not yet ready for violence, so instead of rocks Šolević's men were issued with cartons of yogurt from a local dairy. Soon the parliament building was spattered in yogurt, in what came to be called the Yogurt Revolution. The Vojvodina leadership, fearing violence might be next, resigned and handed power to Milošević's men. In the same month, Šolević moved to Montenegro, again providing the nucleus for demonstrations against the local government. Once more, the local leaders, faced with spiralling violence, resigned, handing over to Milošević's allies.

In November 1988 Milošević turned his attention to Kosovo. Demonstrations by Šolević were not the answer here because Serbs were in a minority. Albanians might feel that their local government was corrupt but they would not join a Serbian protest against it, so Milošević tried different tactics. On 17 November Serbia announced that the Kosovo parliament contained traitors and sacked the entire leadership, replacing it with Milošević loyalists.

The ethnic Albanian public in Kosovo reacted angrily and miners marched on the capital, Priština, joining with students to stage protests. Milošević responded by organising a demonstration of his own in Belgrade. His television put out the message that the Albanians in Kosovo were intent on gaining independence, and called on Serbs to protest to stop this. To make sure that there was a good attendance he instructed factory managers, the men he had appointed in that year's purges, to send their workers to the rally. The managers, wanting to show loyalty, did as they were told. Fleets of buses were assembled.

On 19 November 1988 tens of thousands of workers were driven to Belgrade, given sandwiches and drinks, and directed to make their protest in front of the federal parliament. Many needed little encouragement, believing the television propaganda that they must protest to protect Kosovo. Milošević made a speech, informing them that: 'Every nation has a love which warms its heart. For Serbia it is Kosovo.' The rally turned into an outpouring of nationalist sentiment, with one poet declaring 'The people have happened'.[18]

Milošević went a step further in February 1989, calling for a new constitution which would transfer the powers of the Kosovo parliament to Belgrade. Once more the Albanians protested, this time with the miners barricading themselves inside their mines to demand that the leaders sacked in November of the previous year be reinstated. The Albanian protest was supported by the leaders of the northern republic of Slovenia, which feared the growing power and xenophobia of Milošević's Serbia.

On 28 February Milošević replied to a demonstration in Kosovo with one of his own, busing tens of thousands of Serb workers to

Belgrade, with a near-hysterical Serbian Television claiming that not just the Kosovo Albanians but now also the Slovenes wanted independence from Yugoslavia. That night downtown Belgrade filled with Serbs who were instructed to surround the federal presidency. Milošević did not yet have control of the eight-man presidency, but he told the members that unless they sent the army into Kosovo province the demonstrators would not leave. The presidency members, nervous about the crowds outside, decided they had no option but to follow Milošević's instructions. The following day tanks were sent onto the streets of Priština, and the miners gave up their protest. A key Albanian leader, Azem Vllasi, was arrested and the resistance was crushed. On 28 March Serbia passed a new constitution that stripped the Kosovo and Vojvodina parliaments of most of their powers, transferring them to Belgrade. In Kosovo there was a day of rioting that left twenty-two Albanians and two Serb police officers dead. It was a last, desperate gesture by the Albanians, but it made no difference to the new law.

Milošević now controlled Montenegro and Serbia, and could pick four of the eight Yugoslav presidency members, one vote short of having total power. In May he installed himself as president of Serbia. A month later he decided to celebrate.[19]

In June 1989 Milošević organised a gigantic celebration of the 600th anniversary of the Battle of Kosovo. An enormous stage was erected at Gazimestan on the grassy plain that stretched south of the capital. A crowd of more than half a million Serbs came by train, bus and car from across Serbia, camping out in the bright sunshine in numbers not seen since the original battle. Milošević arrived by helicopter, to the roars of the crowd. Perhaps he reflected that less than two years before he had arrived in Kosovo to meet fifteen thousand Serbs shouting him down. Now he delivered a speech dripping with emotion, reminding his huge audience of the battle fought on this very soil 600 years before.

'Serbs in their history have never conquered or exploited others. The Kosovo heroism does not allow us to forget that, at one time, we were brave and dignified and one of the few who went into battle undefeated,' he boomed. 'Six centuries later, again we are in battles and quarrels. They are not armed battles, though such things should not be excluded yet.'[20]

Gazimestan was a defining moment for all Yugoslavia. For the Serbs, it seemed that they would be saved so long as they followed Milošević and stuck together, but other Yugoslav nations were worried. Bosnian Muslims, Croats, Macedonians and Slovenes all felt that they faced a grim choice: either live on in a Serb-dominated Yugoslavia or else push for independence, and possible war.

While other republics worried about the possibility of a war, Milošević spent the time after Gazimestan planning for one. The rally marked a high point in his career and a change in his direction. Until then, his rise to power had been based on the attempt to gain control of five of the eight presidential votes, thus enabling him to rule the country. But this campaign, and the Serb nationalism it whipped up, also had the effect of alienating the other Yugoslav nationalities. It was clear after Gazimestan that even if he could somehow grab a fifth presidency vote, Milošević would never be accepted by non-Serb Yugoslavs. In that case, his path seemed clear: to fall back on another, older plan to carve out a Greater Serbia within Yugoslavia.

The genesis of the Greater Serbia plan went right back to the Načertanije of the nineteenth century, and it followed a logic that any Serb could understand. If Yugoslavia could no longer serve the Serbs, then the Serbs must create a new state. Greater Serbia would include Serbia and Montenegro, plus large parts of the neighbouring republics of Bosnia and Croatia that were occupied by Serbs. Although a simple idea, it presented a serious problem. Serbs in Bosnia and Croatia lived side by side with other ethnic groups. The lands claimed by the Serbs contained more than two million non-Serbs. In the autumn of 1989 Milošević sat down to plan how to get rid of them.

'There will not be the kind of war that they would like,' Milošević's ally, army commander Veljko Kadijević confided in a meeting on 13 February 1990. 'But there will be the kind that there must be, one where we do not allow them to beat us.'[21]

The kind of war that was envisaged would not be one in which one army took on another. Instead, it would pit a Serb army against defenceless civilians, with the object of driving them out of territory claimed by the Serbs. This was a complex operation. Even against an unarmed population, it would still mean forcing more than two million people from their homes.

Milošević set about planning with care. His first priority for this operation was to ensure that when it succeeded he would be left in command. So he divided the operation into two separate command lines, both running back to himself. The first was through the army, and the second through the secret police. Officially, the Yugoslav army was multi-ethnic, so Milošević made private contact with Serb generals sympathetic to his point of view. Through late 1989 and into 1990 he held meetings with this group, termed the military line, and devised a plan which would later be dubbed 'ethnic cleansing' and which had the official name 'ram', meaning 'frame' in Serbian. The army would have the job of providing artillery support for the ethnic cleansing operations in Croatia and Bosnia.

He also recruited a career secret service officer, the wily Jovica Stanišić, to run the secret police line. Stanišić was appointed head of the State Security of Serbia, the equivalent of the secret service.[22] His task was more complicated than that of the army. First, he organised secret Serb groups inside Bosnia and Croatia. These were named Crisis Staffs, and their role was to rise up, at a given signal, and take control of towns and villages in Serb areas. They were to seize town halls, police barracks, main highways and broadcasting stations. Second, the Crisis Staffs were responsible for organising the deportation of the two million non-Serbs, which meant preparing in advance such tasks as the requisitioning of buses. Last, the Crisis Staffs prepared lists of important Croats and Muslims who would be arrested, making it difficult for their communities to organise resistance.

Stanišić also had the job of finding a third force to do the actual ethnic cleansing. While the army would provide the artillery, and the Crisis Staffs would take control of the towns, Stanišić would need another force operating on the simple premise that by torturing and murdering a minority of Croats and Muslims it should be possible to persuade the majority to flee. These men would need to be willing to exercise – even to enjoy – indiscriminate violence. For this force, Stanišić turned to the world of football.

The supporters' club of Yugoslavia's most famous team, Red Star Belgrade, was headed by a baby-faced gangster called Željko Ražnatović, nicknamed 'Arkan'. Arkan had had a colourful life. The son of an air force colonel, he had been recruited by Yugoslavia's Communist intelligence service in the 1970s to carry out assassinations of nationalist dissidents living abroad. In the late 1980s he was arrested in Sweden for robbery, but arranged to have a pistol smuggled into court on the day of his first appearance and used it to force his way out to freedom. Western Europe was by now too hot for him, so he returned home. In Belgrade, in the late 1980s, he was contacted by the Communist secret service. At that time the football terraces had become a popular place for nationalists to express their feelings, because it was hard for the police to stop massed ranks of fans from chanting nationalist slogans. Arkan was made chairman of the Red Star Belgrade supporters club, and given the task of weeding out nationalist activists and ensuring that the chanting stuck to the usual football repertoire.

Arkan also set himself up as a drug smuggler in Belgrade and Kosovo, and ran another business respraying cars stolen in Western Europe. He engaged in a complex series of deals with both Serb and Albanian mafias in Kosovo, and opened a pastry shop in Belgrade to act as a cover for his wealth. On paper, this was the world's most profitable patisserie.

In either 1989 or 1990, Stanišić told Arkan that instead of trying to beat the nationalists he should join them, and Arkan immediately agreed. He formed a private army named the Serbian Volunteer Guard, better known as the Tigers, which he recruited from among the Red Star fans.

Milošević's prosecutors would be frustrated time and time again when insiders among the secret police said that they had only ever received orders from Stanišić. Stanišić passed Milošević's orders on to two key secret servicemen, Franko Simatović, or 'Frenki', head of the State Security special operations department, and Radovan Stojičić, nicknamed 'Badža' after the villain in the Popeye cartoons. In 1990 the Yugoslav army seized large stocks of small arms from territorial army units in Bosnia and Croatia in order to prevent them falling into the hands of non-Serbs. Frenki and Badža then distributed these weapons, sometimes from the boots of cars, to the leaders of the Crisis Staffs. By the end of the year the Serbs had in effect two sleeping armies, one in Croatia and one in Bosnia, ready to seize control.[23]

Recruiting for these private armies was made easier because there was a very real fear among Serbs in Croatia and Bosnia of what might happen to them if Yugoslavia broke up. These fears were stoked in part by Milošević's own propaganda but also by the rise of nationalism among Croats and Muslims. In Croatia, a hardline nationalist party, the HDZ, campaigned for independence, with Croats having superior status to Serbs, and a return to the red and white chequerboard flag of the ancient Croatian kingdoms. In Bosnia, the HDZ formed branches among Croats in the south, agitating for union with Croatia. Meanwhile the Muslims formed the Muslim-only SDA, led by Alija Izetbegović, a dissident whose campaigning for Muslim rights had seen him jailed by Tito.

In September 1989 the Slovenes, alarmed by what had happened to the Albanians, declared that they would quit the Yugoslav federation if Serb nationalism was not reined in. The Slovene parliament voted itself the power to secede, while holding back from taking the actual step itself. Milošević reacted aggressively, sending his Kosovo rabble-rouser Šolević and his thugs to hold a protest rally in the Slovene capital, Ljubljana. Fearing a riot, Slovene police blocked the highways. Later, Milošević declared a boycott of Slovene goods in Serbian shops. This struck many Yugoslavs as absurd because most of the country's products were made in more than one republic. Nevertheless, the order went out and state shops in Serbia removed goods with Made in Slovenia stamped on them, sometimes dumping them in the street.

Tensions between Milošević and the Slovenes came to a head in January 1990 when the Yugoslav Communist party held its Fourteenth Congress in Belgrade. The Slovenes arrived in sombre mood. Their delegates proposed a series of amendments to the constitution designed to ensure equality, but were shouted down by Serbs. Deciding that their mission was hopeless, they abruptly got up and walked out. The Croatian delegation, feeling the same way, followed suit.

Milošević ran onto the Congress stage and urged the other delegates to continue with the conference. But confusion now reigned throughout the hall. Congress chairman Momir Bulatović called a 15-minute recess, but once outside the hall the delegates drifted away. The 15-minute pause, Bulatović reflected later, 'lasted through history'.[24]

The growing tensions within Yugoslavia were in contrast to events elsewhere in Eastern Europe, where in late 1989 Communist regimes were tumbling like dominoes. Popular demonstrations saw the Berlin Wall torn down and Hungary, East Germany, Poland, Czechoslovakia, Bulgaria and Romania throw off their Communist masters. The 1990s dawned with new hope right across the continent, with Yugoslavia as the conspicuous exception. In early 1990 the country was set for war. Instead, it got elections. In the spring, Slovenia and Croatia both voted in governments that seemed determined to claim independence. The Serbs in Croatia reacted that summer. Stanišić contacted the chief of the Crisis Staff in the town of Knin, Milan Babić.

Babić was a dentist who declared that he had a powerful reason for being a nationalist. In the back garden of his house near Knin there was a tree with a deep scar embedded in the bark. Babić would explain to visitors that during the Second World War local Croats had come to his house to kill his father, but finding that he had fled, they took out their fury on this tree. After the war Tito had compelled everyone to live side by side, but Babić's father showed his son the tree and said that it should serve as a warning of the true intentions of their neighbours.

In August 1990 Babić, supervised by Stanišić, and through him by Milošević, organised a referendum for Serbs living in Croatia to vote on what they would do if Croatia seceded from Yugoslavia. The result was not in doubt, with the Serbs sure to vote to split from the rest of Croatia. Croatia's government declared the intended vote illegal, then sent police to take control of Knin.

Knin sits amid craggy mountains which form a long range running down Croatia parallel to the Adriatic Sea. This region is called the Krajina, which means 'military zone', and was for centuries used by the Austrians as a buffer against the Turks. The Krajina Serbs were paid to guard this buffer zone and had grown up proud of this tradition of providing a Christian wall against the Muslim enemy. Now they prepared to face the other way, ready, as they saw it, to protect Serbia from a Croat attack.

Babić sent out unarmed Serb volunteers to stop the police. Lacking firearms, they cut trees to block the mountain roads leading to Knin in what was dubbed the 'Log Rebellion'. Croatia's president, Franjo Tudjman, was furious. He ordered police to get to Knin by helicopter. Milošević responded by getting contacts in the air force to scramble fighter jets. The fighters flew low over the helicopters, buffeting them in their slipstream, and threatened to shoot them down unless they turned back. By the end of the day, Babić, slightly to his surprise, was in charge of Knin.

In July 1990 Milošević formed the Serbian Socialist Party (SPS) out of the husk of the Serbian Communist party, taking care to install his placemen at all levels. In December, Serbia held the first fully democratic elections in its long, tortured history, electing the SPS as the largest party and Milošević as president.

By January of the following year Yugoslavia was edging towards disintegration, and the Serbs were not solely responsible. Croatian and Slovenian nationalists were also gradually taking control of their republics. Yet at this late hour a potential saviour of the nation came into the frame. He was Ante Marković, the Yugoslav prime minister. Marković was an experienced economist and now he proposed a series of reforms which, if enacted, would have drawn Yugoslavia back from the brink. The reform package was no more than the obvious route for a country in deep economic trouble.

As a first step, Marković renegotiated repayments of the US$21 billion national debt with Yugoslavia's foreign creditors. Next, he began an austerity programme to cut waste and mismanagement. It was a brave and sensible move, and for Milošević it was dangerous. His political support was based on an appeal to Serb emotions, rather than on practical ways in which the economy could be put on a sound footing. 'The programme was an obstacle to Milošević in his surge for absolute power,' Marković would later complain, when he finally broke a 12-year silence to give evidence at Milošević's trial in 2003.[25]

Milošević derailed the reforms in what Marković called the 'Crime of the Century'. Using his banking contacts, Milošević simply ordered the Yugoslav state bank to transfer the equivalent of 2.5 billion German marks from its coffers to the Serbian national bank. 'I immediately phoned Milošević and accused him of the robbery which he, of course, denied,' said Marković. 'I replied that there wasn't a single thing, not even a worthless thing, that could be done without his knowledge in Serbia, certainly not such a fundamental robbery.'[26]

This not only destroyed Marković's carefully balanced budget, but also gave Milošević a cash windfall. Some of the money was clawed back, but Milošević was left with one billion marks to pay his cronies and finance his military plans. Milošević was not Marković's only obstacle. By now, most of the republics had decided that Yugoslavia was finished. Slovenia and Croatia refused to pay the subsidies to the poorer republics on which the Marković plan depended. This was the final nail in the reformist coffin and Marković resigned in December 1991, by which time the war he had campaigned against had broken out.

Many ordinary Yugoslavs watched the deterioration of the country with alarm. An oft-repeated comment was that everyone at the time expected someone to 'step in' and halt the ever more hysterical war of words between the Serbs, Croats and Slovenes. But there was no one with authority left to intervene.

Yet, as the storm clouds gathered, the sons and daughters of Belgrade's middle classes made a stand. On 9 March 1991, without warning, Serbian students poured onto the streets of Belgrade to protest against Milošević's rush towards war. The protests were led by a writer named Vuk Drašković, who was once a key Serb nationalist voice but who in the early 1990s had distanced himself from the Milošević bandwagon. Instead, he now positioned himself in the liberal opposition camp, demanding an end to Milošević's control of state television and sections of the judiciary.

Milošević ordered riot police to attack, and soon the centre of Belgrade was full of sirens and tear gas. Drašković's supporters had brought batons and iron bars and fought against the police. Drašković was arrested and police raided two independent broadcasters, B-92 and Studio B. State television reported that the protestors, not the police, had been responsible for the violence.

The protestors returned to the streets the next day. This time, Milošević decided to summon the army. A meeting of the federal presidency was called and Milošević's four allies voted for the army to take to the streets. Other presidency members, worried by the riots, backed them. That night, troops from bases around Belgrade were deployed in the city centre.

The protesters quickly adapted their tactics. The following day female students were mobilised, racing up to the soldiers lined up near the federal presidency building to place flowers in their gun barrels, in an echo of American anti-Vietnam War protests of a generation before. The soldiers made it clear that they would not open fire on their own people, leaving the students once more in control of the streets.

Milošević decamped to an army base, and the Serbian presidency representative, Borisav Jović, again summoned the presidency. This time, Jović arranged for the presidency members to meet not in the presidency building but in an underground bunker at an army base outside Belgrade. Croatian presidency member Stipe Mesić jokingly asked if they had been arrested. They had not – only intimidated. Now Jović demanded that the presidency go further than it had on 10 March, and declare a full state of emergency, a move that would grant Milošević dictatorial powers to control Belgrade.

Jović and Milošević's other three presidency allies immediately voted in favour. The Slovenian member had stayed away, and the Croatian and Macedonian members said no. That meant a state of emergency could become law if the last member, a Bosnian Serb politician named Bogić Bogicević, voted with the pro-Milošević faction. Jović appealed to him as a fellow Serb to back Milošević, but Bogicević said he was a Yugoslav first, not a Serb, and refused to support the action. Jović was furious and stormed out of the meeting.

With the army unwilling to take control of the streets and the police unable to, Milošević decided he had no choice but to make concessions. He met with a delegation of students, then gave in to a raft of their demands, sacking his interior minister, four television editors, and the editor of his television propaganda machine, Dušan Mitević. Mitević was shocked, both by the sacking and by the fact that, once it was done, he was shunned by Milošević and his allies ever afterwards. He was the first in a long line of Milošević cronies to find that, once the man had no further use for them, they were simply abandoned. 'It was a very educational experience,' he ruminated later.[27]

Milošević's move worked and the students dispersed, believing they had won. In fact, they were to learn later that this was a hollow victory. Milošević remained in command of the Serb state. The independent broadcast stations B-92 and Studio B came back on line and Drašković was set free. A few days later Milošević took his revenge on the presidency, declaring that he would no longer recognise its decisions. 'Yugoslavia has entered into its final phase of agony. The Republic of Serbia will no longer recognise a single decision reached by the presidency under existing circumstances because it would be illegal.'[28]

In fact, the opposite was true. Milošević was tearing Serbia, Yugoslavia's most powerful component, out of the fabric of federal institutions for no better reason than that the legally constituted presidency had refused to follow his demands and declare a state of emergency. The move to war was now almost unstoppable, but there was one final thing Milošević needed to do, which was to arrange for the dismemberment of Bosnia-Hercegovina between himself and the Croatian republic's president Franjo Tudjman.

In late March 1991, in a moment of supreme cynicism, he met Tudjman at Karadjordjevo, a former hunting lodge of Tito's. Speculation that the two men agreed to carve up Bosnia between them was finally confirmed in 2003 when the former Yugoslav prime minister, Ante Marković gave evidence at Milošević's trial.[29] It went without saying that the two men recognised that Croatia would also break from Yugoslavia.

After the Milošević–Tudjman summit, extremists on both sides began pushing for war. In mid-April 1991, Tudjman's defence minister, Gojko Šušak, swapped his suit for camouflage and crept up on the Serb village of Borovo Selo late one night, firing three anti-tank rockets into the village centre. Nobody was killed but Serbs across Croatia were traumatised, seeing in the attack proof that Milošević's television propaganda had been correct. On 2 May, Croatia sent police to try to retake the village and twelve policemen were killed.

Croatian and Slovenian officials met in early June and decided to declare independence. Milošević told a meeting of Serbian mayors: 'I hope they won't be so crazy as to fight against us, because if we don't know how to work and do business, at least we know how to fight.'[30]

The first serious attempt by the West to intervene took place when on 22 June 1991 America's Secretary of State, James Baker, flew to Belgrade to try to head off the possibility of war. Baker gave mixed signals. First, he told Milošević that he would not accept the use of the army to prevent Croatia and Slovenia from seceding. Next, he told Croatia and Slovenia that America would not support their secession from Yugoslavia. The Croats and Slovenes were left confused, but decided that what this meant was that America would protect them from attack by the Serbs if they broke away. On 25 June 1991 both republics declared independence.

Slovene units were sent to occupy Yugoslav customs posts along their northern border with Austria. The same day, prime minister Marković ordered the Yugoslav army to retake these posts, seeing this as the only way to save the country. Milošević sat on the sidelines. His reasons must be guessed at, but they appear to have revolved around a calculation that there was no point in resisting the Slovenes. There were few Serbs living in Slovenia and the northern republic was not included in his Greater Serbia.

Marković's attempt to retake control in Slovenia was a fiasco. Army units seized the border posts, then found themselves being shot at by Slovene volunteer units. The army units were mostly composed of conscripts, in some cases local Slovenes who had no idea why they were fighting and no desire to die. Television pictures captured these teenage soldiers, frightened and crying, hiding behind their tanks as Slovene sniper bullets pinged off the hulls.

In the capital, Ljubljana, Slovene police units surrounded an army barracks. A federal helicopter tried to fly into the base and was shot down, only for the Slovenes to discover that the machine was carrying a cargo of bread for the trapped soldiers. Marković faced a choice between asking the presidency to launch a full scale invasion or giving up. He decided to stand down the army, and the Slovene war ended after ten days with forty-four federal soldiers killed. Milošević had remained on the sidelines. Now he prepared for a much more important conflict to begin in Croatia.

War came to Croatia not all at once but as a piecemeal process. By 25 June Serb and Croat villages had erected numerous roadblocks, and by the start of July shooting and sniping from these areas was common. In July Milošević gave orders, first to his military line – the Serb generals in the army – and then through Stanišić, to his secret police operatives. Some Crisis Staffs were already operating inside Croatia, making sure that local Croats in areas claimed by the Serbs were being rounded up.

In villages across the country, the Yugoslav army and Serb paramilitaries went into action. Typically, artillery would launch a short bombardment against a Croat village. Then Arkan's Tigers, or another paramilitary unit, would move in, shooting any Croats still offering resistance and rounding up the rest. The villagers would be deported, some might be shot, and the village itself looted and then burned.

The Tigers were not the only paramilitary unit in operation. Other Serb nationalist leaders formed their own armies and went to Croatia. Drašković dropped his liberal credentials from the March student protests and formed his own small unit, though it was not linked to war crimes. Another nationalist, Vojislav Šešelj, adopted the name of the Second World War royalist army, the Chetniks, for his own private army. The Chetniks and the Tigers were a contrast in styles. The Tigers were fit and smart, with short hair and tough discipline. Arkan trained his men to military standards, and punished drinking on duty with one-hundred lashes. The Chetniks dressed as they pleased, wore beards, were unfit and frequently drunk. For their victims, however, the two units were similar: neither took prisoners and both quickly established a reputation for casual violence. By 1994 the UN had identified eighty-four separate Serb paramilitary formations.

On 4 October 1991 a unit of Arkan's Tigers shot dead twenty-eight Croat civilians at a police station in Dalj, in eastern Croatia, then dumped the bodies in the Danube.[31] On 18 October a mixed group of army and paramilitary soldiers forced a group of fifty-one Croat civilians, who had been used as forced labourers to dig trenches, to run through a minefield. A total of twenty-one Croats ran over mines and were killed, or were shot soon afterwards when the Serb soldiers opened fire on the group.[32] The Serbs, however, were not alone in carrying out atrocities. In eastern Croatia, hardline Croat nationalists rounded up one-hundred-and-sixty prominent Serbs, including doctors and politicians, and shot them. Fighting escalated over a broad front stretching across the crescent that forms Croatia. West of Belgrade, drivers could see villages on either side of the motorway to the Croatian capital, Zagreb, now blackened ruins. In late August the army, which until then had clung on to the pretence of being a federal institution, went over to the Serbs and the fighting began in earnest.

Croatian villages that held out were flattened, the army opened an offensive on the town of Vukovar, a strategic post because it was on the River Danube. The attack went badly, with unmotivated conscripts sent in to fight against under-equipped but highly motivated Croats. The

Croats, who were local men, used the sewers to move around under the streets, popping up in the rear of Serb units and pouring fire into their backs before disappearing again. Arkan's Tigers were thrown into the battle and ordered to pour cement into the sewer junctions to cut the Croat lines.

During October a new front was opened when the Serbs attacked Dubrovnik, and suddenly the West took notice. Dubrovnik was a world heritage site and many Western Europeans had been there on holiday. This front was led by units from Montenegro, the traditional ally of the Serbs. They attacked the hinterland around the city, burning a string of holiday hotels. Dubrovnik airport was a popular target for looting. Journalists watched drunken Montenegrin soldiers wheeling away their loot in the airport luggage carts.[33] TV pictures showed Serb shells hammering into holiday yachts and historic buildings, and world opinion turned against Milošević. Economic sanctions against the Serbs were announced.

The battle for Vukovar had meanwhile developed into a Balkan Stalingrad. Among the unhappy discoveries made by Serb generals was that modern concrete buildings could not be easily shattered by artillery. One shell could make only one small hole in a structure. To pulverise a building took days. The Yugoslav army began to fall apart, with whole units of conscripts deserting the front. One conscript showed his anger at the senseless war by driving his armoured personnel carrier away from the town, down the highway to Belgrade, and all the way to the steps of the federal parliament, where he left it abandoned. Later, a new play called *Dark Is the Night* was put on in Belgrade and played to packed houses, dramatising the dilemma facing the city's middle classes over whether to send their sons to die in this war.

As the two sieges ground on, world opinion turned ever more against the Serbs. There was talk of further UN sanctions, even murmurings about armed intervention. In November, Vukovar, a town now largely reduced to rubble, finally fell. Some streets had been hit with so many thousands of bullets that the surviving walls looked pebble-dashed.

Yugoslav army units entered the battered city hospital and found two hundred Croats, sheltering there, some of them wounded. The Croats were marched out of the town and handed over to Šešelj's Serb paramilitaries. They took them to a village called Ovcara, lined them up, and shot them.

In Belgrade, Milošević seemed to understand that there was no point in continuing the war. The Serbs had taken all the territory in Croatia that they were likely to get, approximately one third of the total area. Now the war needed to be brought to a halt.

Since the fighting in Slovenia in June international envoys had been urging peace, and now Milošević decided to choose a peace plan. The best one he could find, in November 1991, was that prepared by a UN envoy, the US diplomat Cyrus Vance. On paper, the Vance plan showed the UN at its most noble. It required Croats and Serbs to stop fighting, accept a UN buffer force to be inserted along the front line, and then to commence peace talks regarding a final settlement. Milošević quickly saw that this plan could be used to cement the gains of the summer: if the Serbs accepted it, the UN would in effect be guaranteeing Serb control of the areas they had ethnically cleansed. Talks could be spun out indefinitely, as was the case with Cyprus which the UN had been patrolling since a 1974 ceasefire between Greek and Turkish forces. Croatia was too weak to offer any resistance to the Vance plan.

Croatian Serb leader Milan Babić, however, rejected the plan, saying that the Serbs should accept nothing less than international recognition of the territory as independent, which he wanted to be guaranteed by the army of the Yugoslav state. Milošević, keen to get the war over, invited Babić to Belgrade and tried to persuade him to change his mind. When this failed, Milošević contacted the Knin police chief, Milan Martić, who agreed to support him. A meeting of the parliament of the self-proclaimed Serb Republic of Krajina was held, without Babić present, and the members, aware of their dependence on Milošević's largesse, voted to accept the peace plan. The war of 1991 came to an end in December.

By the end of 1991, Milošević could feel satisfied. He had initiated a war, and that war had gone to plan, if not quite to timetable, with the Serbs, about one tenth of Croatia's population, now holding one third of its territory. Now it was time to turn to Bosnia.

For Milošević, Bosnia was a much more formidable operation than Croatia. The area to be taken under control was four times the size of Croatia. The territory contained mountains, forests and ravines. It was ideal territory for guerrilla fighters and had been the operating area for Tito's partisans in the Second World War. From Milošević's point of view, any campaign would have to seize a huge area of territory very quickly, before Muslims and Croats could organise resistance.

By early 1992 the Serbs in Bosnia were braced for war. The Yugoslav army, now dominated by hardline Serb generals and under Milošević's command, was deployed in strength across the republic. The Serb Crisis Staffs were organised in towns throughout Bosnia, ready to take control of their designated areas when the command was given. The paramilitary units of Arkan had returned to Belgrade and were hungry for more action. And the spark to commence the war had also been struck, oddly enough, by the European Community.

In November of the previous year, Germany had recognised the independence of Croatia and Slovenia, ripping a hole in the idea of a common foreign policy for the European Community. Europe's diplomats scrambled to patch things up, agreeing that they would recognise the right of any of the Yugoslav republics to leave the mother state, provided that there was a simple majority in a referendum. In the winter of 1991–2 the EC proposed a series of referendums, most of which would have been foregone conclusions. The Slovenes and Croatians confirmed their secession, while Serbia and Montenegro chose to stay inside Yugoslavia. The southern republic of Macedonia also voted to secede and the Serbs let it go – there were few Serbs in Macedonia.

By early 1992, all attention was focused on Bosnia. The country was almost equally divided between Croats, Muslims and Serbs. The fighting in Croatia the previous year had left the republic very tense. Croat and Muslim leaders campaigned for a vote for independence, believing that the outside world would not allow Serbia to attack a sovereign country. The Serbs, seeing this, were nervous about living in a state where they would be in a minority.

The EC had plenty of warning about the trouble that was to come when local Serbs formed a Bosnian version of the SPS under the leadership of Radovan Karadžić, former psychiatrist of Sarajevo Football Club, convicted fraudster and a self-proclaimed poet. In October 1991 he warned Muslims in Bosnia's parliament against any moves towards independence. 'You want to take Bosnia-Hercegovina down the same highway of hell and suffering that Slovenia and Croatia are travelling.'[34]

On 9 January 1992 the SPS proclaimed the formation of a Bosnian Serb republic. The EC, however, was trapped inside its own logic and pressed ahead with its vote. On the weekend of 29 February–1 March Bosnians went to the polls. The Serbs, knowing they would lose the vote, boycotted the referendum and the Croats and Muslims voted overwhelmingly for separation.

On Sunday, 1 March, a sniper, presumably a Muslim, shot dead the father of the groom of a Serbian wedding party in Sarajevo city centre. Barricades were thrown up by Serbs around much of the city. Karadžić declared: 'We warned what would happen in the event of demands for an independent Bosnia-Hercegovina. Northern Ireland would be like a holiday camp compared to Bosnia.'[35]

A hurried round of talks between Serbs and Muslims and Croats on 3 March lowered the tension and the barricades came down. The result of the vote was published, giving the expected massive majority for independence.

On 6 April the EC and the United States recognised Bosnia as an independent state, and this proved the signal for war. Four days before, Arkan and his Tigers had moved into Bosnia, taking control, with the aid of the local Serb Crisis Staff, of the north-eastern town of Bijeljina. He achieved this by the simple expedient of shooting Muslims in the streets, thus clearing the town at once. His men disarmed the police and the local Crisis Staff grabbed the radio station and police stations. This was crucial because the town was a key bottleneck for the bringing of military hardware into Bosnia from Yugoslavia.

Bosnia's new president, Alija Izetbegović, assumed that this was some sort of ethnic confrontation and asked a Serb presidency member, Biljana Plavšić, from the SPS, to go to Bijeljina to try to mediate. Plavšić, a biology professor at Sarajevo University, drove to the town, sought out Arkan and then, with television cameras recording the scene, stepped up to kiss the warlord on the cheek.

With that kiss, the scales fell from the eyes of Muslims and Croats, and they understood at last – and far too late – that the Serbs of Bosnia were operating to a plan. There was no point in the Muslims or anybody else trying to placate the Serb leadership, because the Serb leadership was intent on war.

In Sarajevo a huge demonstration of Croats, Serbs and Muslims paraded through the streets to the parliament building to call for peace. Serb snipers based in the nearby Holiday Inn opened fire on the crowd, which scattered. Izetbegović had only one armed force, the Green Berets, a Muslim militia, and now they stormed the hotel, taking control and arresting the Serbs. Muslim militias then spread out across the city centre. Besides the Green Berets, these were made up of two forces: the city police and local gangsters. The cops and robbers joined together and spread out a thin defensive cordon around the city centre.

Karadžić, now operating from Pale, a village in the nearby hills near to the 1984 Olympics ski resort of Jahorina, ordered an attack on the city. Serb units of the former Yugoslav army drove into Sarajevo in armoured vehicles. But the attack was badly coordinated. Muslim volunteers with rocket launchers disabled the leading armoured personnel carrier of one column, causing a traffic jam, and the other vehicles retreated. The operation to grab Sarajevo had been botched, and Karadžić would spend the rest of the war outside the city looking in. But he took his revenge with artillery placed in the mountains. The guns were commanded by a rotund general named Ratko Mladić, a former colonel in the Yugoslav army who was now appointed commander of the new Bosnian Serb army. Mladić's father had been a partisan in the Second World War and was killed storming a position held by pro-German Croats. Now Mladić showed his nationalist colours. A radio intercept later captured his orders to begin bombarding Sarajevo:

'General Mladić here.'

'Yes, sir.'

'Don't panic. What's your name?'

'Vukasinović.'

'Colonel Vukasinović?'

'Yes, sir.'

'Shell the presidency and the parliament. Shoot at slow intervals until I order you to stop. Target Muslim neighbourhoods – not many Serbs live there.'

'Look at all the smoke.'

'Shell them until they're on the edge of madness.'[36]

The artillery commander did as he was told. The Serbs had failed to capture Sarajevo, but they took out their frustration with an indiscriminate barrage that would hammer the city for nearly four years, leaving eleven-thousand dead, including twelve-hundred children.

In southern Bosnia, Serb forces failed to hold the country's second city, Mostar, with a Croat–Muslim force blasting its way in to push Serb units out. Elsewhere, the Serb plan went more smoothly. Crisis Staffs in dozens of towns quickly took control from the surprised local authorities. The Yugoslav army was officially withdrawn from Bosnia, but handed over its equipment to the new Bosnian Serb army. And now the paramilitaries set to work.

Ethnic cleansing came to the Muslim village of Prhovo, in north-west Bosnia, on 26 May 1992. On that day, according to a farmer who appeared in The Hague as protected witness Bt-77, a unit of armed Serb farmers, led by two brothers, arrived in the village and demanded that the Muslims hand over any hunting guns. When they did so, the Serbs set fire to one of the sixty houses that made up Prhovo, then marched out.

Not knowing what else to do, and hearing radio reports of fighting in the area, the villagers stayed where they were. A few days later they saw pillars of fire from the direction of two neighbouring villages. Then one morning a shell slammed into a field near one of the houses. The villagers came out of their houses, and minutes later Serb soldiers in black balaclavas arrived in the village.

The soldiers separated the men from the women, and a list of men was produced and the names called out, one by one. Each man was taken round behind the village, then they heard someone shout 'Run'. A few moments after that there was a single shot. Panic seized the villagers, but there was nothing they could do. One by one, the terrified men were called out and led away. Eleven times the procedure was repeated. Then the rest of the men were ordered to form a column and marched out of the village, where they now saw their eleven friends lying dead by the road.

Then someone called out the name of Bt-77. He was ordered to step out of the line, take out his documents, put them on the ground, and then take off his jacket. He did as he was told. A soldier seemed about to take aim with his rifle but then another soldier, a man the witness thinks must have been a schoolfriend, shouted 'Don't hurt him'.

Spared from execution, Bt-77 rejoined the rest of the men and they were marched away down a road. At a nearby junction some Serb soldiers were struggling with a truck that had got stuck in a ditch. Bt-77 and four neighbours were ordered to push it out. But the wheels were jammed tight and they could not move it. They walked back towards the road and one Serb soldier, furious, opened fire on them. Three men were killed, one wounded, but Bt-77 was untouched. The Serb who fired had also hit and killed a Serb soldier. The Serb commander shouted that one of his men should go back to the village and kill any men still there. As Bt-77 was marched away with the survivors, he heard gunfire and then explosions from the direction of Prhovo.

As the men marched, their guards kicked at them and hit them with their rifle butts. They came to a Serb village, and as they marched through it some Serb women came out and began shouting that they were 'Balia', a Serbian insult for Muslims.

On the far side of the village, they were ordered off the road and into a field and told to take off their shoes and strip to the waist. The men put their shoes into a bag and left it under a tree. Then they were told to form a group and, when they were assembled, their Serb guards suddenly levelled their weapons and opened fire. Bt-77 threw himself to the ground.

After less than half a minute the firing stopped and the Serb commander shouted for anyone left alive to stand up. Fourteen men did so. Then a discussion began among the Serbs, with the commander saying 'fourteen was too many, it was not enough for revenge'.[37] Bt-77 had no idea what the commander meant. He then demanded that the two youngest Muslims step forward. These men, Senad Hadzić and Ismet Mesić, did as they were told, and were both shot by a Serb soldier with a pistol. They marched on and their unprotected feet soon became bloody from the hard tarmac, while their throats were parched from lack of water.

In the evening they reached a small municipal building in another village, were taken inside and had their hands tied behind their backs with wire. A Serb soldier told them they would all be shot in the morning. Inside the building other Muslims were also gathered. None of the twelve men could sleep. One of their number, an elderly man, died in the night from beatings he had sustained on the march.

In the morning, instead of being shot, the men with Bt-77 were ordered into a van and driven to the town of Ključ where they were led to a school gym. Inside there were about five hundred other prisoners, and the walls were smeared with blood. After waiting there for much of the day, they were moved to another school building nearby and finally given water and a salami sandwich. They stayed in this school for five days, without being told why they were being held, and were then marched on. This time their destination was a large detention camp which had been built at Manjaca.

From Bijeljina, Arkan's Tigers drove south on 9 April 1992, arriving in another strategic town, Zvornik, which was on the Drina River border with Serbia. They were joined here by Šešelj's Chetniks, but met resistance from lightly armed Muslims. Yugoslav army artillery was set up on the far river bank and blasted the city. Then the paramilitaries moved in. Civic leaders were arrested, using lists provided by the Crisis Staff, and either shot or deported to prison camps. The rest of the Muslim population was told to stay at home and await transport out of Bosnia.[38]

Next, Serb units headed south, arriving at the small town of Foca, where the Crisis Staff had already seized control. There was no fighting, and once more the Muslim population was quickly rounded up. Men were separated from women and put into camps. Many of the women were kept in a school gym.

The paramilitaries reached Visegrad in late April. The town's bridge was made famous in a novel, *Bridge Over the Drina*, by Nobel-prize winning Yugoslav author Ivo Andrić. For centuries the Muslim and Serb communities had lived separate, but interwoven, lives. Serb army units took control of the bridge, and many Muslims fled into the hills.

A paramilitary unit went after them, rounding them up and gathering two hundred civilians into a clearing. They feared the worst when a helicopter appeared and landed nearby. A Yugoslav army major got out and demanded to know what the paramilitaries were doing with the civilians. The paramilitary commander was non-committal, so the major ordered him not to harm the civilians and to escort them back to Visegrad, warning that he would check later that this had happened. Bemused, the Muslims were taken back to their homes.

This move undoubtedly saved many lives. For two weeks the Muslims lived in a state of fear in the town, with Serb units holding the Drina River bridge. Many Muslims slipped away before the paramilitaries got the green light from the Bosnian Serb authorities to move in and kill them.

The campaign took place amid great brutality. The commander of a Zvornik prison camp forced Muslim fathers and sons to perform oral sex with each other. Tiring of the game, he then told several to bite off the other men's penises. In Foča, local Serbs installed the Muslim women in a sports hall and the emptied houses, and turned them into sex slaves over the months that followed. Girls as young as twelve were raped, some were later killed, and several women were raped repeatedly for many weeks. In Visegrad, two Serbian cousins drove around the town with a list of prominent Muslims. These people were arrested at gunpoint, driven in the cousins' red VW Passat to the famous Drina bridge, and made to stand on the parapet. Then they were shot and their bodies thrown into the water.

Meanwhile, a second arm of the ethnic cleansing operation pushed out westwards across northern Bosnia. As with the southern arm, the progress of the paramilitary units was assisted by the Crisis Staffs who had already seized a swathe of towns. Resistance was minimal and Muslims, fearing they would be killed, were only too ready to hand over money and cars. Arkan would later open a transport company in Belgrade with trucks stolen from Muslim firms.

In each town, the campaign followed an almost identical routine. Serb artillery would throw a few shells into the town to frighten the people. Then the paramilitaries would come in. Milošević's war crimes indictment lists crimes of extermination – the killing of people on the basis of their ethnicity or nationality – by Bosnian Serb forces in thirty-three separate towns or municipalities – a list that reads like a tour guide to the towns of northern and eastern Bosnia.[39]

In the north and west of Bosnia, Serb units encountered a new problem. There were too many people to be deported. Hundreds of thousands of Muslims were instructed to stay in their homes and show white flags until buses could be found to deport them.

The paramilitary units became drunk with their own power. One woman, who was fifteen at the time, described how Arkan's men had arrived at her village near Brčko. They had marched the Muslims from the locality into one village. Then the men were separated from the women. The men were driven off to death or deportation. The women were gathered into six buses. The woman's mother feared her daughter would be raped, so she covered her face in dirt from the floor of the bus, and an old woman lent her a shawl and scarf so that she might be mistaken for an old lady. For several days the buses remained parked outside a wood, with the women allowed off only to urinate. The Serbs provided neither food nor water. Every few hours Serb soldiers came onto the bus and selected a teenaged girl who was taken into the woods and raped.

Eventually, the buses were driven into a darkened Muslim village, already cleansed and empty. The women were ordered off the buses and lined up. Now there was no way for the woman's mother to hide her daughter and, being tall and blonde, she was quickly selected and taken to a nearby house. The door had already been forced by a previous paramilitary unit and she was taken inside and upstairs to a ransacked bedroom. She was told to undress and then raped on the bed by one soldier. Afterwards he went downstairs and another, younger soldier came in and raped her. He was followed by a third soldier, before the first man returned, told her to dress, and took her downstairs. Outside, the rape victims were brought back and all the women were ordered onto the buses.[40]

By the middle of May 1992, a rough front line had formed across Bosnia. The Muslims and Croats had not collapsed, but had formed scratch units which held on to Sarajevo and a thumb-shaped piece of territory anchored on Bosnia's southern border with Croatia. The Serbs held about two thirds of the country.

The ethnic cleansing operation had been a success, with Serbian artillery, Crisis Staffs and paramilitary units working well together. In late May, Serb commanders began to remove all traces of Croat and Muslim presence in Bosnia, dynamiting Catholic churches and hundreds of mosques. In Banja Luka, the authorities blew up all the mosques, then bulldozed the ruins flat and turned several sites into car parks. The whole country was a seething cauldron of human misery. American satellite photographs from the period sometimes showed what looked like a view of the night sky sprinkled with stars – in fact they were the campfires of Muslim refugees who had fled to the forests.

However, despite their success in grabbing territory, the Serb planners had not anticipated how much time it would take to move nearly two million Croats and Muslims, even when those people were living in terror. The Crisis Staffs could not mobilise enough buses to drive the refugees away. The practice of telling communities to stay at home with white flags draped from their windows was widespread.

The Serbs were presented with the problem of what to do with the Muslim and Croat menfolk. If they deported them, they could join the army of the Bosnian government, which had not collapsed but was instead determined to fight. The Serbs decided that it would be better to keep these men captive than set them loose to fight a war of revenge. Improvised holding camps had been set up in the earliest days of ethnic cleansing to gather up the Muslims and Croats. Now they took on a permanent air.

Conditions in the camps quickly deteriorated as a result of overcrowding. The soldiers charged with guarding the prisoners were poorly paid and resented their work. With a shortage of guards, Serb commanders were happy to accept the sadists and perverts that any society includes, who gravitated to the camps for the chance to indulge themselves on utterly defenceless men. Typical was Duško Tadić, a café owner and former karate instructor living near the town of Prijedor. He volunteered to be a part-time guard at the Omarska camp. One of his predilections was to set off fire extinguishers inside the mouths of Muslim prisoners, rupturing their lungs.

In his cynical exploitation of the insecurities of a nation under stress, Milošević had much in common with Bismarck, the nineteenth-century German chancellor. Like Milošević, Bismarck was an opportunist who took advantage of a time of chaos to seize control of a troubled state. Like Milošević, Bismarck was happy to launch wars to further his own career. The two men differed predominantly in their attitude to guilt.

Bismarck unleashed three wars, and chose to tour his battlefields to see the horrors that followed. It did not stop him ordering further battles, but it made him uneasy. Back in Berlin, he wrote to a friend: 'From this window I look down on the Wilhelmstrasse and see many a cripple who looks up and thinks that if that man up there had not made that wicked war I should be at home, healthy and strong.'[41]

Milošević never toured his battlefields. If he harboured any feelings of guilt or remorse, like those felt by Bismarck, he kept them to himself.

New World Disorder 4

Now we can see a new world. A world in which there is a very real prospect of a New World Order. A world where the United Nations, freed from Cold War stalemate, is poised to fulfil the historic vision of its founders.
President George Bush, speech to US Congress, 6 March 1991

There was ferocious activity on Wall Street in 1989. Young lawyers were making fortunes in the business of mergers and acquisitions. Jim O'Brien, however, was not one of them. On graduating from Yale Law School, inspired by a high-minded professor and keen to do some good in the world, he had joined the State Department.

After working in different departments, O'Brien was given a unique job as head of war crimes. This was a one-man operation and he was tasked with advising on legal issues involving Status of Forces Agreements. Like their acronym, SOFAs were regarded by many in the foreign service as a comfortable backwater, involving sorting out legal tangles over who had jurisdiction when servicemen and women got into trouble overseas. The work was uninspiring. O'Brien's chief perk was having an office window that looked down on the internal State Department courtyard, where he could gaze on young women sipping drinks in the summer months.

O'Brien's friends called up from Wall Street telling him what he was missing out on. His then-girlfriend was making big money handling leveraged buyouts and advised him to drop his idealism and think about doing the same. In October 1989 he watched the fall of the Berlin Wall on television and a black cloud descended. 'I remember thinking that the most interesting thing that will happen in my time in government has happened,' he told me when we spoke in Washington.

In August 1990 Iraq invaded Kuwait and an international coalition, led by the United States, was mobilised to go to war to push the Iraqis back. British prime minister Margaret Thatcher called for the Iraqi dictator, Saddam Hussein, to face the same justice the Nazis had faced after the Second World War, at a Nuremberg-style war crimes court.[1] American president George Bush echoed that call, and plans for an Iraq war crimes court were drawn up by Germany. Early in 1991 the US-led coalition pushed Iraqi forces out of Kuwait, but the prospect of a war crimes court faded because there was no way to arrest Hussein short of invading Iraq. The war ended with President Bush proclaiming that a 'New World Order' had come into being. The decades of stalemate between the two nuclear superpowers were at an end, and instead the world could look forward to a bright future in which America would take the lead in opposing aggression. Bush declared: 'The Gulf War put this New World to its first test, and, my fellow Americans, we passed that test.'[2] Perhaps, after all, O'Brien had made the right choice by opting to work for America's foreign service in this bright new era.

In June 1991 a new war exploded on the world's television screens, this time in Yugoslavia. Media reports spoke of atrocities committed against civilians, and O'Brien was tasked with reporting on America's legal position regarding possible war crimes prosecutions. The United States, in common with most of the world's democracies, was a signatory to the Geneva Conventions and the Genocide Convention, both of which meant, in theory at least, that America could hold war crimes trials in its domestic courts. O'Brien dutifully wrote reports commenting on the laws that could be invoked in the unlikely event that a Balkan warlord might arrive on United States territory and therefore fall within American legal jurisdiction.

The war crimes issue faded from sight in December 1991 when the United Nations arranged a ceasefire for Croatia. In April 1992, however, fresh fighting broke out in Bosnia, and once more media reports about atrocities flooded in. This time the scale of the violence seemed much greater than the year before. Bosnian Serb forces launched waves of attacks against hundreds of thousands of civilians.

Refugees were arriving in the West with stories of murder, rape and torture on a grand scale. Television news broadcast pictures of the indiscriminate shelling of Sarajevo. Bosnian Serb commanders were not shy about declaring that their aim was to 'purify' Serb land by expelling Croats and Muslims. They began to refer to their campaign as 'ethnic cleansing'. It was language last heard in Europe fifty years before, and O'Brien waited expectantly for America to make good its pledge to defend the New World Order.

However, America's reaction to the slaughter in Bosnia in the spring of 1992 was very different from its reaction to the Iraqi invasion of Kuwait in 1990. The White House issued strong condemnations of the Serb violence and demanded that the fighting stop, but when the Bosnian Serbs ignored this criticism America made no threats of military intervention.

For the US administration, the problem with the fighting in Bosnia was that this was a civil war, not the invasion of one country by another. While the Bosnian Serbs were getting a great deal of help from Yugoslavia, it was nevertheless their war, and they could not be 'pushed back' out of the country in the way that Iraqi forces had been forced from Kuwait in 1991. The Pentagon in particular was nervous about any kind of military intervention. It was true that air strikes could silence the Serb shelling of Sarajevo, and a ground invasion could certainly smash the Bosnian Serb forces, but the American generals worried about what would come next. To prevent the fighting starting up again, they felt that they would need to retain a large force on the ground. Another worry was that American bombing that targeted Serb forces might encourage Croat and Muslim forces to counter-attack, possibly even carrying out reprisals against Serb civilians. What, then, should America do? Should it respond by bombing the Muslims as well?

A military campaign to smash the Serbs would not be easy because the terrain was one of forests and mountains. American planners worried that in such a scenario Serb forces could adopt the guerrilla tactics that they had used so successfully against the Germans in the Second World War. Above all, they worried that their forces would be sucked into an interminable conflict, a second Vietnam War. Britain, which had been fighting a low-level war with separatist guerrillas in Northern Ireland, and France with its memories of fighting, and losing, against guerrilla armies in Algeria and Vietnam, experienced the same apprehension. American anxieties about the long-term problems of launching a military intervention were summed up two years later by the Democrat Defense Secretary, William Perry, when he said: 'If air strikes are Act One of a new melodrama, what is Act Two? What is Act Three? What is the conclusion?'[3] America knew that air strikes would only solve the immediate problem in Bosnia.

While this caution among Pentagon planners was understandable, what followed was hugely controversial. America, Britain and France spearheaded a UN Security Council resolution that imposed an arms embargo on the Former Yugoslavia. This was intended to starve all the combatants of weapons in order to lessen the fighting. The Bosnian Serb forces, however, already had plenty of weapons, supplied by the Yugoslav army, and did not need arms imports. The effect was simply to starve the Bosnian government, which had no army, of the means to defend itself. 'I completely agree with Mr Bush's statement that American boys should not die for Bosnia,' said Bosnian president Alija Izetbegović, marooned in his shell-shattered capital in June 1992. 'We have hundreds and thousands of able and willing men ready to fight. But unfortunately they have the disadvantage of being unarmed. We need weapons.'[4]

Journalists covering the slaughter faced the same question from Bosnians day after day: why was the West not helping? Instead of stopping the war, the UN was refusing either to fight for Bosnia or to allow Bosnia to arm herself. Legally, the Security Council was on shaky ground, as UN law compelled the organisation either to defend a member that had come under attack or at least not to deny it the means of defence.[5]

A few voices in America's Republican administration were raised against the embargo policy, notably that of Senator Robert Dole, who demanded intervention. He had visited the Balkans and felt that the

Pentagon's fears of the capabilities of the Serb forces were overstated. 'I knew the Serbs, and they bore no resemblance to the Vietnamese Communists. Theirs wasn't a holy crusade, theirs was a land-grab. They were weekend warriors and many of them were drunk a lot of the time.'[6] Dole pushed for a policy called 'lift and strike', the idea being to lift the arms embargo and use air strikes to silence the Bosnian Serb artillery. However, the US government was adamant that America would stay out of the war.

O'Brien watched all this with incredulity, wondering where President Bush's 1991 promise of a New World Order had gone. Many State Department officials felt angry at their administration's inaction. One official, Tom Westen, was an analyst in the same building, working for the Bureau of Intelligence and Research. Day after day, photos of horrors and atrocities arrived on his desk. Some stories he struggled to believe. One was a newspaper account of Serb paramilitaries who raped a nine-year-old Muslim girl in front of her parents. She was left lying in a pool of blood on one side of a fence while her parents watched, helpless, on the other side. The soldiers refused to let them help their daughter and she died two days later. Westen could believe the story only when he saw a second report of the same incident.[7]

Westen's intelligence gave him the eerie feeling of being able to predict future atrocities. 'We could see the attacks coming by watching our computer screens,' he said. 'We knew exactly what the Bosnian Serbs were going to do next... You just sat there, waited for it to happen and dutifully reported it up the chain.'[8]

The problem for O'Brien was, what could an idealistic junior lawyer in the State Department do to make things better? He kept writing memos about America's duties under the Genocide and Geneva Conventions to prosecute any warlords who happened to come there. In August 1992, with the slaughter now entering its fifth month, the Human Rights group Helsinki Watch published a 359-page report listing thousands of individual atrocities in the Bosnian war, almost all of them committed by Bosnian Serb forces. The report condemned the US government's stance as 'inert, inconsistent and misguided'.[9]

America's politicians may have decided that, in the absence of public demonstrations, there was no real appetite for military intervention. During the Vietnam War, tens of thousands of protesters had marched through Washington. During the Bosnian conflict, however, protests were rare. Opinion polls showed that the public was concerned, but not concerned enough, apparently, to go out and demonstrate. In Britain, some generals at least felt that growing public support for intervention would drain away if British troops started to get killed.

One of the few demonstrations in support of the Bosnian Muslims in Washington that summer was staged by American Jews, angry that the outside world was ignoring the slaughter. The decision of Jews to support Muslims, despite tensions in the Middle East, was heartening to State Department officials, yet it made no difference to the Bush administration's decision to stay firmly out of the war.

In late July 1992 reports began to appear in the media about Serb-operated prison camps inside Bosnia. One of the first was brought out by a Muslim man who had been freed from a camp and had escaped from Bosnia with the aid of a Serb Orthodox priest. At that time US journalist Roy Gutman managed, in the company of the Red Cross, to visit a detention camp at Manjaca. He reported for *New York Newsday* that the Serbs were holding thousands of innocent Croat and Muslim men in grim conditions. Food was sparse, beatings were common. Most disturbing were quotes from some of the prisoners who claimed that conditions were far worse at another camp, at Omarska, near the town of Prijedor.

In Washington, Gutman's story caused a media sensation and later earned the journalist a Pulitzer Prize. US officials, however, stuck to the line that the Bosnian war was too complex for America to intervene. Some government spokesmen tried to muddy the waters by suggesting that, despite the one-sided nature of Serb ethnic cleansing, it was in fact only the latest episode in an inter-ethnic conflict that stretched back for centuries. 'It's tragic, but the Balkans have been a hotbed of conflict . . . for centuries,' Defense Secretary Dick Cheyney told CNN.[10]

Media pressure for intervention intensified in the last days of July and State Department spokesman Richard Boucher, asked about the

Bosnian Serb camps, said: 'I should also note that we have reports that the Bosnians and Croatians also maintain detention centres'. The following day, Assistant Secretary of State for Europe Tom Niles stood before Congress and contradicted Boucher, saying that the statement of the day before had been wrong because the administration had no certain information on any camps operated by Serbs or anybody else. Congressman Tom Lantos, a Holocaust survivor, stood up and waved a copy of the *New York Times* which carried Boucher's statement. 'Either Mr Boucher is lying or you are lying,' he thundered. 'We are not going to read Boucher's statement in the *New York Times* and listen to you testify to the exact opposite.'

In fact, the US government had received reports of camps in May 1992 but had chosen not to disclose them, fearing that public opinion might demand military action. On 6 August 1992 television pictures of the Omarska and Trnopolje camps were aired on British television, triggering a fresh media outcry. President Bush gave a press conference, expressing shock at news about these camps and demanding that they be closed. But he stopped short of threatening action against the Serbs. Opinion polls in America in the days that followed showed support for air strikes against the Bosnian Serbs jump from 35 to 53 per cent.

The drive to impose some sort of accountability for war crimes began that month. On 13 August 1992 the UN Security Council passed a resolution ordering all parties to 'desist from all breaches of humanitarian law'.[11] The Council also announced a conference, to be held in London at the end of the month, to look afresh at the war in Bosnia.

On 18 August France's minister for humanitarian affairs, Dr Bernard Kouchner, led a delegation to visit the camps and described conditions as 'hell on earth'. Serb officials in Prijedor claimed that the emaciated prisoners 'were just ill'.[12] Yet the UN said nothing about military intervention, and the war continued.

Frustration at the inaction of the US government boiled over in the State Department that month, and acting Yugoslav desk officer George Kenney resigned. The front page of the *Washington Post* quoted his resignation letter: 'I can no longer in clear conscience support the administration's ineffective, indeed counterproductive, handling of the Yugoslav crisis.'[13]

By the time of the London conference, opinion polls showed the public slightly less supportive of military intervention. America's acting Secretary of State, Lawrence Eagleburger, told the conference: 'The fact of the matter is that the conflict was willed by men seeking to perpetuate Europe's last Communist regime by manipulating age-old hatreds and fears.'[14] The conference agreed to send a UN force, named UNPROFOR, to Bosnia to protect aid supplies, and to support a UN no-fly zone to prevent Bosnian Serb aircraft from operating. There was no mention of military intervention. Among other measures in the final communiqué of 31 August 1992 was acceptance of a German motion, listed as point 7b, calling for examination of the idea of the creation of an international war crimes court.

After the London conference, diplomatic support for a war crimes court gained momentum. In September 1992, German foreign minister Dr Klaus Kinkel called for the UN to form such a court. In October, a French-sponsored Security Council resolution set up a Commission of Experts to go to Bosnia and report back on any evidence of 'Grave Breaches of the Geneva Conventions'.[15]

Winter saw the Bosnian Serb ethnic cleansing campaign peter out among the early snows, and America's attention was focused on the November presidential election. This ended in a victory for Democrat candidate Bill Clinton, ending a twelve-year term of office for the Republicans. The government did not immediately change, however, because under the terms of the American Constitution the old administration continued in office until the new president was sworn in in early January.

In December human rights campaigner Elie Wiesel, a survivor of the Auschwitz concentration camp, visited Manjaca and then flew to Washington to brief Secretary of State Eagleburger, now in his final weeks in office. Wiesel made two points: first, that the horrors he had witnessed were not on the same scale as the Holocaust; second, that the camps were nonetheless a dreadful atrocity which the civilised world could not allow to continue. His arguments appear to have swayed Eagleburger.

A few days after the meeting with Wiesel, the phone on O'Brien's desk, one floor below Eagleburger's office, buzzed. It was one of the Secretary of State's assistants, who explained that he was phoning because Eagleburger had decided to go to a human rights conference in Geneva in two days' time, to make an important announcement. At that conference, the assistant explained, he would throw America's weight behind the idea of an international war crimes court administered by the United Nations. He would also list ten Bosnian warlords who should be brought before it. O'Brien was delighted. 'It was great news. I remember asking him, "Where did you get the names from?" And he said, "We're getting them from you."' O'Brien was astounded. Being a junior official, he had no access to intelligence information and his requests for such information had gone unanswered for months, possibly because none of the US intelligence agencies had collected anything of substance. O'Brien had no staff working for him and no data bank, and he had just two days to produce a list of Bosnia's 'Most Wanted' which could stand up to scrutiny at the United Nations.

He spent the rest of the day making frantic phone calls. Intelligence, however, was slight – and the CIA and Pentagon were not about to give up their key information to a lowly State Department officer. In desperation, he skimmed through human rights reports and press cuttings. In two days O'Brien and a team of helpers cobbled together a list of ten names, including Serbian president Slobodan Milošević, Bosnian Serb president Radovan Karadžić, and Bosnian Serb army commander Ratko Mladić. 'We had very little evidence that would stand up in court,' he told me later. 'We wrote the worst memo in the history of the State Department with forty different points of view. What it boiled down to was just to say these are people who there are reasons to believe can be accused of war crimes.'

The speech that followed in mid-December 1992 was a key moment in the development of the war crimes court. Eagleburger's so-called 'Naming of Names' speech saw a senior statesman from a major power blaming specific individuals for war crimes. The speech emphasised that the men he was naming were the leaders who were perpetuating the ethnic cleansing of Bosnia. 'This is really where Eagleburger was right and maybe a little ahead of the rest of the politicians, that the people who were guilty of war crimes were the ones who were going to keep the war going,' O'Brien said.

Journalists and advocates of the prosecution and punishment of war crimes were ecstatic. Back in Washington, O'Brien was nervous, worrying that some legal expert might call him up wanting to know what evidence he had for the names he had chosen. At the time his information was mostly gleaned from dog-eared clippings out of *Newsday*, the *New York Times* and the *Washington Post.*

After the 'Naming of Names' speech, O'Brien's job suddenly changed. Now people answered his calls and his memos were read and passed from hand to hand. He found that he was valued as one of a handful of people in the building with an understanding of war crimes issues. At the end of December the Republican politicians moved out of the State Department. The Democrats had yet to move in, with Bill Clinton not due to be inaugurated until 19 January 1993. Officials met at water coolers and in coffee rooms and decided that it was now up to them to make sure that the incoming Democrat administration was given no excuse not to support a war crimes court. 'I thought, we couldn't afford to let it fail. I wasn't part of the policy-making apparatus. I tried to focus on what I could do; on the war crimes, it was essentially creating an issue. We decided; there are war crimes, we at least have a duty to investigate.'

Privately, O'Brien was not sure that the UN war crimes court would ever happen, because the warlords who were ordering the atrocities were the same men with whom the UN was negotiating to try to achieve a peace settlement. 'The smart political money was that this issue would just go away – I mean that the peace talks would open an amnesty all round, the war would stop and people would gradually lose interest. I'm pretty sure that many people turned off on creating the Tribunal on the expectation that it would be traded away in a peace agreement. I thought that was the wrong approach. The argument I used for them was that, in the first instance, if you are going to give something away you have to have it first – you are creating leverage for yourself.'

In January 1993 French foreign minister Roland Dumas appointed a commission of jurists to design, at lightning speed, a complete blueprint for how such a court should work. That same month, a second blueprint for a war crimes court was published by the Conference for Security and Cooperation in Europe. January also saw the publication of a report on Bosnian atrocities collated by a small team of UN investigators, named the Commission of Experts, who had toured the country's battlefields since the autumn of 1992.

It all added up to a powerful momentum building towards the establishment of an international court. When the first Clinton officials began to arrive in the State Department, O'Brien made sure he had all the arguments in favour of the court. That way, he hoped, the incoming politicians would find it difficult to refuse to support the idea. 'The way it worked was that by pushing this and showing it was possible, people were in a position where they had to say no, and nobody wants to say no to justice. The decision to go ahead with the war crimes tribunal depended on two things. One, is it practical? We had shown it was. Second, is there the political will? That was something else.'

O'Brien's doubts were answered on 22 February 1993. At a meeting of the UN Security Council, France proposed a resolution calling for a war crimes court and America, perhaps emboldened by the French, supported the motion, which was then passed unanimously. UN Secretary-General, Boutros Boutros-Ghali, was instructed to draw up a plan for the court. The plan needed to be ready for the middle of April, when the Security Council would meet again to decide if it would go ahead with it.

On 23 February a thirty-three-year-old American lawyer named Larry Johnson came back to his hotel room in Iowa City, where he had been lecturing students on his work for the UN legal office. He found a message at the front desk telling him to phone his headquarters urgently. The chief of the UN legal affairs office asked him to return immediately because he had a big new project – which was to design, from scratch, an international war crimes court. Johnson had been selected as one of six officers for the design team.

Johnson was one of the youngest senior members of the UN legal office, but he was full of confidence in his ability to navigate his way through international law. A Nebraskan, he had studied law at Harvard and in the mid-1980s found himself a place on the International Law Commission in Geneva. International law fascinated Johnson, as did the chance to work with the top people in the field. 'For a guy from Nebraska to be in Geneva for twelve weeks a year is not a bad deal. I was working with the greats which gave me the feeling that I was working on something important,' he told me when we met in his office at the Hague Tribunal in 2004.

Johnson's boss warned all the team members that it would be extremely hard work. Nobody had ever tried anything like this since the victorious allied powers had set up the Nuremberg and Tokyo war crimes trials after the Second World War.

In the great concrete slab of the UN's New York headquarters, Johnson and the other five lawyers set to work. One important problem was that this new court would be trying crimes already committed, so it was no good designing new laws because international law could not work retrospectively. Instead, the team would have to sift through existing conventions and treaties and draw up war crimes laws based on them.[16] 'It was tremendous, a great challenge,' said Johnson. 'Pretty big responsibility too.'

His job was to be the collator of everyone else's work. Framing the laws was only one problem they had to deal with. Another was whether the proposed court should follow the Anglo-Saxon system of justice, where prosecutor and defence slug it out in open court, or the continental system, where an investigating magistrate sifts the evidence. The team decided on the Anglo-Saxon model, simply because most of them were familiar with it. As with many other decisions, this was not set in stone because the Security Council could always reject it when the draft plan was delivered.

The team tried to borrow different pieces from different legal systems around the world, and fundamental decisions were being made on a daily basis. 'When we were writing it we were taking so many decisions; there were so many possible ways to organise the thing – you know, sometimes it was "flip a coin".'

There were encouraging words of support from the new American ambassador to the United Nations, Madeleine Albright, but many other UN staff thought the team was wasting its time. The mood in the UN was that the court was being created by the Security Council as a fig-leaf to cover its failure to stop the Bosnian ethnic cleansing. Johnson, like O'Brien in Washington, felt the whole project could be dropped if there was a peace settlement in Bosnia.

'I always wondered what the policy makers were going to do with it,' he said. 'It seemed like a schizophrenia, like a discord. I mean, either you call for a war crimes court and go at it, or you take the diplomatic route and negotiate a peace settlement. But both? Cynics in the Assembly said this was a Madeleine Albright initiative to defend European criticism of the US for not putting troops on the ground in Bosnia.'

Nevertheless, he and the rest of the team worked late into the night to build their court, determined that if it failed it would not be for legal reasons. 'We were definitely committed to doing our job the best we could do. We wanted to do ourselves and the legal profession proud. If the politicians had a problem with it, that's their problem.'

In the end, the project was too much and they did not make their April deadline, with the legal office asking the Secretary-General to give them more time. This was embarrassing for Boutros Boutros-Ghali, who had to ask the Security Council to reschedule its deliberations. Finally, in mid-May 1993, the war crimes court plan was ready. On 22 May Johnson and the others squeezed into the UN Security Council meeting room, which was not the major hall where motions are debated under the glare of television cameras but a smaller room, hidden from the public, where the real deals are done.

Johnson imagined that his work was half done – that his draft plan would now be sifted and argued over, and then the legal team would be sent away to make a host of changes and recommendations. 'They just asked for a draft; I never thought that it would be adopted without changes. I thought it would be rehashed,' he said. But fate decided otherwise. When the meeting started, one ambassador, whom Johnson will not name, rose to give his comments and launched into a long, detailed appraisal of the war crimes court plan. 'Lo and behold, we had one guy, from a country we won't mention, and he gave a two- to three-hour academic and scholarly dissection of the statute. And everyone was looking at their watches. The US told the French, we can't have this going on or we'll never get out of here. Albright and the French wanted this thing done pronto.'

The conference took a break and, outside the meeting room, US and French officials conferred. They came back in, sat down, and then the two countries made a quick proposal. To save time, they suggested that the Council end debate about the plan. It could accept it or it could reject it, but there was no time for debates and negotiations that might drag on for months. Some of the ambassadors around the table nodded. Then there was a call for a vote, a show of hands, and in the blink of an eye it was settled. The United Nations Security Council, the most powerful decision-making forum on earth, representing five nuclear powers, approved the plan for a war crimes court as written, with no modifications.

'It felt like that Frankenstein movie,' said Johnson. 'You make this creature by borrowing bits and pieces of different things – a bit from the Geneva Conventions, something from Hague law, other bits from other places. Then you sew the thing together, and inside a castle you stick this monster onto an iron bed, then hoist him up to the sky. And instead of a bolt of lightning, this thing gets a Chapter Seven energy infusion from the Security Council. Then you bring it back down, and damn it, the thing's alive!'

Yet the new court might never have been born if Serbian president Slobodan Milošević had been successful in persuading the Bosnian Serbs to sign a peace deal only a few weeks earlier.

In April 1993 Milošević met with European Community envoy Lord David Owen, who told him that the only way to get sanctions against Yugoslavia lifted was to end the Bosnian war. The United Nations would never accept that the borders of Bosnia could be changed without consent from the country's Croats and Muslims. So the two men supported a peace plan, drawn up jointly by Owen and UN envoy Cyrus Vance, that called for Bosnia to remain a single state but divided into ethnic 'cantons'.

In late April, under huge international pressure, Bosnian Serb president Radovan Karadžić agreed, at a conference in Athens, to support the plan. However, a few days later, back in Bosnia, he changed his mind and said the Vance–Owen plan must first be approved by the Bosnian Serb parliament.

Milošević went to the Bosnian Serb capital, Pale, on 6 May to address a meeting of the parliament called to consider the plan. For want of a better venue in this small town, the MPs met in a hotel, cramming into the assembly room to make their momentous decision. Milošević addressed the MPs and told them that the Vance–Owen plan would give them most of what they wanted, with self-government and UN protection. The MPs stared him down. They wanted independence, not autonomy, and saw no reason why, with their military superiority, they should settle for less. When the vote came, it was a massive fifty-one to two against signing the Vance–Owen plan.[17]

While no one will ever know for sure, the chances are that if the Bosnian Serb parliament had voted that day for the Vance–Owen plan the UN war crimes court would never have come into being. It would have been a simple matter for the Serbs, with Milošević's backing, to demand, among other concessions from the UN, that it shelve its idea for a war crimes court. Faced with a choice between watching the shelling of Sarajevo end, or a war crimes court being established, the probability is that the Security Council would have shrugged its shoulders and told Secretary-General Boutros Boutros-Ghali that his six-strong legal team, already late with its plan, could stop work and forget the whole idea. And then Milošević and Karadžić and Mladić, and more than a hundred Bosnian warlords, would have lived to enjoy a prosperous retirement.

On 25 May 1993, three days after being presented with a draft statute by its office of legal affairs, the United Nations Security Council met in a full public hearing and announced that, acting under Chapter Seven of its rules on peace and security, it was establishing the International Tribunal for the Prosecution of Persons Responsible for Serious Violations of International Law Committed in the Territory of the Former Yugoslavia Since 1991. Johnson watched the decision: 'I was surprised, pleased, amazed, scared. I thought, gee, this thing is going to operate, they are actually going to do it.'

Habemus Papam   5

When you were in law school you had some noble ideas of what a lawyer should
be... then after you practice for six months you realise we're nothing but hired
guns, mouthpieces for sale to the highest bidder. Yeah, Mitch, you'll get cynical.
And it's sad, really.

John Grisham, The Firm

In the summer of 1993 Italian law professor Antonio Cassese broke two
promises to his wife. The first was to clear from his basement a
collection of torture implements he had seized as part of his job
inspecting Europe's police stations. The second was to return to
teaching law in his native Florence after four years on the road as
president of the Council of Europe's Torture Commission.

Cassese has a soft round face and an easy manner and was regarded
as open and accessible by students at Florence University, where he
had specialised in international law. After two decades at the university
building a reputation as an innovator in human rights law, he was
picked to lead the Torture Commission in 1989. The Commission was
a revolutionary concept because its inspectors were given passes
allowing them instant access to the cells in police stations across
Europe. They could go where they wanted and mount no-notice
inspections at any time of the day or night.

Cassese's speciality was to visit a city and spend the day with
ministers and police chiefs, then spring spot checks on the police
stations in the early hours of the morning, when they were often at their
busiest. The job called for a fine mix of diplomacy and stubbornness in
dealing with station chiefs who were often ignorant of the
Commission's power. The last thing some police commanders would
want to see, as they coped with the Friday night fallout from city pubs,

was a team of inspectors turning up with clipboards. One night Cassese inspected the office of a Turkish police chief and refused to leave until the officer unlocked a filing cabinet. When he at last consented, it was opened to reveal a rubber truncheon kept for beating prisoners. It was immediately confiscated, to join Cassese's private collection. 'You had to push it,' he told me when I interviewed him in Florence, 'To show that you had a lot of, I don't know how you call it – to be cheeky.'

Cassese returned home from his trips with blindfolds, an electric cattle prod, and a wide variety of truncheons, including an inscribed wooden baton belonging to the Turkish police. 'My wife said why do you keep this awful instrument?'

His reputation as a successful president was sealed with a piece of diplomatic chutzpah. Although his team had wide-ranging powers to inspect cells, the Council of Europe had decreed that the results of these inspections should remain secret. Cassese wanted to change this practice and decided he would start by trying to get states with good records to publish his reports. The task called for flattery, and he deployed his Florentine charm to full effect when visiting the Lord Chancellor, Britain's top law officer, in London. The Torture Commission, Cassese announced, had given Britain full marks for the state of its jails. Why not make its report public? 'We said, well, but you are a great country, a great democracy, why don't you set an example and make our report public? They started smiling and said they would have to consult, but in the end they did it. Now, thanks to the UK, each time we would go to a country we would say: "You know the UK set a wonderful example by breaching themselves the rule of confidentiality." It was a sort of domino effect.' Within a year all member states, bar Turkey, had agreed to publish the Torture Commission's reports.

The work was intense and when Cassese was asked to do a second term in 1993 he said no. 'It was wonderful, but very exhausting. So I had to throw in the towel.' Back in Florence, he was just picking up the threads of life as an academic when he got a phone call from Italy's justice minister. He was an admirer of Cassese's work and asked him if he would agree to be Italy's nominee as a judge in a new UN war crimes court. The minister warned that there were eleven places for judges and it was by no means certain that the Italian nominee would be chosen. Cassese agreed, assuming that even if he were chosen, life as a Hague judge would be 'a more relaxing job' than the Torture Commission. His first surprise was that the UN, meeting in the early summer, chose him as one of the eleven judges. The second surprise, when he turned up for the first meeting in The Hague in November 1993, was that, thanks to his reputation on the Torture Commission, he was picked by the other judges as the first court president. It meant that, unlike the other judges, he could not go home and wait for the first cases to begin. He would have to live in The Hague full-time and build up the court from scratch. Not everybody was happy. 'My wife got very angry. I phoned to say look, I've been elected. She said, "Ah". That was all she said – "Ah".'

Cassese set to work. That winter, the UN war crimes court consisted of five people: Cassese, an assistant, and three secretaries hired, at the UN's insistence, on short-term contracts. 'Many judges told me we don't have anything, we have no budget, we have no headquarters, we have no seat for the court, we have no procedures and evidence. Most of them said let's go back and wait. I said, "No, I'm sorry, this is a wonderful thing." I thought we are going to miss a wonderful opportunity. They said you are too naive and so on.'

His anxiety stemmed from the need to get the court started in time to halt the slaughter in Bosnia which was being shown every night on television. The siege of Sarajevo was now a year old, with Bosnian Serb artillery hammering the city each day. In April 1993 the war acquired a new dimension when Bosnian Croat forces turned on the Muslims in the south of the country. In a copy of the Serb ethnic cleansing of the year before, Croat paramilitary units attacked Muslim towns and villages, creating a new wave of refugees. The Croat leadership proclaimed their own statelet, Herceg-Bosna, anchored on the south of the country. In May 1993 Croat forces attacked their former Muslim allies in Mostar, the southern town that the leaders of Herceg-Bosna wanted as their capital. The Muslims, caught between Croat infantry attacking from one direction and Serb artillery pounding them from another, held out. The Croat besiegers bombarded the town in a siege more intense than Sarajevo because the area was much smaller. Almost every building on the east side of the city, the Muslim district, was damaged or destroyed. One technique that the Croats tried in order to dislodge Muslims from homes on the west side was to fill oil drums with explosives and then roll them down a steep hill to explode against the houses below. The Croats opened their own version of Omarska, a detention camp where torture, murder and beatings were routine, at the Mostar heliport.

In Central Bosnia, Croat forces rampaged along the broad green Lašva Valley, torching Muslim villages. The worst atrocity came at the village of Ahmići, which was famous before the war for producing large numbers of young Muslim clergy. A Croat paramilitary unit, nicknamed the Jokers, stormed the village, killing Muslims in the streets and gardens. The women and children hid in basements, and in several cases they were sealed in their homes and burned alive. British troops of the UN protection force were based in valley, at the town of Vitez, with the task of protecting the food convoys that were keeping nearly a million people from starvation. UN rules stipulated that the British soldiers could protect the aid shipments but not the people they were intended to feed. They had to stand and watch, biting their lips, as the one-sided slaughter took place in the valley around them.

The British commander, Colonel Bob Stewart, decided to stretch the UN mandate to the full and sent his troops into Ahmići. The first white-painted armoured vehicle drove up the narrow main street to see a column of Muslim civilians being marched in the opposite direction by Croat soldiers. One Muslim woman threw herself in front of the British vehicle, shouting that they were being marched away to be executed. The British deployed and the Croat soldiers melted away. Because snipers were operating in the village, journalists stayed outside and television footage was taken by a camera fixed to the viewfinder of a Warrior armoured vehicle. The pictures brought back from Ahmići that day showed a Dantesque scene with homes burning and twisted corpses strewn around the roads, gardens and ditches, all under a grey, brooding sky. Moving always on the fringes of the scene, trying to keep out of view, were small bands of camouflaged Croat soldiers.[1]

Later, BBC newsman Martin Bell filmed a television report from one of the Ahmići basements amid the twisted, charcoaled limbs of women and children burned to death. A few days after the massacre British soldiers returned to the burned village looking for a baby abandoned by its panic-stricken mother. It was found where she had left it, on the window sill of a now-burned house. The sergeant who found it decided the remains were too small to need a body bag and brought it out in a black rubbish sack instead.[2] If there were a silver lining to the great black cloud of Ahmići, it was that UN forces were right on top of the massacre and saved civilians who could later testify against those who carried it out. Many similar atrocities carried out by Serb forces the previous year had been far from the eyes of international monitors.

In the months and years ahead testimony from the Ahmići survivors, and from British army officers on the scene, would be a major boost for the war crimes prosecutors. But in November 1993 such help was far in the future, and Cassese, newly installed in the cold, damp Hague, had the job of finding a home for the court. With speed his key consideration, he decided against trying to build a courthouse and scouted around for somewhere to rent.

An obvious place for the new court was in the imposing Peace Palace, headquarters of the UN's International Court of Justice, which settles disputes between UN member nations.[3] The International Court of Justice lent Cassese a couple of offices but made it clear that there was not room for two courts in its building. The Hague is a small city, sandwiched between The Netherlands two main metropolises, Amsterdam and Rotterdam, and large, empty office buildings are in short supply. Cassese decided to rent two floors in an insurance company headquarters building, built of white brick and shaped like an A for the initial letter of the company's name, Aegon. This was hardly the setting for such a momentous enterprise, located far from the city centre in The Hague's leafy northern suburbs. For a man used to the glories of Florentine architecture it was, he told me, a 'dull awful building'. Also, it would need major work to create space for the courtrooms and a jail in the basement. Finding a detention centre was also a problem because there was not enough money to build one. The Dutch government pitched in, agreeing that it could be built inside the existing Scheveningen prison on The Netherlands windswept North Sea coast.

In early spring 1994, Cassese had a courthouse and a jail but money was in short supply. The Security Council had allocated its new court just a quarter of a million dollars for its first year, barely enough for the courthouse and jail. To save cash, Cassese spurned the offer of an official car. 'I went by bike. We had no car. We had no money. I felt hopeless, also because I was all alone. I felt as a duty that I should be there, the captain of the ship. The ship was not sinking but it was stuck.'

Some UN bureaucrats back in New York were hostile to the court, seeing it as an added burden on their workload. The Security Council, preoccupied with other things, lost interest in its new legal creation. Cassese had a sympathetic friend in the Secretary-General, the Egyptian Boutros Boutros-Ghali, but their regular phone conversations were hardly reassuring. 'First he would say I see some light at the end of the tunnel and then later he would say I don't see any light,' said Cassese.

The Italian judge used his first annual report, in early 1994, to make an emotional appeal for the Security Council to give more money. 'How could a woman who had been raped by servicemen from a different ethnic group, or a civilian whose parents or children had been killed in cold blood, quell their desire for vengeance if they knew the authors of these crimes were left unpunished?' Cassese pleaded. 'The only civilised alternative to this desire for revenge is to render justice.'[4] This was a departure from the dry style favoured by UN bureaucrats, but it worked and later in 1994 the budget jumped to US$10 million.

More cash rolled in from private donations. The Chicago-based MacArthur Foundation and billionare philanthropist George Soros provided a total of US$1.4 million.[5] The Netherlands gave a further US$300,000 and Pakistan, keen to show support for Bosnia's Muslims, donated US$1 million. This was still way short of the money the tribunal would need to track down and prosecute Bosnia's war criminals. All kinds of expertise were needed by the court and there was no money to pay for it. The International Criminal Tribunal for the Former Yugoslavia needed extra help, and in May 1994 America stepped into the breach. The US ambassador to the UN, Madeleine Albright, took a personal interest: her family had escaped as refugees from the privations of the Second World War and she often talked about the importance of human rights.

On Albright's instructions, in the summer of 1994 the State Department collected desks, tables, computers and law books and shipped them across the Atlantic.[6] With them went twenty-two top legal experts, FBI investigators and Justice Department specialists, all seconded to work at the new court. Jim O'Brien, the State Department officer in charge of war crimes, said: 'You had three cabinet ministries sending people to work on this thing. It was a sign that the administration was serious. Albright deserves enormous credit for this. Each time there was a problem she would just say we're going, we're going, and whenever there was a problem she would just hammer at it. Our help was a sign that the Clinton administration was serious about war crimes.'[7] Money was still tight, as Albright saw for herself, when she visited in the autumn of 1994. 'She came with ten people. I was there with a secretary,' said Cassese. 'I thought the whole meeting would be recorded but then we realised that this secretary was so bad at taking shorthand that we had no record. This was at the outset – not even a good secretary.'[8]

By then the world had a second war crimes court – built, like the first one, on the back of a colossal UN failure. In 1993 the UN had mediated a ceasefire that ended the civil war in the small African country of Rwanda where two tribal groups, the Hutus and Tutsis, had clashed. On 6 April 1994 Rwanda's Hutu president, Juvenal Habyarimana, was killed when his plane was shot down over the capital, Kigali.[9] The killing was carried out by Hutu extremists, who then blamed the country's Tutsis and began a campaign of slaughter. Hutu death squads, named the Interahamwe, or 'those who fight together', had been secretly trained and armed for several months, and were told to rise up by instructions from Hutu leaders broadcast on the national radio.

The UN had a 2500-strong peacekeeping force in the country, but when the killings began the Security Council decided, incredibly, to pull them out. The Belgian force commander had been warning about the genocide plan since January 1994. When he was told to withdraw, he protested that he should be saving the Tutsis not abandoning them, but the UN was adamant. In late April 1994 his troops pulled out, with Tutsi civilians running after their trucks, begging them to stay. Leaving for home, some of the Belgian soldiers, seeing television cameras filming them, shredded their blue UN berets on the tarmac of Kigali airport.

In the following hundred days at least eight-hundred-thousand Tutsis, and possibly up to one million, were killed, mostly hacked to death with machetes. Piles of bodies were left on main roads and rivers became jammed with corpses. In one instance, Hutu leaders issued safe-conduct passes to local Tutsis, telling them they would be safe in a Roman Catholic mission house. But it was a trap. Once the Tutsis had gathered inside, two truckloads of Hutus arrived to hack them to death.[10] The Security Council decided not to label the slaughter genocide, because to do so would compel the UN to intervene under the terms of the Genocide Convention. As with Bosnia, the organisation's fine words about fighting for peace were exposed as a bluff. For the Security Council members, the decision was a shame that they were willing to bear rather than risk the lives of their soldiers. They also found they could deflect the blame by claiming that they were bound to seek collective action and were unable to act alone. When convenient, the major powers resorted to blaming the UN itself for its failures, as if the organisation had a life beyond the collective will of its members. The killings stopped when the Hutus ran out of Tutsis to kill, and on 26 May 1994 the Security Council declared that genocide had indeed taken place. A war crimes court was established on the same model as that in The Hague, not out of any enthusiasm but because of public pressure.

By the summer of 1994 America's largesse had allowed the Hague Tribunal to begin work. Cassese now felt energised and began work on tasks ranging from the rules of the new court to the design of the judge's robes – he opted for red as being the most dramatic colour. 'I was so excited, I would wake up at six o'clock each morning. I thought this must become reality, this must become something.'

One asset that helped Cassese recruit staff was the novelty of the court itself. Nothing like it had ever been attempted, and for some lawyers this was a chance not to be missed. A senior French judge, Claude Jorda, forsook a high salary and comfortable position in Paris to come to The Hague, telling Cassese the Tribunal was 'a splendid intellectual adventure.'[11] Young lawyers were also inspired to join. British barrister John Jones was called to the bar in 1992 and heard about the war crimes court when he was in Washington in 1994. He met an American lawyer while queuing at a cashpoint machine. 'She told me about this new war crimes tribunal. It sounded like a very worthwhile project, and a chance to be a part of history,' he said.[12] He applied for an internship and later went to work as law clerk to Cassese. South African law graduate Rod Dixon was in the United States studying constitutional law when he got to hear about the new court. He had campaigned against his country's apartheid regime in the late 1980s, and when South Africa converted to democracy in the early 1990s he decided it would need constitutional lawyers. In 1994 the American university where he studied put up the money to pay for a Hague Tribunal intern, knowing the court was short of money. Dixon, like Jones, thought this was a chance to be a part of history and applied, later working as a prosecutor. For both men, the experience was a life-changing event. They would later co-author the two main legal texts on war crimes law.[13]

For many Hague lawyers these early years were an exciting time. Everything was new and the energy of the young pioneers spilled over into after-hours parties and all-night discussions about law and idealism of a kind both Dixon and Jones thought they had left behind at university. Idealists mixed with secondees, all of them frantically busy, none of them sure whether the court would last a decade or a few months. 'It was a mixture in those days – you have the pioneer types and there were others who had lots of experience, but they didn't fully grasp the ramifications, just how much this court could change things,' said Dixon. 'We knew the critics were waiting for a failure so they could say it's impossible to have these trials. So we had to go in full throttle.'

Had Jones remained a barrister in London chambers, he would have had a successful but predictable start to his legal career. Instead, he found that, even as a junior, he was making key decisions that would shape not just the court but the future of war crimes justice. On one occasion, walking on the Cornish coast, he mapped out a simple filtering system for appeal hearings so that not every case would require the full, and cumbersome, five-judge appeals panel. On his return to The Hague, Cassese liked his plan, the judges approved it, and it became law, with Jones then tasked as the official in charge of administering the system. 'In those days, major decisions were being made all the time; you had the feeling you were creating something big,' he said. Newcomers were also horrified by the administrative mess they sometimes found. The first legal officer for the registry, responsible for adminstration, was American lawyer David Talbot, who had joined wanting to do some good. His great-grandfather had had his home burned down by the Ku Klux Klan for defending blacks in America's deep south. He arrived to find that the court did not, in fact, own its own jailhouse. 'The previous registrar had signed the lease, but he had no authority to do this. In the beginning there were these basic kind of administrative things.'

The sense of excitement and energy that former court staff remember from those early days can seem odd, given the nature of the work they did and the horror and sadness to which they were exposed on a daily basis. Of the early pioneers, many have gone on to greater and better-paid things, with Jones and Dixon both now being consulted as legal experts in a fast-growing field. But talk to them about the early days and they grow wistful for the sense of mission that they felt then, despite working for a court that at the time had few cases, huge problems, money shortages and an uncertain future.

In her account of her time sifting through mass graves in both the Balkans and Rwanda, forensic expert Clea Koff says that she was inspired by an earlier generation of investigators working with the remains of Argentina's 'disappeared' – innocent civilians kidnapped and killed by the military junta of the 1970s. Like those early volunteers, she says that she was inspired to 'help reduce oppression by making the bones talk'.[14]

Cassese tried to encourage his staff with a bright and breezy style. When they came to his office to complain he had a reply ready, with a quotation borrowed from Bertolt Brecht: 'I told them I am busy preparing my next mistake. I would tell them that I knew every day I would make at least one mistake, the minimum. But I told them this is human. You can't help making mistakes if you start something which is brand new.'

In the summer of 1994 The Hague's priority was to find a prosecutor. More than any other official, the prosecutor would set the tone for the new court and determine how aggressive it would be in hunting down war criminals. The decision rested with the Security Council and its members began squabbling over who should get the job. America, under Albright's influence, wanted an aggressive prosecutor. Other nations, led by Britain, favoured caution. America nominated the chairman of the UN's Commission of Experts, Cherif Bassiouni, who had seen Bosnia's atrocities at first hand. Britain blocked the nomination, partly on the grounds that as an Egyptian-American he was a Muslim and might be seen as hostile to the Serbs. The Hague's first prosecutor lasted less than a week. Venezuela's attorney general, Ramón Escovar Salom, took the job in November 1993 and asked for a three-month delay. He turned up at The Hague in February 1994, stayed a few days, then announced to Cassese that he had changed his mind and was quitting.

Cassese was furious that there would now be another delay before the court could start its mission. That same month a mortar bomb exploded in Sarajevo's Markale market, killing sixty-nine civilians and leading NATO to threaten to bomb the Serbs. If the Serb commanders of the besieging forces were worried about the threat of The Hague's war crimes court, they had a funny way of showing it.[15]

Cassese already knew about South Africa's judge Richard Goldstone, famous for combating the former apartheid regime through the law courts. He had made his reputation by using the state's own laws to prosecute it for crimes against blacks and white protestors. Later, as the country began its move towards democracy, he set up what came to be called the Goldstone Commission to investigate human rights abuses in the late 1980s. His big breakthrough was to discover the identity of a 'third force', disowned by both the white government and black activists, which was killing blacks. It proved to be a splinter group of the defence ministry. Goldstone had limited experience as a prosecutor, but Cassese felt he was ideal. For one thing, he was Jewish, so he could not be accused of bias by Bosnia's Christians or Muslims.

Cassese got hold of Goldstone's home phone number in South Africa, rang him up and asked him to be the chief prosecutor. Goldstone thanked him but said he already had a job offer, to be a judge of South Africa's new constitutional court.[16] Cassese was not deterred and phoned the office of his friend in New York, UN Secretary-General Boutros Boutros-Ghali. 'The people in New York were not very happy. They said: "It's not for you to decide." I said: "Yes, but you have not done anything."' Boutros-Ghali was sympathetic, knowing the problems the Security Council had had with the previous nominee, and not wanting to see the whole process repeated. He agreed to help secure Goldstone as chief prosecutor and phoned South Africa's president, Nelson Mandela, to make a personal request for Goldstone. Mandela was in a difficult position because Goldstone was one of a handful of law officers in South Africa who had earned the respect of both blacks and whites, and he wanted him for the constitutional court. On the other hand, he told Boutros-Ghali that he found it hard to turn down a personal appeal from the head of the UN, an organisation that had campaigned against apartheid for so many years. So a secret deal was struck between the two men, whereby Goldstone would serve only two years of the expected four-year term of The Hague's chief prosecutor.

That way he could get back to South Africa in good time for the constitutional court. 'Boutros-Ghali arranged everything. They made arrangements, a secret deal. Not even people in the Security Council knew that the secret deal was for two years only,' said Cassese.[17]

The plea to Mandela was made on a Wednesday. On the following Friday the Security Council met to approve the deal. Cassese waited in his office in The Hague long after everyone else had gone home. At 10.30 p.m. the news came through from New York. Goldstone had got the job. He wanted to fax his colleagues but could find no Hague Tribunal headed notepaper, so he simply took a plain white sheet from a computer printer, wrote 'Dear Friends, *Habemus papam!*' (Latin for 'We have a pope'), and fed it into the fax machine. 'I was so happy. I had a good drink, a glass of red wine. To me this was the turning point, I thought from now on we are in business.'

Richard Goldstone had an early indication of how tight money was when he flew to UN headquarters in New York to accept his new appointment and was told to pay his own air fare. The UN was in debt as it tried to pay the huge costs of the aid and peacekeeping operation in Bosnia, and bureaucrats told him that they had no standard procedure for paying someone like him, who worked for the UN but was not a UN staff member.

Things were no easier when he arrived in The Hague, having travelled economy class. America was embroiled that year in a long-running row with the UN over the non-payment of more than US$1 billion in dues. Congress was refusing to pay the money, saying it must first have more control over how it was spent.[18] The row spilled over into an argument about the Hague court. It was normal practice for states seconding staff to the UN to pay an additional 13 per cent in order to cover expenses such as flights. America was refusing to pay this money, and the UN bureaucracy was refusing to waive the rule, so Goldstone was now worried that the US secondees he was depending on would be withdrawn or even ordered home by the UN. He flew back to America to meet both the US government and the UN bureaucrats.

His meetings with the US administration went badly. America felt that it had done enough in giving The Hague twenty-two highly skilled people for nothing, and it would not stump up the 13 per cent fees as well. He met with UN officials who were adamant that, this being the case, the 'gift' would be refused. As a last resort, he threatened to make a statement on the issue to the press. The UN backed down, waived the 13 per cent rule, and the Americans were allowed to stay.[19]

Arriving to take up his post as chief prosecutor, Goldstone's first problem was where, in the great pool of Bosnia's suffering, should he start? Certainly not with Milošević, though even then he was aware of the Serbian president's pivotal role in the Balkan wars. The problem with indicting Milošević was that he was too far up the chain of command. A prosecution would need to prove not only the war crimes themselves but also the long series of links from battlefield to presidential office.[20] 'Nothing would have delighted me more than to have an indictment against Milošević. It was well known what he did. The thing was to get the evidence to prove it beyond doubt – that's something many people have difficulty in understanding. They sort of assume that you can use what's in the media as proof,' Goldstone told me.[21]

For his first prosecutions Goldstone decided to focus on the atrocities at the prison camps. For one thing, there were plenty of witnesses, as in Europe and America refugees had formed their own associations which were keen to help the prosecutors track down survivors. By the time Goldstone arrived in The Hague, one camp guard was already under arrest in Germany. Duško Tadić, former karate instructor and guard in the Omarska camp, had fled the country at the end of 1993 when he was called up for the Bosnian Serb army. Tadić had a brother who ran a night club in Munich, so he moved there. Germany was home to the largest population of Bosnian refugees, totalling six hundred thousand, and one day one of them recognised Tadić in the street. The refugee had been one of his victims in Omarska, and now tailed him to the night club, then doubled back to alert the German police. Tadić was arrested and Germany considered prosecuting him in its own courts under the terms of the Geneva Conventions. In the summer of 1994 Goldstone applied for him to be sent to The Hague; Germany agreed, but needed to change its constitution first, which took more than a year.[22]

Goldstone began fourteen separate prison camp investigations, but gaining cooperation from UN member states proved difficult. Pentagon officials dragged their feet about handing over reconnaissance photographs and signals intercepts, not wanting to compromise their intelligence information. Goldstone wrote a memo asking Washington for speedier action which was leaked to the press, causing a storm when he was accused, in effect, of biting the hand that fed him. Afterwards, under media pressure, the Pentagon released some intelligence information, but the relationship with Goldstone was not improved.

Progress was slow and tension built up between Goldstone and the judges in The Hague. They wanted trials to begin, or at least the first indictments to be issued, so that they could become a working court. By the autumn of 1994 events in Bosnia were moving fast. The Americans, through pressure on Croatia, had persuaded the Bosnian Croats to give up their campaign for a separate state, signing the Washington Agreement in February 1994 which committed them to living again with the mostly Muslim Bosnian government.

Goldstone insisted on caution, saying that he did not want to issue an indictment until he had rock-solid evidence.[23] Making things worse were the contrasting personalities of Cassese and Goldstone, with the Italian's easy flamboyance grating on the dry, meticulous South African. 'I had a fair number of quite difficult differences with Cassese. They [the judges] were angry, frustrated, embarrassed and they wanted work as soon as possible,' said Goldstone.

Cassese told me a similar story: 'I had many clashes with the prosecutor Goldstone. He felt that the president was simply a judge and as a judge he should exercise what they call judicial restraint. Which is quite correct for a judge. But the role of president in an international tribunal was totally different.'

What prevented the spat from getting out of hand was the knowledge that failure for either the prosecutor or the judges would mean failure for the whole court. To sort out their problems, the two men began the practice of taking long walks together in the leafy lanes around the Tribunal building, sorting things out away from the hothouse atmosphere of the court. 'You know, it all worked out, and I think it all worked out because primarily we respected each other,' said Goldstone.

One bonus for him was the willingness of witnesses to give evidence. Despite the terrible ordeals of many camp survivors, they were able to give lucid, accurate evidence which could be cross-referenced with other witness statements. Also, it seemed that even in the most appalling massacres, some people always survived to tell the tale. 'It wasn't difficult to get the pieces at all. The witnesses wanted to come forward, both for themselves and for their families.'

In the early winter of 1994 Goldstone was summoned for a December meeting with the UN in New York and heard rumours that the organisation was making across-the-board cuts. Fearing it might cut, or even close, his war crimes prosecution department, he decided he must have at least one charge filed. Once an individual was publicly indicted, he must be tried.

On 4 November 1994 Goldstone made the first indictment in the Tribunal's history, charging former Bosnian Serb prison camp commander Dragan Nikolić, with Grave Breaches of the Geneva Conventions. Nikolić, witnesses told the investigators, had revelled in his god-like power of life and death over the inmates. He had taken one teenaged Muslim girl, Saha Berbić, for his sex slave.[24] Over a period of several nights he had left with the girl to go to an empty house outside the camp. What happened there she never said, but each morning he brought her back to the camp bruised and bleeding. Finally, one night he took her to the house and never brought her back, and Berbić remains missing, presumed dead.[25] Four days later, Goldstone heard from Germany that formalities were complete for the handover of Omarska prison guard Duško Tadić.

In New York in December, Goldstone met with the Security Council and told them about Nikolić and the crimes of which he was accused. He was surprised to find the Security Council supportive. There was no talk of closing the Tribunal down, or even of cutting the budget, and he flew back to The Netherlands feeling he had got the court over a potential crisis.

It was February 1995 by the time the other prison camp investigations were finished, and Goldstone announced indictments against twenty-one Bosnian Serbs, some on the same indictment. These should have been cause for celebration but instead they highlighted the biggest problem of all for The Hague, which was the lack of a police force to arrest the suspects. The Hague court ordered the Bosnian Serbs to hand over the twenty-one suspects, but no one was surprised when the instruction was ignored. An arresting force was needed, but none existed.[26] As 1995 went on, more indictments were issued, but they only emphasised the failure of the court actually to put anyone on trial. One British official, who remains anonymous at his own request, visited the empty jail in early 1995 and remembered the bizarre spectacle of a prison complete with guards but without a single inmate. 'There were no prisoners and morale was on the floor. The Dutch guards in the regular prison used to tease the UN guards about having nothing to do and it got them down.'

The arrival of Tadić in April 1995 meant the Tribunal's detention centre now had a single prisoner, but his trial was still a year away. Two years had passed and the Tribunal had made no difference to the war it had been set up to combat. And three months later, its staff would find out just how little they meant to the Bosnian warlords they were supposed to be combating.

Srebrenica is a long, narrow town which sits in the bottom of a steep, prettily wooded valley. The town took its name from the old word for silver, which was mined in the surrounding hills. Under Tito, factories had been built at the base of the valley and the town thrived.

In April 1992 Serb units swept into the town as part of the push to clear eastern Bosnia of Muslims. Most of the population ran into the hills. However, the Serbs had too few men to hold the town, and by summer 1992 it was one of three enclaves in eastern Bosnia held by government forces, the other two being Goražde and Žepa. Serb forces began to bombard the enclaves, and only in November 1992 did the first UN food convoy get into the town. The Muslim population of fifteen thousand was swollen by the arrival of twenty-five thousand Muslims fleeing ethnic cleansing in the surrounding area. To stay alive, raiding parties went out to snatch food from Serb farms.

In February 1993 Srebrenica was declared a UN Safe Area, and a force of Canadian soldiers was sent in to enforce a ceasefire. Both sides broke it immediately. The Serbs kept up an intermittent bombardment and imposed tight restrictions on food and supplies entering the enclave. Bosnian government units positioned most of their weapons in the forests, out of sight of the Canadians, and continued to run raiding parties out of the enclave, striking at Serb farms. Along with the thousands of Muslims slaughtered in the region, Serbs began to be killed in a vicious tit-for-tat war. At Christmas 1992 Muslim forces killed thirty Serb civilians around the village of Kravica – said by some to be in revenge for the annihilation of several local villages and the torture and murder of a seven-year-old girl by Serb paramilitaries.

Attacks out of the enclave also had a military purpose, tying down Serb units that might have been used elsewhere against government forces. The Muslim guerrillas were followed into action by a small army of hungry refugees, keen to grab what food they could to take back for their starving families.

Conditions in the town deteriorated, with the Muslims who had come from outside complaining that the local residents were taking more than their share of the UN food supplies. The Canadians suggested that the outsiders elect a leader who could negotiate on their behalf. A few days after an election had been organised, the leader was shot dead by a Muslim in the town. The outsiders complained no more about mistreatment.

By summer 1995, with a Dutch battalion now in the enclave, events were conspiring against the little town. As exhaustion with the war spread across Bosnia, the Serbs began to consider a peace settlement. It was realised by all sides that the enclaves were an anachronism. In Sarajevo, government officials whispered that in any final deal the enclaves would be traded away in return for territory elsewhere in Bosnia. Srebrenica's commander, Naser Orić, once a bodyguard of Slobodan Milošević in pre-war days, was ordered to Sarajevo for consultations and then refused permission to return. It certainly seemed that the Bosnian government had given up on the town.

In June the commander of UN forces in Bosnia, the French general Bernard Janvier, proposed pulling out of all three enclaves, saying that the troops were too few to make any tactical difference. He was, in effect, giving the UN Security Council a choice between giving up the enclaves or allocating sufficient forces to mount a meaningful defence. The Council simply ignored the issue. It was obvious to all that the fall of Srebrenica would tidy up the map of Bosnia, suiting everybody apart from the forty thousand people trapped in the town.

A Serb offensive started on 6 July. Tank shells hit Dutch outposts. The Dutch formed a line with their white-painted armoured personnel carriers and called for the air power that the UN had promised. On 11 July, with Dutch commanders screaming into their radios that they could not hold the town, NATO jets were scrambled. Two Dutch F-16s appeared over Srebrenica. The pilot of the lead plane destroyed a Serb tank. The Serbs reacted fast, threatening to kill captured Dutch soldiers if there was more bombing. Then, in one of the great unexplained decisions of the Bosnian war, General Janvier called off the air strikes. NATO planes circled helplessly above. Down below, the Dutch decided that they could not fight without heavy weapons and surrendered. What everyone seemed to expect was that the town would now surrender and its population be deported. But the Serbs had other plans.

A gigantic extermination began to unfold around Srebrenica. The women and children were separated from the men and bused to safety. But the men were rounded up and detained. Many had already left, staging a desperate break-out which managed to punch a hole through Serb lines and strike north-westwards towards government positions. They took heavy casualties and might have been wiped out, except that

Orić, kicking his heels in the northern Bosnian town of Tuzla, assembled a scratch force of government troops and attacked eastwards, linking up with the column.

The first sign to the world at large that something was wrong in Srebrenica came when busloads of women and children began arriving in government territory without their menfolk. As the days passed and no men arrived, their families became worried. Some of these women got off their buses to report seeing men dead or kneeling, trembling with fear, by the roadside. The UN contacted the Serbian Red Cross but this organisation could give no answer. Some days later, a few Muslim men arrived in Tuzla, having escaped through the woods. They told of watching the Serbs slaughtering men on a huge scale. One unit had even used a Dutch armoured personnel carrier to fool Muslims hiding in the woods into coming out. The Dutch, for reasons best known to themselves, had not immobilised their vehicles but simply handed the Serbs the keys. On 9 August, America's representative to the United Nations, Madeleine Albright, displayed a series of photographs of farmland around Srebrenica taken by American military satellites and high-flying reconnaissance jets. One set of two pictures showed an empty field outside the town: the first picture was simply of the field; the second showed it a few days after the town fell, covered in freshly turned earth. It was the first official confirmation of mass graves.

In fact, the Bosnian Serbs had planned a meticulous operation to wipe out Srebrenica's male population. This involved not just mobilising death squads but putting in place all the machinery to enable the killing of such a large number of people. Documents later seized by the war crimes court showed that the Serbs had used the military and civil authorities to organise a fleet of buses to take the men to their killing sites, then arranged fuel and bulldozers for the job of digging mass graves. When the killing was over, more than seven thousand Muslim men were dead.

For Judge Antonio Cassese, the news of the Srebrenica massacre was a devastating blow. It was confirmation that his court had made no difference at all to the Bosnian war. 'All of a sudden came Srebrenica.

Imagine our anguish, watching on television what was happening in Srebrenica and feeling so impotent. Absolutely, utterly, impotent.'

For Serbian president Slobodan Milošević, the killing at Srebrenica was an opportunity to end the Bosnian war. Since May 1993, when the Bosnian Serbs had refused his appeal to stop the war, he had been trying to get them to do so. This had nothing to do with altruism, but was based on his desire to have sanctions against Yugoslavia lifted. He was by now the supreme ruler of the country, having changed the constitution in his own favour in April 1992. Out had gone the old power structure, and now supreme authority rested with a three-man defence council. This consisted of himself, as Serbian president, plus two yes-men installed as the presidents of Montenegro and of Yugoslavia itself. The leaders of the Bosnian Serb and Croatian Serb republics wanted Yugoslavia to incorporate their statelets. But the UN made it clear that this was impossible because it would mean redrawing the borders of Bosnia and Croatia, and that could only be done with the consent of all parties.

Perhaps a more committed nationalist would have ignored the trade sanctions and incorporated these lands into a new Greater Serbia, even at the risk of economic collapse. But Milošević was not like that, and in 1993 he had dropped the idea of nationalism as fast as he had that of Communism in Kosovo in 1987. What he wanted was an end to sanctions, and if this meant sacrificing the old dream of Greater Serbia, so be it. This surprised some of his supporters, but not his closest advisers. Former Serbian presidency member and key adviser, Borisav Jović, would later tell the Milošević trial: 'There was nothing stronger for Milošević than the urge to stay in power. Principles did not matter to him as much as political success and staying in power, that had priority over everything else. The main definition of Milošević would be – political pragmatism.'[27]

Milošević had tried to get the Bosnian Serbs to sign the Vance–Owen peace plan which called for a united Bosnia. Afterwards, he had had the option of cutting their supply of cash, weapons and oil, but had chosen not to do so. The most likely explanation is that, had he done this and the Bosnian Serbs had fought on and been crushed by Bosnian government forces, his own supporters in Yugoslavia would have blamed him.

Having lost leverage over the Bosnian and Croatian Serbs, Milošević spent the rest of the war trying to hold on to power at home. Under sanctions the economy sagged. Oil-fired power stations had to close, starving factories of power.

While sanctions shut down legitimate enterprises in Yugoslavia, crime flourished. Paramilitary units began to come home from Bosnia laden with booty. They also found lucrative new work as smugglers, finding ways to bring in cigarettes, coffee and petrol. Sometimes this was from clandestine trucks offloaded at the borders; sometimes it was more elaborate. Marko, Milošević's son, now in his early twenties, went into the smuggling business along with senior customs officials.

Government coffers, never very full in the first place, soon emptied. Milošević then used his banking expertise to raid the estimated £5 billion worth of savings held by individuals, largely from long years spent as guest workers in Western Europe. Ordinary people found banks telling them that their savings accounts had been temporarily frozen, when in fact the money was being gradually spent. At the end of 1993 Milošević encouraged hyperinflation as a way of forcing Serbs to spend any hard currency they were hoarding. By December 1993 inflation, already high, had gone into a government-assisted free fall. In January 1994 it peaked at a rate most easily expressed as 851 followed by 78 zeros. Each night the national bank printed fresh banknotes worth double the value of those printed the day before, the largest being worth 50 billion dinars, or about £2, when it was issued in early January. Having sucked in people's savings, Milošević then called a halt and the currency was revalued, with inflation falling to a more manageable 50 per cent.

Milošević ran the economy like a juggling act, constantly finding new ways of acquiring the cash he needed to pay his army of state workers and pensioners at least a part of their salaries, along with subsidies to the Bosnian and Croatian Serbs. But Yugoslavia only had a limited amount of hard currency, and poverty crept over the population. It came in another form, too, as the social fabric deteriorated and public morals collapsed. Serbia became a society where honest work was impossible and criminality became a necessity simply to buy food for the family table. In Belgrade the bars and restaurants were full of gangsters and would-be gangsters, who were nicknamed 'Diesel Guys' because they were the only ones able to afford a pair of smuggled jeans bearing the Diesel logo. In 1994 the city saw a spate of mobster turf wars which arose because there were now too many gangsters chasing a dwindling market for smuggled goods. Independent television station B-92 made a documentary about this problem and found that between filming and the programme going on air, three of its interviewees had been gunned down.

While corruption was rampant, Milošević himself stayed aloof from it. No records have been found showing that he personally enriched himself, though he did help direct millions of German marks into bank accounts in Switzerland and Cyprus, presumably for his own use. His personal style remained modest, although he wore fine suits. It seemed that power, rather than wealth, was his ambition. He did, however, ensure that his family lived well through the war years. In 1991 they had swapped their comfortable city centre flat for a huge three-storey villa at 33 Tolstoyeva in Belgrade's smartest suburb, Dedinje. He lavished state money on new decorations and carpets, and on an elaborate security system. His daughter Marija was given her own radio station to operate, while Marko used his privileged position to become a racing car driver. The Yugoslav air force was instructed to clear airbases of planes in order to let him race down their runways. The family remained close. Milošević's wife Mira recorded in her diary in 1994: 'Early this morning, very early, with the first rays of the early morning sun, my son came into my room and announced with a radiant smile: "Mama, I'm twenty years and one day now." I know, as did he, that he was being facetious. Incorrigibly cheerful, sometimes sad without reason, walking on clouds, wrapped up in his dreams of adventure, he will never grow up. He will be forever young, like Peter Pan.'[28]

While the Milošević family fiddled, their Rome burned. From its high water mark in December 1992, the territory held by the Serbs shrank. In January 1993 Croatia attacked across the UN buffer zone, seizing the bridge at Maslenica. Two French soldiers were killed but the UN issued only a mild protest, which was interpreted by the Croats as a signal that they could attack again once they had the strength. In September Croatia retook another piece of Serb-held territory at Medak, south of Zagreb, again breaching the buffer zone and this time murdering twenty-five Serb civilians and burning the village.

In February 1994 the United States pressured Croatia into forcing the Bosnian Croats to give up the idea of an ethnically pure state and make peace with the Bosnian government under the terms of the Washington Treaty. That same month saw the Sarajevo market mortar bombing and the ensuing threat of NATO air strikes. From then on, the Bosnian Serbs went into decline, coming under attack from Bosnian government forces which were now freed from having to fight the Croats.

NATO planes hit Serb units when they attacked Goražde, one of the three eastern Muslim enclaves, in May. In October Bosnian government forces displayed their new strength by storming a rebel Muslim enclave at Bihać in the north-west and then attacking Bosnian Serb forces. The offensive was pushed back by Serb armour, but it was evidence of the changing balance of power in the country.

In May of 1995 Serb forces began shelling the so-called Blue Route, a land corridor bringing goods into Sarajevo. NATO jets bombed two ammunition dumps near the Bosnian Serb capital, Pale, and in retaliation the Serbs took 375 UN monitors hostage, chaining some to the railings of strategic targets. That same month, Croatia launched Operation Flash in which a force of thirty tanks retook Serb-held territory near Pakrac. In anger, Croatian Serb leader Milan Martić fired a ground-to-ground rocket at Zagreb, which killed eleven civilians including visiting dancers from Russia's Bolshoi Ballet. This rocket attack could not obscure the new strategic reality, with the Serbs in both Croatia and Bosnia losing their superiority to their Croat and

Muslim foes. This was partly due to Milošević who, although he dared not cut supplies to these statelets, was careful not to give them the most modern equipment.

This change in the balance of power was not apparent to either side at Sarajevo, where the out-gunned government forces were still being hammered by Serb artillery on the mountains above the city. The main road to Pale from Sarajevo wound up the side of a mountain where, during the siege of the city, Serb soldiers had some emplacements. One bunker had a commanding view of Sarajevo and was nicknamed the Pale Press Centre by journalists because if they wanted a quote from the Serb side of the line, this was the nearest place to get it. Serb soldiers there insisted that they were the victims not the victors in the war, complaining that the cycle of revenge had begun not with their ethnic cleansing in 1992 but long before, with atrocities against Serbs during the Second World War and under the Ottoman Empire. For these men, at least when talking to the Western media, the present war was simply one in a long chain of episodes in which the Serbs had battled against oppression by their neighbours.

Further up the hill, artillery units could be seen hammering at the city. The soldiers manning some, though not all, of these guns were often drunk. They would rise late, drink slivovitz, a plum brandy, and then in the late afternoon and early evening blast away at the city, aiming at nothing in particular. The shelling was heaviest at weekends, when eager volunteers would arrive by car and bus from Belgrade to man the guns until Sunday night when they went back home to their regular jobs.

Inside Sarajevo, large parts of the city could not be used because they were in sniper zones, though residents often ignored these warnings. One of the first things foreign journalists were told when they arrived was not to follow the routes taken by local people. 'The locals,' one journalist was told by a seasoned veteran, 'don't care.' This was wide of the mark, yet it is also true that after so much death and suffering over nearly four years the city's inhabitants were fatalistic. The authorities in Sarajevo were far more tolerant than the Bosnian Serb leadership, and Croats and Serbs continued to live on the government side throughout the war – including the Serb commander of a Bosnian government special forces unit who told me that he had stayed in the city, breaking with his Serbian friends, because he was in love with a Muslim girl.

Yet the Bosnian government had its cynical side. Sarajevo was not evacuated, although the Serbs might have allowed it, because the government knew that the UN would not feed a city unless it had civilians within it. Families were not even allowed to leave the most vulnerable place, Dobrinja, though it was surrounded on three sides by Serb artillery and large areas were destroyed.

The Croatian Serb and Bosnian Serb leaderships were widely accused of corruption, many of them spending most of their time in Belgrade rather than in the statelets they were supposed to control. In the summer of 1994 Bosnian Serb troops in Banja Luka staged a protest, using tanks to block main roads in protest at the smuggling profits amassed by their president, Radovan Karadžić. Karadžić was known as a compulsive gambler, with opposition newspapers in Yugoslavia reporting that he squandered fortunes in the casino of Belgrade's Metropol Hotel. Back in Pale he became almost nocturnal, rising at 5 p.m. and working or drinking all night, with journalists often summoned to see him at four in the morning. Milošević turned to drink, with one British diplomat, arriving to meet him in early 1995, recording that he was slumped in a chair and 'almost incoherent'.

The most important change, and one that the Bosnian and Croatian Serbs either missed or chose to ignore, was that public opinion in Yugoslavia had changed. At the beginning of the Balkan wars, Serb patriotism was strong. By 1995 Serbians were poor and desperate, and just wanted the war and the sanctions to end.

In June of that year Milošević delivered a warning to the rebel leaderships not to expect his help, using his wife Mira as the messenger. In a newspaper column she wrote of her disgust that the Bosnian and Croatian Serb leaders were living in Belgrade, getting rich. 'Did they expect someone else to defend their homes?' she wrote. 'Or the youths from Serbia's towns and villages who are supposed to prove their patriotism by getting killed for the homes of those who left them and came to Belgrade to run their restaurants and firms?'[29]

After the Bosnian Serbs had eventually freed the UN monitors whom they had held hostage for more than a month, the UN quietly moved all its monitors out of Bosnian Serb territory. Meanwhile, NATO moved its Rapid Reaction Force, spearheaded by British and French combat units, into government-held Bosnian territory, ready for a showdown with the Serbs. It had been decided that the next time the Serbs launched a provocation, there would be a harsh response.

Extra bombers were deployed in bases close to the Balkans. Croatian forces commenced a mass mobilisation along the front line facing the Croatian Serbs. Diplomats began speaking about an endgame in Bosnia, when the Serbs would be forced to choose between ultimate defeat and accepting a peace deal in which Bosnia would be reunited. This was truly the last chance for both the Croatian Serb and Bosnian Serb leaderships to make a deal, if only to save their own people from the suffering to come. The UN asked the Croatian Serbs, now badly outnumbered in Knin, to sign a deal to live inside Croatia, offering generous terms. It was on 11 July that the Bosnian Serb commander, General Ratko Mladić, changed the rules of the game by not just seizing Srebrenica but killing the male inhabitants, the worst single massacre of the war.

On 4 August 1995 Croatia opened its long-awaited offensive, named Operation Storm, against the Krajina Serbs. Armoured units slammed into Serb defences along a broad front. Most Serb commanders, including Martić, had run away a few days before, abandoning their people to their fate. Milošević, as his wife had indicated, did not offer military assistance. Serb defences, outnumbered five to one, buckled and then collapsed. By 5 August Croatia's red and white chequerboard flag flew over Knin castle, which had fallen without a fight. Several dozen Serb civilians were murdered by vengeful Croatian soldiers. There was no orchestrated campaign of ethnic cleansing by the Croatian army command, for the simple reason that the Serbs did not stick around to wait for the invaders to arrive. In the space of a day, almost the entire Krajina Serb population took flight, leaving their homes and racing for the border with Bosnia. The highway from Krajina across the north of Serb-held Bosnia, and all the way to Belgrade, was clogged with cars, carts, tractors, trucks and buses, carrying a quarter of a million people into exile.

It was the greatest Serb migration since the retreat from Belgrade in 1915, and recalled the earlier migrations following the failed rebellions of 1690 and 1737. It also punctured in spectacular fashion the myth of the invincibility of the Croatian Serbs, who had been proud of their tradition of fighting for centuries in the Krajina, the military zone of Croatia. Until now they had taken courage from a heritage of bloody resistance stretching back to the great, sacrificial battle fought by St Lazar at Kosovo Polje in 1389. Yet now they took flight. 'The Serbs, caught up in Lazar's myth, believe that they always stand and fight. When defeat looms though, they are as prudent as other people. They run,' wrote Tim Judah in his historic study, *The Serbs*.[30] A British army officer told the author that the Serbs in Bosnia reacted in much the same way. A government offensive had only to seize one town for the entire Serb line to pull back, so worried were the soldiers about being surrounded and captured. Serbs had fought doggedly in the Second World War for something they believed in. But in 1995 it seemed that Senator Bob Dole had been correct in seeing this war as opportunistic.

On 24 August five Serb mortar shells slammed into Sarajevo's Markale market killing thirty-seven people – the same market where sixty-nine civilians had been killed the year before. Two days later, NATO jets bombed ammunition dumps and Tomahawk cruise missiles fired from US Navy ships in the Adriatic destroyed Bosnian Serb air defence sites, radio transmitters and telephone exchanges. 'Finally the decks were cleared for a real military response, not some piece of garbage,' proclaimed America's Balkan envoy, Richard Holbrooke.[31] British and French artillery hammered Serb artillery positions around Sarajevo.

NATO bombed the Bosnian Serbs for ten days, and the Croats and government forces took their chance and launched ground attacks. By the end of August government forces were at the gates of Banja Luka, the largest Serb-held town. Milošević, already struggling to find homes for a quarter of a million Croatian Serb refugees, complained to the UN that he could not absorb a similar number from Bosnia. America decided to call a halt and Richard Holbrooke instructed the Croatians to pull back their artillery. Croatia had been helped in Operation Storm by a group of American mercenaries called Military Professional Resources Inc., most of them retired US Army generals. Although a private company, MPRI only undertook contracts approved by the US government, so Croatia understood that it had the support of Washington. Not wanting to lose it, the Croats did as Holbrooke instructed. Starved of artillery support, the mostly Muslim units around Banja Luka were pushed back by a Serb tank attack. NATO stopped its bombing campaign, and a sudden lull fell over Bosnia.

The Bosnian Serbs knew that only prompt action would save them from the fate of their Croatian counterparts. Milošević summoned Bosnian Serb president Radovan Karadžić to Belgrade and told him that this was the time to sign a version of the deal he had rejected in May 1993 – a deal that would mean Bosnia was united as a single state. Milošević also demanded that he give him the right to negotiate a peace deal on behalf of the Bosnian Serbs. Karadžić, tired and stressed, decided he had no choice, and accepted. On 5 October a ceasefire went into effect in Bosnia. In November, Milošević joined Croatian president Franjo Tudjman and Bosnian president Alija Izetbegović at Dayton airbase, in Ohio, to sign a peace deal. This deal, a well-constructed piece of realpolitik, was crafted by Holbrooke and was in essence simple. Bosnia was to become one country but divided into two entities: one for the Serbs, and the other for the Croats and Muslims. Tudjman and Milošević were there to guarantee that the Croats and Serbs would observe the agreement. Izetbegović, for whom the deal was less than he wanted, was told that it was the only one on offer. There was nervousness in The Hague that key leaders might be offered immunity deals over war crimes, but in fact this was never considered. Right in the middle of the Dayton process, chief prosecutor Goldstone charged Karadžić and Mladić with genocide for the Srebrenica massacre, adding to an earlier charge of war crimes for the 1992 ethnic cleansing.

While hard talking went on at Dayton, Milošević seemed to understand that a deal was now inevitable. The Dayton peace agreement gave the Bosnian Serbs more or less the same territory as the Vance–Owen plan had offered them more than two years before, except that now NATO troops occupied their land and they had to disarm. Radovan Karadžić, indicted for war crimes, was forced to step down as president.

Milošević began to enjoy himself at Dayton airbase. He joked with American diplomats, used a flight simulator for recreation and even flirted with his favourite waitress, Vicky, at Packy's All-Sports Bar. His attitude was in studied contrast to the gloom of Bosnian president Alija Izetbegović who seemed unable to forget the suffering his people had endured. 'Milošević knew us very well as a people, he was able to play with us,' said one US official. 'He had an uncanny ability to judge how serious we were, and in most cases he would be right.'[32]

Milošević achieved an astonishing trick at Dayton. Having started the war in the first place, with his crusade for Greater Serbia, he now emerged with the thanks of a grateful world for having stopped it.

The judges and prosecutors in The Hague were pleased to see the end of the war, but they also felt a profound sense of failure. For all its hard work, the Tribunal had yet to hold a single trial or to make any appreciable difference to the war in response to which it had been created. There were just five suspects in jail awaiting trial and seventy-three more, mostly Serbs, on its wanted list.

When he first came to The Hague, Cassese said that the Tribunal's mission was 'to do justice, to deter further crimes and to contribute to the restoration and maintenance of peace'. It was hard to see how the court had achieved any of these things. Bosnia's slaughter had gone on for four long years. What was worse, from the Tribunal's point of view, was that Milošević appeared to have got away with murder.

Operation Tango   6

I know this agreement would not have been possible without you.

You made Dayton possible.

President Bill Clinton to Slobodan Milošević, November 1995

In early July 1997, by means that remain classified, a team of British SAS soldiers took up positions in undergrowth overlooking a small lake outside the north-western Bosnian town of Prijedor. The lake was the favourite fishing spot of Prijedor's police chief, Simo Drljača, and the soldiers had orders to wait until either he showed up to go fishing or they ran out of food. On the morning of 10 July they looked out from their hiding place to see a car bumping down the dusty track that led to the lake shore. It stopped, a door opened, and out stepped Drljača. The soldiers looked at each other. Upon their mission hung the future of the war crimes court.

In September 1996 the International Criminal Tribunal for the Former Yugoslavia had acquired a new chief prosecutor with a new mission. Feisty Canadian judge Louise Arbour arrived determined to persuade the outside world to make the arrests needed to allow the court to work.

Arbour was the personal choice of retiring chief prosecutor Richard Goldstone, which surprised many because the two were very different people. Whereas Goldstone was dry and serious, Arbour was charming and even flirtatious. On holiday shortly before taking the job, she had decided on a whim to have a tattoo on her ankle – not a common habit among the world's most senior judges.

As a judge in Ontario she had made a name for herself with a report blaming police for inciting a riot in a women's prison. She had come to the notice of the Hague court for ruling in favour of a suspect accused of war crimes. In the 1980s Canada had tried a man, originally from

Germany, who was charged with having deported Jews to the gas chambers during the Second World War. He was found not guilty, and the prosecutors appealed. Arbour backed the decision of the original trial. It seemed strange to some that Goldstone would want a prosecutor who had taken the side of the defence in such a case, but he felt that she was someone committed to justice. 'I took the job because Richard Goldstone told me about it. He portrayed it very accurately as this great intellectual challenge. We never had much of a conversation about what you actually do there,' Arbour told me.[1]

When Arbour arrived at The Hague she found morale low. Just five suspects were held in the thirty-six-cell Hague prison. Indictees were refusing to come to the court. 'The tribunal was in its whining mode. It was constantly whining, nobody's helping us, why are we so abandoned? I said, what are you talking about? Sometimes it takes an outsider to turn a situation completely on its head.'

The chief problem was that the Hague court had no police force. It had to rely on outside nations to arrest suspects. And in 1996 nobody wanted to do this. Since the end of the Bosnian war a sixty-thousand-strong Implementation Force, led by NATO, had garrisoned Bosnia. But the commander, the American admiral Leighton Smith, was adamant that his troops would not be used for arrest missions. 'Remember Mogadishu,' he declared early in 1996, in a reference to the botched operation in Somalia three years before in which US forces had attempted to snatch the warlord Mohamed Aidid. The mission had failed to find him and in the resulting battle eighteen American soldiers had been killed, along with nearly three hundred Somalis. NATO generals feared that arrest operations would cost the lives of their soldiers and might also trigger unrest among the Bosnian Serbs.

Officially, NATO's rules were that soldiers should arrest a war crimes suspect if they found one 'in the course of their duties'. In practice, even if a NATO soldier met a suspect, it would be difficult to recognise him from among the galaxy of faces depicted on the court's Wanted posters distributed across Bosnia. 'There was this obsession about a backlash, there was this reluctance to get stuck in,' said Duncan Bullivant, a former British army officer working with the senior Western envoy in Bosnia, Carl Bildt. 'The psychology was that if we arrest Karadžić, there will be rioting, we will lose lives.'

Radovan Karadžić, realising that NATO was not going to arrest him, began living openly at his villa in Pale in the hills above Sarajevo. This was a twenty-minute drive from NATO's headquarters but at no time did NATO troops bother him. Journalists were able to drive up to his villa and chat to his security guards. One typical summer's day his security detail were sitting in the shade of a tree, one of them using his bayonet to open a fat watermelon. A green armoured car from the nearby Italian garrison rolled by and Karadžić's men waved to the driver. The guard commander, hefty muscles bunched under a black T-shirt, told the journalists they were welcome to hang around but that Karadžić was not at home. Asked what, in that case, the guards were doing there, one of them shouted 'eating watermelon'.

For Louise Arbour such scenes were not a joke, but the outside world had lost interest in Bosnia. The war was over and most Western governments were happy to forget about the country.[2] Arbour turned elsewhere to try to find her police force. While NATO would not help, there was a small force under UN command in north-east Croatia, based around the town of Vukovar. In October 1996 she came up with a bold plan to use this force to arrest a war crimes suspect.

In 1991 Serbian forces had massacred two hundred and fifty Croat civilians outside the town of Vukovar and one of the commanders blamed was the former Serb mayor, Slavko Dokmanović. In 1996 Vukovar was handed over from Serb to Croatian control, with the UN force deployed to prevent violence, and Dokmanović had fled to Yugoslavia. Arbour received information that he was still living in the region, in a house on the Yugoslav side of the border. If he could somehow be lured a few miles north into Croatia, the UN could arrest him.

Arbour contacted the local commander, a large, bullish American diplomat called Jacques Klein, who said that he would be happy to use his troops to make the arrest. The problem was how to persuade

Dokmanović to come into Croatia. A Hague prosecutor made contact in the autumn and asked him if he could give information on war crimes committed by Croats against Serbs. He agreed and the prosecutor said that, because he could not get a visa for Yugoslavia, perhaps the meeting could be in Croatia. Dokmanović refused, fearing that he would be arrested by Croatian police. The lure appeared to have collapsed.

In November the main powers concerned with peace in Bosnia held a meeting in London called the Peace Implementation Council. For Arbour, this was a chance to change some minds about using NATO to make war crimes arrests. However, the Hague court received no invitation to attend – a reminder of its lowly status in the eyes of the outside world. Tribunal president Antonio Cassese was furious and complained, and the British organisers relented and issued two invitations. Cassese said he was insulted and would not go, sending his clerk, John Jones, to represent him. Arbour went too, anxious to make her case on the world stage. 'It was an absolutely critical time, the end of '96 and beginning of '97. It would not have been unthinkable then that the Tribunal would be dismantled or sort of left to fizzle with lack of support,' she told me.

The conference took place in a large, oak-panelled room in the British Foreign Office, but Arbour arrived to find no place for her at the meeting table. Instead, she was told to sit with the spectators. 'It was very clear we couldn't get the Tribunal to get a seat at the table of this London conference, which frankly was a bit cheeky. They were still treating this institution as at worst an irritant and at best as irrelevant.'

Her luck changed when she was spotted by Dutch foreign minister, Hans van Mierlo, a keen supporter of the Tribunal. He had presided over The Netherlands substantial financial contribution to the establishment of the Tribunal, and the Dutch also felt considerable guilt over the surrender of their troops at Srebrenica the previous year. He put up his hand and proposed that the meeting make space for Arbour. Without visible enthusiasm, the ministers shuffled along to make room and a chair was found for her. 'Nobody had the nerve to say, well, no she can't,' she remembered.

Van Mierlo again put his hand up, this time to call for Arbour to have the right to speak. Again, a quick vote was taken and it was agreed that she could make a short address after the first morning break. She was alarmed because she had not expected to make a speech and had nothing prepared. Now, she sensed, she was being asked to deliver an address that could make or break the international court, with only half an hour in which to prepare it. 'It was a brilliant idea, except these delegations were there with fax machines, with ministers, each with four helpers in the background,' she said. 'And I'm there all by myself. All I had was a pen.'

Outside the meeting room, she sent Jones to phone Cassese in The Hague and ask him for any points he wanted made. Meanwhile, she sat at a small table and scribbled notes on spare pieces of paper.

Armed with these, and suggestions from Cassese, Arbour walked back into the room feeling all eyes upon her. She knew that everyone would expect an emotional appeal for support. But she decided to go one better. She would not appeal for support – she would demand it. She stood up and said that the UN Security Council had mandated the war crimes court and now the world's powers must support the decision. 'I told them this is not a matter of political choice, it's the law and you have to do it. I told them, "You are required by law to execute these arrest warrants. The Security Council resolution says all states shall cooperate, and shall execute the orders issued by the court."'

She sat down to a polite silence. There was no applause from the statesmen sitting around the table, nor did she find offers of help pouring in during the weeks that followed. But at least she had made her mark. 'It didn't happen overnight but this made the foundation, this was the critical part. It was very important that we should assert ourselves, not as a political player but as the only judicial one.'

Arbour spent the winter trying to build on these foundations. She flew to European capitals, pointing out that the people she wanted to arrest, such as Karadžić, were also political figures standing in the way of the Bosnian peace process. Elections the previous September had produced big gains for Croat, Muslim and Serb nationalist parties – including many of the same Croat and Serb warlords who had masterminded the ethnic cleansing. These men could not be beaten at the ballot box but, she suggested, some could be arrested for war crimes. 'I wanted them to give justice a chance to play its hand in the peace process by removing people who, in many cases, were common criminals before the war, war criminals during the war, and had reverted back to essentially being common criminals, racketeers and black marketeers. I told them it's not as though everything else was working so beautifully. It was more plausible to say well, at least give justice a chance, as opposed to give peace a chance.'

She also introduced a new kind of indictment, called the sealed indictment, which was made in secret so that a war crimes suspect would not realise they were being targeted. A sealed indictment, Arbour explained, would give NATO commandos the element of surprise if they chose to make an arrest.

In Washington, Madeleine Albright, moved from the UN to become Clinton's Secretary of State after his 1996 re-election, was sympathetic. But she was a lone voice. The Pentagon was against war crimes arrests, and no European power would support Arbour's demand. 'The first time that we went outside the Tribunal with these sealed indictments, the first response was one of shock and dismay I think it is fair to say, because it took only a few minutes for people to understand the implications. So the reaction was not all that positive.'

In May 1997 everything changed and the fortunes of the Hague Tribunal were revived by a single, apparently unrelated, event, which was the election in Britain of a Labour government. The Labour Party of Tony Blair arrived in office promising an 'ethical foreign policy'. The new Foreign Secretary, Robin Cook, was aware of Arbour's bold stance at the London conference of the previous November. Now he won cabinet approval to use the SAS to go after war crimes suspects. With Cook backing the idea, Albright pushed America to give its support.

By early June an arrest plan was taking shape. A massive operation was proposed to round up twenty top suspects, including Karadžić. According to Madeleine Albright, it was called off when an unnamed nation changed its mind. 'We had in mind a Bosnia-wide sweep designed to net Karadžić and fifteen to twenty other suspected war criminals in a single day,' she wrote in her memoirs.[3] 'I was angered when, at the last minute, a key country whose identity remains secret opted out.'[4]

The identity remains secret but many war crimes officials believe that it was France that pulled out of a joint operation also involving America, Britain and The Netherlands. Instead, Britain and America decided to go ahead with the arrest of two suspects, with Britain providing the ground troops and America the air support. For the SAS this mission was unusual because, far from going in with all guns blazing, they had to make sure that their target was taken unharmed. Arbour offered the SAS two suspects who seemed the perfect choice. Simo Drljača and Dr Milan Kovačević had been the architects of the Omarska prison camp during the Bosnian war, so few could dispute that they had crimes to answer for. The two men were also powerful political figures in post-war Bosnia, Drljača as Prijedor police chief and Kovačević as director of the town hospital. The Dayton peace plan called for Prijedor's surviving Muslims to be allowed to return home, but few dared to do so with their former tormentors still in power. Finally, intelligence from British units based nearby reported that the two men were not popular among local Serbs because of their links with corruption and organised crime, so arresting them should not provoke too much anger.

The operation took several weeks to organise. The most difficult aspect was not the arrest, but tracking the movements of both men so that the snatch could be planned with the lowest possible risk of bloodshed. A senior source involved in the planning, speaking on condition of anonymity, said that the hardest part was piecing together the movement patterns of the two men. 'The operation had three phases – starting point, surveillance, lift. The key in these operations is to get a starting point. It's immensely difficult in the sense that before you can start planning an operation to lift someone you actually need to find a start point from which you can gather intelligence and information that will allow you to mount the operation to pick him up. Sometimes the surveillance gets under way only to discover you have not found a start point at all – that the suspect in fact lives somewhere else.'

British commanders wanted to snatch the men in a situation in which they would not be armed and would be alone. This ruled out raiding their homes because in the time it took to kick in a door a suspect could pick up a gun and shoot one of the soldiers. There was also a secondary risk that the men's families could be caught in the crossfire.

It was decided that Kovačević could be arrested while at work in his office at the city hospital. The arrest of Drljača was more difficult because his workplace, Prijedor police headquarters, was full of armed Serb police and the SAS could walk into a firefight. They were also unhappy about trying to snatch him while he was driving to or from work. Reconnaissance showed that he was always armed, and in the time it would take to get vehicles in front of and behind his car, and for a soldier to wrench open the door, he would be able to draw his weapon.

'The surveillance is to try and identify an opportunity to lift the guy in such a way as to do no harm to and with minimal involvement of others. Maybe his work routine. Maybe out and about. That surveillance can go on for a long time; you can wait for the circumstances to be right. We would always pull away from any option that was potentially controversial. Frustration is a major part of it,' said the source.

After several weeks of observation, the SAS finally hit on a solution for capturing Drljača. It was realised, as the weather grew warmer, that he liked to fish, and observation showed that he often went to the same spot, a small lake south-east of Prijedor, not far from Omarska. From an operational point of view the spot was perfect. It was far from the town, so there would be no angry crowd to protest or to get caught in any crossfire. The open countryside around the lake would also mean that helicopters could swoop in. The only problem was predicting when he would turn up. It was possible that the SAS could insert a team at a moment when he had a heavy workload, or was called away, or perhaps took a summer holiday. They decided that this was a chance they had to take. A small team, believed to be less than half a dozen, was positioned by the lake in early July and told to wait.

Slobodan Milošević in court at the war crimes tribunal in The Hague
(Corbis)

Kosovan refugees in Albania (Corbis)

Bosnian Serb camp, shed interior (Ron Haviv / VII)

Starving prisoners in Bosnian Serb detention camp (Ron Haviv / VII)

Bosnian families bury victims of Srebrenica massacre (Corbis)

Srebrenica refugees (Corbis)

The Siege of Sarajevo: wrecked multi-story buildings tower above the city
(Corbis)

Arkan and his troops, known as 'the Tigers' (Ron Haviv / VII)

Hague Tribunal former court president Judge Antonio Cassese (Courtesy: International Criminal Tribunal for the former Yugoslavia (ICTY)/UN)

Hague Tribunal former chief prosecutor Justice Louise Arbour (Courtesy: International Criminal Tribunal for the former Yugoslavia (ICTY)/UN)

Hague Tribunal chief prosecutor Carla Del Ponte (Courtesy: International Criminal Tribunal for the former Yugoslavia (ICTY)/UN)

Hague Tribunal building (Courtesy: International Criminal Tribunal for the former Yugoslavia (ICTY)/UN)

Hague Tribunal former chief prosecutor Justice Richard Goldstone, Prosecutor, ICTY (Courtesy: International Criminal Tribunal for the former Yugoslavia (ICTY)/UN)

John Jones, ICTY Defence Counsel, In Lincoln's Inn, London (Chris Stephen)

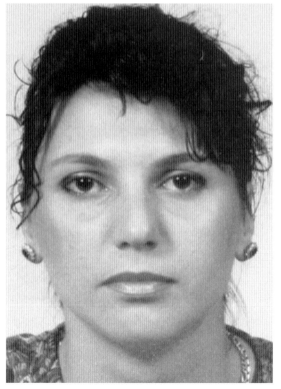

Above:
Nusreta Sivac
(Chris Stephen)

Left: Edna Duatović
(Chris Stephen)

Hiding for extended periods in enemy terrain is a prized skill among the SAS. The Hollywood image of special forces soldiers jumping from helicopters with guns blazing is only one side of their job. Less publicised is their training in long-range reconnaissance. For the team sent to catch Drljača the waiting was something for which they were well prepared. Many pieces of kit, such as compass and knife, are attached to the uniform with pieces of string so that they cannot be dropped and left behind to be found by enemy soldiers. They even defecate into cling film, taking this away with them, along with any other litter, so as to leave no traces of their presence. Meanwhile, two American helicopters, piloted by specialist crews, were put on permanent readiness at a NATO airfield in northern Bosnia.

One more problem remained to be solved before the operation could begin. Although the undertaking was to be Anglo-American, the authority for it to take place in Bosnia belonged to the Implementation Force which involved more than fifty nations, and this meant that each NATO member would need to be informed and to give its approval. Alliance leaders were likely to be nervous about authorising such a mission. A demonstration was needed that such arrests could take place without triggering civil unrest among the Serbs.

Here luck played its part. In neighbouring Croatia the plan to trap Slavko Dokmanović, the former mayor of Vukovar, suddenly came back to life. Having refused to come to Croatia to meet war crimes prosecutors, he changed his mind and got in touch with the Hague prosecutors. He told them that he would come to Croatia to meet them on one condition. As mayor of Vukovar he had owned a nice house, and now he wanted to sell it to the incoming Croatians and needed the UN to establish his property rights. So he asked if they could fix a meeting with the head of the UN mission, Jacques Klein. This was a tall order. The plan was for Klein's commandos to arrest Dokmanović, so the promise of a meeting would be a straight lie. Nevertheless, Klein agreed, and the trap was set. After months of talks, Dokmanović agreed to walk across the border and meet the prosecutors in their car. A senior American Hague prosecutor, Clint Williamson, flew to Croatia. Klein had only one special forces unit under his command, a Polish commando company. These troops were now alerted.

Shortly after three in the afternoon of 27 June, Dokmanović arrived at a bridge over the Danube River which marked the Yugoslav border with Croatia. A car was waiting with two men inside. As arranged, Dokmanović walked across from the Yugoslav side into UN-administered Croatian territory. One of the men got out of the car and held the door open for him. He gave a curt greeting and then got in, to find himself looking not at a middle-aged prosecutor but at a young Polish army officer. Quickly, his arms were pinned, then tied, and a canvas sack was pulled over his head.

Trussed like a chicken, the two men, both Polish special forces soldiers, drove Dokmanović from the bridge to a nearby UN base, where the car was surrounded by a cordon of soldiers. Walking through their midst was prosecutor Williamson, holding in his hand a war crimes indictment with Dokmanović's name on it. The sack was removed and Dokmanović immediately began protesting that he had been kidnapped. Williamson read him his rights, and later that day he was on board a Belgian air force plane heading for The Hague.

With the success of this mission, the fears among NATO chiefs about their own arrest operation subsided. The SAS men were cleared for what was named Operation Tango. When the team saw Drljača arrive at the fishing lake they were apprehensive because their quarry was not alone. Along with him was his 14-year-old son. As they watched, Drljača took out a fishing rod and wandered over to the lake. He stripped off his shirt, but then jammed a pistol into the waistband of his shorts.

Nevertheless, the decision was taken to make the arrest. The SAS signalled their second team to go after Kovačević in Prijedor. Another signal went to the American helicopters. Meanwhile, troops across Serb parts of Bosnia were put on alert and told to prepare for possible civil unrest.

On the lake shore, one of the SAS team broke cover and ran towards Drljača. He heard the noise of the footsteps, turned, and reached for his gun. He had got the weapon cocked as the SAS man reached him. The

British soldier grabbed him, but Drljača fired off a shot, the bullet grazing the man's thigh. A second soldier sitting in the bushes had Drljača in his gunsight. He had a split second to make a decision, and there was little hesitation. Before Drljača could take a second shot, the sniper opened fire and the Prijedor police chief fell dead.

At almost exactly the same time, in the centre of Prijedor two men in civilian clothes walked quickly up the steps into the town's main hospital. One of them carried a package under his arm embossed with a red cross. They told a receptionist that they had a delivery for the hospital director, Dr Kovačević. The receptionist assumed they were from one of the dozens of aid groups and charities working in Bosnia at the time. She showed them Kovačević's office. Once inside, it was almost an anticlimax. One of them produced a gun, introduced himself, and the doctor was hustled outside to a waiting vehicle.

At the lake shore, two American helicopters arrived. The SAS men loaded the body of Drljača into one machine and forced his son in beside him. Then the rest of the team boarded the second helicopter and both flew away. Operation Tango was over.

In The Hague, chief prosecutor Louise Arbour was pleased. Operation Tango had been less than a perfect success, with one suspect dead and one soldier wounded. The Red Cross asked NATO to explain rumours that the SAS men in Prijedor had been posing as Red Cross members. There were also claims that Drljača's son had been forced to lie on the floor of the helicopter next to the dead body of his father. However, the operation had worked, and there was no public protest. British units in the Prijedor area reported in the weeks that followed that many Serbs were not sorry to see the two men gone, blaming them for running rackets in the town.[5]

With this one operation, the fortunes of the Hague court were transformed and it was now taken seriously. 'In the region everybody felt a little chill,' said Arbour. 'The next time we arrived in town, so to speak, we were no longer perceived as this kind of pathetic, spin-their-wheel, NGO type. We were perceived as pretty serious and pretty scary people. Which is what we are supposed to be.' Others put it even more strongly: 'There was a long period in which the Tribunal was hanging on a knife edge between success and failure. It wasn't until NATO made those arrests that the future was secure,' said John Jones.

More raids followed in the coming months. Dutch troops swooped on two Bosnian Croats charged with the massacre of Muslims at Ahmići in 1993. American troops made several arrests of Serbs in the north of the country.[6]

In the summer, America pressured Croatia into handing over ten Bosnian Croats living on its soil. The leverage was international loans, which the Croats desperately needed. So Zagreb handed over all ten on the same day, some of them wanted for the Ahmići massacre.[7]

Immediately he heard news of Operation Tango, Karadžić vanished from his villa in Pale, and as of March 2004 he remains on the run, believed to be living in the mountains and forests of south-eastern Bosnia and northern Montenegro, from where his family originates. In 1998 NATO arrested seven more suspects, and the Hague court found that these operations had a knock-on effect, with more than a dozen more people giving themselves up because they feared arrest and thought it would look better if they turned themselves in. The arrests did not always go smoothly. One suspect was killed and another blew himself up, and the SAS once arrested the wrong pair of Bosnian Serb twins, their innocence only being established after the poor men had been flown, under restraint, to The Hague.

In 1997 the Hague judges passed their first sentences. Duško Tadić, the camp guard charged with sadistic acts against prisoners, was jailed for 20 years. Dražen Erdemović, who had turned himself in for crimes committed at Srebrenica, was jailed for 10 years. A new mood of confidence swept over the war crimes court and the year ended on a high note. The more her investigators probed into the crimes of the Croatian and Bosnian wars, the more evidence Arbour saw pointing to Milošević as the man in charge. However, indicting Milošević was a tricky proposition because of the difficulty in finding definite proof. The crimes in Bosnia and Croatia were carried out by local Serb forces and, officially at least, Milošević, as president of Serbia, had no control over them. Piecing together the chain of command would take a long time, and Arbour doubted whether she yet had sufficient evidence.

However, early in 1998 something happened in the Balkans that changed this equation in dramatic fashion. On 5 March something strange began happening in the woods south of the town of Mitrovica, in Serbia's Kosovo province. From among the trees, wandering alone or in small groups, came women and children from the ethnic Albanian village of Prekaz. They were tired, some were in nightclothes, and many had tear-stained faces. They told townspeople that their village, on the far side of a line of hills, had been attacked in the early hours of the morning by Serb soldiers and helicopters firing rockets. Their menfolk, most of them unarmed, had stayed behind, ordering their families to flee.

On that day Serb forces surrounded, and began obliterating, the farmstead at Prekaz occupied by a well-known man, Adem Jashari. Big, bearded and boisterous, he saw himself as heir to the kachaks, Albanian guerrillas cum bandits who had made war on the Serbs, and occasionally on each other, for centuries. Prekaz sat deep in the rolling hills and woods of Kosovo's central Drenica region. Jashari had been accused of shooting a Serb policeman several years previously, but the authorities were frightened of trying to arrest him because he would open fire when police vehicles approached. In late 1997 the first signs of a guerrilla organisation called the Kosovo Liberation Army had appeared. Albanians identified as collaborators with the Serbs were found dead. Others discovered bags of coffee or chairs left outside their front doors, traditional signs of a house where someone has died, which were considered as a warning to the occupants to leave town. While the KLA remained secretive, Jashari went public, being photographed as a KLA leader in army uniform and brandishing weapons.

In January 1998 armed Serbian police tried to arrest him, but he turned his farm into a fortress and fired back. Then on 5 March troops of the Serbian Interior Ministry surrounded his house, then opened fire with heavy weapons. The battle was one-sided and after two days it ended with the farmstead in ruins. Jashari was killed along with fifty members of his family, among them twelve women. The only survivor was his 11-year-old granddaughter, who survived because she had been placed beneath a thick oak dinner table which withstood the impact when the roof fell on top of her. One of her last memories was of her grandfather singing songs as shells crashed into the building.

The attack had the opposite effect from that intended. Instead of subduing Kosovo's Albanians, they were galvanised. The KLA, at the time a tiny guerrilla organisation struggling to find members, was transformed almost overnight into a mass movement. Within a week of the Jashari attack, a small 'free zone' was established around a cluster of Drenica villages. Within a month, attacks on Serb police posts had become daily events. By May, the 'free zone' included several huge pockets covering almost a quarter of the province.[8] These lightning victories were won mostly because Serb forces withdrew without fighting. Yugoslav army units stayed out of the fighting, while the police were content to let the Albanians grab large chunks of territory in areas where few Serbs lived.

In June, all this changed. Milošević ordered Interior Ministry troops into the province under the command of Franko Simatović, head of the special forces of his secret service and one of the original planners of the ethnic cleansing in Bosnia. These units, equipped with armoured vehicles and heavy weapons, smashed the KLA defences. By early July 1998 great columns of smoke were rising from Albanian villages. The KLA had grown too fast and was disorganised, with no central command. As in previous Serb wars, civilians bore the brunt of the suffering. In September the British politician Paddy Ashdown, leader of the Liberal Democrats, stood watching Serbian artillery hammering ethnic Albanian villages.

In The Hague, Louise Arbour had to decide whether to investigate Kosovo or ignore it. The decision was difficult because by 1998 her investigations into Bosnian and Croatian crimes were making good progress. To divert staff to look at Kosovo would mean closing down some of the Bosnian investigations. 'By the time Kosovo happened we were in full flight; we were starting to be very focused. For the first time we felt we knew where we were going; we had no spare resources to devote to it, so if we were going to pay attention to Kosovo we had to take people off these ongoing investigations.' Yet with the television news showing the slaughter each evening, she felt she had no choice. She remembers telling her staff: 'We are called upon to operate as a real-time law enforcement agency and for us it is a test we cannot fail.'

Slobodan Milošević seemed unsure how to act when fighting flared in Kosovo in 1998. In the wars in Bosnia and Croatia, he had been the orchestrator. Now the KLA was dictating the pace. The end of the Bosnian war had seen economic sanctions lifted but, at American insistence, a so-called outer wall of sanctions remained, denying Serbia credit. This outer wall was intended to ensure that Milošević kept his word and respected the Dayton agreement. The effect was to keep Yugoslavia impoverished and Milošević struggling to run the country.

A different politician might have decided to normalise Serbia, allowing normal democratic parties to flourish. Instead, Milošević continued to hold on to the levers of power. Possibly he felt trapped by the system he had created. He had made many enemies over the years and feared that if he relaxed his grip on the state, or relinquished control of the security service, he would be in trouble. 'What you have to understand,' a British intelligence official told me at the time, 'is that Milošević is riding the tiger. He is the only one of the Balkan leaders who cannot retire. Can you see him in a little house in the country? Impossible.'

In November 1996 demonstrations had broken out in Belgrade after the authorities refused to recognise the election victory of opposition mayoral candidate Zoran Djindjić. Soon two hundred thousand, mostly young demonstrators poured onto the streets. The protests continued right through a freezing winter with all the colour and passion of 1991 – and humour too. Students threw thousands of paper planes at the government headquarters.

Milošević reacted by organising a counter-demonstration of workers loyal to his rule. But only sixty thousand workers turned up, and soon opposition began to spread. The Orthodox Church signalled support for the demonstrators, protesting against a 'Communist, godless and satanic regime'.[9] Finally, an elite paratroop unit published a joint letter signalling its support, while army commander General Momčilo Perišić staged a public meeting with student leaders. At this point, dissent broke out within Milošević's SPS party, with the Niš branch joining the protestors. Reports appeared in the media that the chief of the secret service, Jovica Stanišić, had refused Milošević's demand that he use force against the protests. Shortly after this was made public, Milošević gave way and the election commission suddenly announced that it was recognising Djindjić's victory in Belgrade.

In July 1997 Milošević, having served his two terms as Serbian president, stood instead for election as president of Yugoslavia. The democratic opposition had fallen into one of its bouts of squabbling, and he won the election. The problem of how to run a country that was bankrupt remained. In Belgrade there was a series of gangland killings which reached even his confidants. In April 1997 Radovan Stojičić, or Badža, one of Milošević's inner circle who had organised the 1992 ethnic cleansing, was shot dead in a Belgrade restaurant.

Milošević went to the funeral, but many thought he had authorised the killing in order to rid himself of a potential witness at The Hague war crimes court. In October gunmen killed another of his inner circle, Zoran Todorović, leader of Yugoslav Left, or JUL, a political party created by Milošević's wife, Mira. Milošević moved house, from 33 Tolstoyeva to Tito's former palace. This was situated in the best suburb, Dedinje, and within its grounds were two grand residences and Tito's tomb. On Mira's orders, furniture was thrown out and smashed and the Persian carpets taken outside and burned. The workmen were forbidden to take them home. Inside, Mira redecorated the bathroom with navy blue tiles.

The world was indebted to the Croatian secret service for an insight into what was going on, as disclosed in a bugged phone call between Mira and Marko:

Marko: 'When I walked in, I couldn't believe it, honestly.'

Mira: 'That's because your mommy chose everything. It has been closed for seventeen years, ever since Tito died. I threw everything out.

Literally everything. Except a few chandeliers downstairs and one chandelier here. Look at our living rooms on the first floor. Look at the dining room, the kitchen. Also go upstairs and to the penthouse.'[10]

Mira took to wearing imported designer labels – this at a time when ordinary Serbs, not least the half million refugees from Krajina and Bosnia, were mired in poverty. She hired image consultants. She was reported to have had liposuction at Belgrade's military hospital.[11] Marko opened a disco called Madona (*sic*) in his father's home town, Požarevac, and began work in the same area on Serbia's answer to Disneyland – named Bambiland.

In October 1998 Richard Holbrooke, the US envoy who had negotiated the Dayton peace treaty, flew into Belgrade. He threatened Milošević with NATO air strikes unless he agreed to stop fighting in Kosovo. A deal was signed, international monitors were brought into the province, and NATO jets were kept on standby at bases in Italy.

As winter drew in, the Albanian guerrillas in Kosovo continued to attack Serb positions. Serb forces responded, often with artillery, and often targeting civilians rather than the guerrillas. By January 1999 only heavy snow was keeping the KLA from launching large-scale operations. NATO commander US general Wesley Clark warned that major fighting would begin in the spring unless diplomats could think up a political solution.

One of the KLA base areas was in a large area of territory in south-eastern Kosovo. This area bordered onto a highway that ran past the village of Račak. Ambushes against Serb military convoys driving by were common. In January two Serb policemen were shot and killed in the area, and Serb police launched a counter-attack. They met light opposition from the surrounding hills and moved into the village of Račak. This was not a guerrilla stronghold, being too near the main highway. Exactly what happened there on 15 January 1999 is still unknown, but at the end of the day aid workers stumbled on the bodies of forty-six civilians lying in ditches, having been shot at close range. None was armed. A few days later, an American newspaper carried what it said were transcripts, apparently acquired by US intelligence, in which, in a conversation with a senior officer in Belgrade, a Serb officer admits to having massacred the men. The senior officer orders him to cover this up.

A few days later, The Hague's chief prosecutor, Louise Arbour, arrived in the province to investigate. She was turned away by Yugoslav customs officers, apparently on Milošević's orders. NATO, having threatened bombing if there were further Serb atrocities, now backed down. In February, France and Britain, with America's blessing, held peace talks at the chateau of Rambouillet outside Paris. They summoned the ethnic Albanian and Serb leaderships to come and make a deal on Kosovo. Milošević refused to turn up, and many of the KLA senior leadership also stayed away. The talks became bogged down, with the Albanians demanding independence and the Serbs refusing to consider it. A second issue was NATO's insistence that it should deploy peacekeepers in the province to ensure that both sides adhere to a ceasefire.

In the end, US Secretary of State Madeleine Albright intervened, asking that the ethnic Albanians give up, at least for the moment, the demand for independence. Their leadership agreed to this, leaving the ball in Milošević's court. He sent instructions to his delegates at Rambouillet that they must not sign a deal that allowed a NATO occupation force into Kosovo. The Rambouillet talks collapsed and the delegates went home. Now, once again, America stepped into the breach. Its Balkan envoy Richard Holbrooke flew to Belgrade and met with Milošević, telling him that he must either agree to allow a NATO force into Kosovo or else NATO, as it had promised, would start a bombing campaign.

Milošević replied that his position remained firm and that Kosovo was the most sacred Serb land and must not be occupied by a foreign power. Holbrooke got up and said that there was nothing he could add. As he left, Milošević asked: 'Will I see you again?' Holbrooke replied: 'You have my phone number.' Two days after their final meeting, at 8 p.m. local time on 24 March, bombs began to fall on Belgrade as NATO launched the first war in its history.

A week before the bombing began, Serb security forces had commenced a massive ethnic cleansing of Kosovo Albanians. They began by attacking and burning a long chain of villages near the strategic highway that linked Priština to the rest of Serbia. The attack was an awesome sight, with an entire mountain ridge on fire for more than fifteen miles.

When NATO began its bombing, this ethnic cleansing was accelerated into a campaign to remove the majority of Kosovo's population. The old techniques, seen in Croatia in 1991 and Bosnia in 1992, returned to the Balkans. Yugoslav army units shelled Albanian villages, then Interior Ministry troops would attack, rounding up the people, separating men from women, and sometimes exacting revenge for KLA attacks in preceding months. One Serb soldier told of what happened when his unit entered an ethnic Albanian village during the operation.

'A reservist nicknamed Crni ['Black'] went up to an old man who was holding a child aged around three or four. He grabbed the toddler form the man's arms and demanded a ransom of 20,000 German marks. The Albanian only had 5000. Crni took the child by the hair, pulled out a knife and hacked off its head. 'Five thousand is only enough for the body,' he said, and walked off past the other villagers, carrying the child's head by its hair. All of this took place in front of dozens of people. We were all in a state of shock. Some soldiers vomited, while our young second lieutenant fainted at the terrible sight of the headless body writhing in the dust. Crni was later declared insane, discharged and sent home. But he is still free to walk the streets.'[12]

Outside the capital, Priština, a group of men and women were ordered from a collection of farm buildings and herded into the downstairs room of the largest house. Then hand grenades were thrown in. Two months later the stone floor of the cool, dark basement was still sticky with the blood which had poured through the cracks in the floorboards. In the room above, pieces of flesh had been pasted onto the walls by the force of the blasts. Relatives identified some of the dead by the watches and rings found among the tangle of corpses.[13]

Across Kosovo a vast exodus of refugees got under way. It was dubbed Operation Horseshoe by the UN because Serb forces were deployed in a horseshoe shape around the province, propelling the Albanian population out through the open end which faced the border with Albania.

In Priština, the Serb authorities ordered Albanians to leave the town and the road was soon choked with cars. South of the capital, Serb villagers moved among the vehicles, women as well as men, shouting at the drivers and demanding money. Thousands more Albanians were herded onto trains which were sent to the Macedonian border, then offloaded into a field between the two states.

This ethnic cleansing was a public relations disaster for Milošević. NATO had begun the campaign expecting it would be brief, leading to his quick capitulation. Instead, he held out. Public support in the West might have drained away were it not for the fact that television screens were now filled, night after night, with the weary faces of so many Albanian civilians expelled from Kosovo. As the bombing campaign stretched into April, NATO's war aims changed, at least publicly, from attempting to enforce a peace agreement to enforcing a demand that the eight hundred and sixty thousand Kosovo Albanians forcibly expelled be allowed back.

In The Hague, chief prosecutor Louise Arbour began a bout of frantic activity. The massacre at Račak seemed a good atrocity to pin not just on local Serb troops but on Milošević himself. He was commander-in-chief of Serb forces. This was his country, these were his men, and there was strong evidence that the forty-five civilians had been killed in cold blood.

Arbour told her investigators to move fast. At the back of her mind was the fear that, unless she had an indictment ready early, the UN might make a peace deal with Milošević that would include immunity from prosecution for war crimes. 'I felt when we have that strong a case we must move rapidly so that there's no risk that some deal will be made providing him with a kind of de facto amnesty. If the Security Council didn't want us to do that they could stop us any time. Until the phone rang I felt I have been asked to do something and I'm going to do it.'

Making life harder for the investigators was her insistence that Milošević be charged with other crimes, not just Račak. She wanted them to find witnesses and evidence to tie him to a string of killings and attacks on Kosovo villages. If she were to indict a president, she needed a big case. 'We had three hundred killings, mass deportation. I didn't think it would have been appropriate to try and catch him on tax evasion type counts,' she said.

In late May everything was ready. A Hague indictment only becomes law once judges have confirmed it – in other words, once they have looked at the charge and decided that it appears to be based on real crimes. That would take four days from the time it was handed to them. Arbour decided to give the judges the indictment on 22 May and then make it public on 27 May, assuming that the judges confirmed it. In the meantime, she decided to inform key world leaders and also senior UN officials, partly because there was a UN monitoring team in Belgrade which had to have time to leave before the indictment was made public lest they be taken hostage.

By this time NATO, keen to destroy installations but not to kill large numbers of people, was running short of targets. The bombing of airbases, bridges, oil plants and power stations had sapped Serb morale, but Yugoslavia still held out. In Kosovo, to NATO's frustration, most Serb tanks were hidden under trees. Then Tony Blair and US president Bill Clinton conferred and decided that, if there were no peace deal, they would consider a ground invasion of Kosovo. More than ten thousand NATO troops were already in Macedonia and now the president prepared to send US Marine forces to the region. Milošević knew he would be defeated. Two peace envoys, Russia's former prime minister Viktor Chernomyrdin and Finland's president Martti Ahtisaari went to see him. The Russian told Milošević that, while Moscow was sympathetic to his plight, there was nothing his country could, or would, do to protect him from a NATO ground invasion.

As the talks went on, chief prosecutor Arbour feared a deal was close. She was determined to have her indictment out first. One of her senior prosecutors, Clint Williamson, wrote the indictment. Just after

8 p.m. on Saturday 22 May, with Arbour waiting downstairs to see the finished draft, his computer crashed. As he watched, the indictment text on the screen in front of him was transformed into meaningless symbols. He had no back-up. 'I was sitting down and I was typing and then all of a sudden it just went to like these symbols on the computer, on the monitor, instead of letters,' he said, 'and we were like, oh no.'[14]

The Tribunal's technical department was closed for the weekend. Frantically Williamson phoned around, finally tracking down a technician who was on the beach at nearby Scheveningen. Not wanting to tell the man what it was all about, he simply pleaded with him to come straight to the office to fix a computer. 'He walks in and sits down and he sees "Prosecutor vs. Slobodan Milošević" and he goes, "Oh shit, I see why this is important,"' Williamson recalled.[15]

The technician set to work. Later that night he finished tapping the keyboard, smiled, and changed the symbols back to letters again. Williamson saw that the most famous document he would ever write was still there, intact on the screen. He quickly finished it, not forgetting to make a copy, printed it and delivered it to Arbour.

On Sunday it was authorised by a judge and on 26 May, strictly against precedent, details were leaked to CNN. The leak ensured that the next day the parkland in front of the Hague court was packed with television crews. These were anxious days, and the media was alive with speculation that Chernomyrdin was at that very moment brokering a peace deal between Milošević and NATO. By the morning of 27 May there had been no news of either a peace agreement or an immunity deal, and a relieved chief prosecutor made her announcement to the world. Standing on the front step of the Hague court she announced that, for the first time in recorded history, a court claiming to represent, through the United Nations, 98 per cent of humanity was indicting a serving head of state for war crimes.

The news shot around the world, provoking mixed reactions. For many of the ethnic Albanian refugees, for the residents of Sarajevo, Vukovar, Prijedor, Foča and Zvornik, for the wounded, the dispossessed and the relatives of the dead from three separate wars, there was relief, surprise and even hope. Many Western diplomats had a very different reaction, complaining that Arbour had just made it much harder to negotiate with Milošević who would surely now feel he had nothing to lose by holding out against NATO bombing. In fact, the very next day Milošević met with Chernomyrdin and agreed that he would pull his troops out of Kosovo and let NATO in. The war was over.

On that spring day Arbour looked outwardly confident. She made her announcement to the world's media, then strode back inside the court building. But once behind the security doors, she did an unusual thing.

The offices used by prosecutors and judges are on separate floors in The Hague and the two groups are kept apart in order to preserve the integrity of the court. Each floor has a glass security door leading to the main stairwell, and even the chief prosecutor has no access to the floor used by the judges. On this day, however, she walked to the door leading to the judges' floor and tapped on the glass. John Jones, clerk to court president Antonio Cassese, saw her. Cassese, wearing his judicial robes, had just come out of his office and now he strode down the corridor and opened the security door. He knew about the indictment. Arbour looked at him and asked, 'Have I done the right thing?' Cassese smiled and said. 'Yes,' then added, 'It takes a woman to be that courageous.'

Prisoner 101980 7

Those who say it can't be done should get out of the way of those who are doing it.

Inscription on a photograph showing Louise Arbour signing the indictment of Slobodan Milošević

In September 1999, four months after she had indicted Slobodan Milošević for war crimes, the Hague's chief prosecutor Louise Arbour left her job. Canada had offered her a place as judge on its Supreme Court. She still had a year of her prosecutor's job to run, but she knew that such positions came up only infrequently since they depended on a judge retiring. So, like her predecessor Richard Goldstone, she left before her term was up.

Arbour's replacement was Swiss investigator Carla Del Ponte, who was just over five feet tall, had spiky white hair cut short and chain-smoked. Where Arbour had been impishly charming, Del Ponte revelled in being tough and abrasive. She had made her name in the toughest arena of all, as an anti-Mafia investigator. In the 1980s she teamed up with Italy's Emilio Falcone to probe the Swiss bank accounts held by Sicilian Mafia families. In 1988 she was staying in Falcone's Italian home when police found a bomb made of Semtex hidden in the foundations. Del Ponte told him she was not intimidated, and he labelled her 'the personification of stubbornness.'[1] Three years later Falcone and his family where killed by a massive bomb which destroyed his car, which the authorities were quick to blame on the Mafia. Del Ponte was given a bodyguard and remained on the case. Later she was promoted to become Switzerland's attorney general. From that base she launched a series of high-profile investigations into organised crime in Switzerland, naming among others Russia's president Boris Yeltsin, Pakistan's former president Benazir Bhutto, and former Italy's former premier Bettino Craxi.[2]

Del Ponte had her critics, with some lawyers complaining that she did not follow through on her investigations and that in the end the famous names were never prosecuted. She also worried the Swiss establishment because, until she came on the scene, Switzerland had had a long history of not looking too carefully at the origins of the money that rolled into its bank vaults. The bankers, the so-called gnomes of Zurich, feared that she was asking too many questions and there was relief when she was named as the new war crimes prosecutor and departed for The Netherlands.

Arriving in The Hague, the 53-year-old chief prosecutor knew that, whatever else she did, the case for which she would be remembered would be the trial of Slobodan Milošević, dubbed 'the Big Fish' by staff in The Hague. In Del Ponte's early months, however, it was not possible to start this case because Milošević remained secure in his presidential villa in Belgrade. Short of a full-scale invasion of Yugoslavia, there was nothing the UN could do to bring him to justice. Del Ponte announced in the autumn of 1999 that she would add to the original charges against him, which related to the Kosovo war, further indictments covering the wars in Bosnia and Croatia.

Her inability to bring Milošević to trial did not mean that Del Ponte was inactive. She arrived in October, just as The Hague war crimes court finally began a series of major trials. The long years of work by its first president, Antonio Cassese, and the prosecutors Richard Goldstone and Louise Arbour, had at last paid dividends. In December 1999 a Serb detention camp commander, Goran Jelisić, was jailed for forty years for a string of murders and atrocities against Muslim prisoners. Jelisić had named himself 'the Serb Adolf' and boasted of his atrocities. Then in February 2000 a Bosnian Croat general, Tihomir Blaškić, accused of responsibility for the Ahmići village massacre, was jailed for forty-five years. The same month, the trials of the commandants of the Omarska and Keraterm prison camps began.

In December 2000, NATO commandos working in Bosnia arrested a Bosnian Serb general, Stanislav Galić, who had commanded artillery units besieging Sarajevo. Bosnian Serb general Radislav Krstić, one of the Serb generals blamed for the massacre at Srebrenica in 1995 went on trial in March 2000, and would later be jailed for forty-six years for genocide.

The UN increased the court's budget to almost US$100 million, and a donation from the British government paid for a third courtroom to be built. The detention centre at Scheveningen, still situated inside the existing Dutch prison, was expanded from 36 to 48 cells, and The Netherlands seconded fifty-seven prison officers to add to the staff. The old days when jailers from the Dutch prison would tease the UN guards about their lack of prisoners were a distant memory. Now each day prison vans would depart shortly after 8 a.m. for the ten-minute journey to the court building. Armed Dutch police patrolled outside the Tribunal and kept watch from three white cabins built nearby.

Del Ponte found Milošević uncooperative on the issue of war crimes arrests, but had more success in bullying Croatia into giving up suspects. Two Croat former paramilitary commanders, Mladen Naletilić and Vinko Martinović nicknamed Tuta and Stela, who had used their private armies to terrorise Muslims in Bosnia in 1993, were handed over in 1999. The Croatian national press labelled her 'the Bitch' but Del Ponte announced that she was proud of her abrasive style: 'It makes many enemies, but that doesn't matter, that's what we're here for.'[3] There was more good news from the other UN war crimes court, dealing with the 1994 genocide in Rwanda. A young American prosecutor named Pierre-Richard Prosper, previously an investigator into drugs gangs in Los Angeles, secured the first conviction against one of the Hutu warlords who had supervised the massacre of more than eight-hundred-thousand Tutsis.

Del Ponte was bolstered by having on her staff many tough young prosecutors whose enthusiasm for the task made them go the extra mile in their investigations. Typical was Stephanie Frease, a young American who was first attracted to the court because her parents had emigrated from Yugoslavia. She told me: 'There were times when I thought I can't believe I'm being paid to do this, there is nothing I'd rather be doing. We were very motivated. We cared very much about doing a good job.'[4] She was one of the first investigators to work on evidence relating to the 1995 Srebrenica massacre. She worked with French police superintendent Jean-René Ruez, and the pair were dubbed the Ghost Team because of the amount of time they spent sifting through bodies in mass graves in the hills around Srebrenica.

Bosnian Serb forces had buried the bodies of many of the victims and then dug them up again and moved them to new burial sites in order to avoid detection. When NATO forces took control of the area after the Dayton peace agreement, war crimes investigators began fanning out, probing the soil. One bonus was that no matter how thorough the death squads thought they had been, often even the worst massacres had left survivors. The worst single atrocity at Srebrenica is a case in point: more than a thousand Muslim men were herded into an abandoned warehouse on the main road running out of the town and then cut down with grenades and machine-gun fire. Later, Serb soldiers went in and began walking around the mass of bodies calling out for survivors, promising them they would not be harmed. Several men who had been hidden among the corpses on the warehouse floor got up, were taken outside, and shot. A few hours later a second appeal was made and, amazingly, another group of men got up. They, too, were taken outside and killed. One man survived, lying all day amid the dead and dying, and crawling away at night to reach government lines. Later he told his story.

Many months were spent locating the killings and finding the bodies. One day, at the site of a grave, surrounded by decaying corpses, Frease was working with another investigator when she was hit by a wave of depression. 'It wears on you after a while. You run into situations that sort of hit you. It just makes you very sad sometimes. One day, you know, it was just, boom, I can't do this, I can't do this today, too much.' She said the second investigator provided a reason for her to keep going. 'He said, "You know, you've got to be able to think about giving these people a voice. In doing this you are allowing them somehow to speak again."'

Witness interviews could be emotional affairs. The massacre of seven thousand men was traumatic not just because of the numbers but because they all came from the same small community of Muslims living in and around Srebrenica. In these emotionally charged interviews, Frease had to retain her legal detachment, remembering the need to ask seemingly mundane questions about such things as the unit markings on the shoulders of the Serb soldiers. 'People have a need to talk about what happened to them. You would ask, did you see people, did you see badges on uniforms, did you see vehicles – you want to get identifying stuff. Questions like: when you walked in the door did you notice a plaque on the door, did you notice the name on it?'

Often witnesses to a particular killing could not give accurate descriptions of where it had taken place. 'A muddy field is a muddy field. People would describe this dirt road. We couldn't find this location. Where could it be, where could it be? But finally we found it,' said Frease. Some of the Ghost Team's methods were innovative – Ruez found that one way of establishing the date of execution was to look at the dates on the wind-up watches of the dead. He learned from the manufacturers that the mechanism would allow a maximum of 36 hours, meaning that the date of death could be no more than two days before that shown on the dial.[5] Usually witnesses did not know the soldiers who had attacked them, but even here there was a breakthrough. 'Sometimes you get amazing nuggets. One survivor recognised the voice of the person who was in charge of the execution squad because he had worked with him for twenty years in Belgrade. So he knew his first name and his last name without a doubt.'

Frease's strategy was to assemble the evidence in layers, one on top of the other. There was the evidence of the bullets found in the bodies in the mass graves, then that given by the survivors, then Serb documents showing unit movements, and finally reconnaissance photographs from US planes and satellites provided by the Pentagon. 'It's piecing it all together, then laying one layer on top of the next, and the final layer is deciding who are the perpetrators,' she explained.

Frease brought bullets, clothing, wire bindings and other evidence from the mass graves back to The Hague but found nowhere to store it, so it was left in crates in the big, open-plan prosecution office. 'It was rancid, it came out of the grave, blindfolds, ID cards, and we didn't have an evidence locker, so it would stay in the office. We didn't have any place to put it and our colleagues complained. We put it in a closet downstairs but that didn't work because it was next to the women's bathroom. So we found a metal container at the back of the building.'

By 2000 the Tribunal was bustling with activity, and one case above all others caught the imagination: the prosecution of three Bosnian Serbs charged with keeping dozens of Muslim women as sex slaves during the 1992 ethnic cleansing campaign.

Foča is a little town tucked away amid hilly, wooded farmland in eastern Bosnia, not far from the Yugoslav border, south of Srebrenica. Serb forces quickly captured it in the early days of the war, rounded up the Muslims, and then moved on. In the months that followed, left to their own devices, unsupervised and unseen, some of the Serb soldiers who remained in charge of the town regressed. Instead of releasing the dozens of women prisoners, they kept them as sex slaves. At first the rapes were random and one-off – a girl seized, raped, then sent back to her detention camp. But then things got worse: the Serb commanders decided to set up 'rape camps' in the town. One was at the sports hall, where sixty Muslim women were being held. Instead of being released along with thousands of other prisoners, these women were kept back.

News of their availability quickly spread and visiting Serb soldiers were also given the chance to rape them, sometimes paying their captors for the service. The rapes ranged from regular sex, albeit under the threat of violence, to beatings and killings. Indicting the men was the easy part, because many of the women were willing to give evidence and they had learned the names of their tormentors over the months of captivity.

In 1998 prosecutors charged eight former Serb soldiers with multiple rapes. The indictments were handed to the NATO-led Implementation Force in Bosnia and arrest operations commenced. For the first time, French troops were ordered to make war crimes arrests, following the reluctance of Paris to allow them to join earlier raids by American, British and Dutch troops.

One suspect was shot dead when he tried to run down French soldiers who had surrounded his car. Another, targeted by German special forces working in eastern Bosnia, blew himself up with a hand grenade. Three suspects could not be traced, but two more, Radomir Kovač and Zoran Vuković, were arrested. Finally, the alleged commander of the rape camps, Dragoljub Kunarac, gave himself up.

Their trial produced some of the most disturbing testimony ever heard in the Hague courtrooms. One woman, appearing as protected witness 48, told the court: 'He took me to a room and when I refused to take off my clothes, he tore them off me and raped me once, twice, three times, orally the third time. He said that we would no longer give birth to Muslim babies, but to Serb children. I was conscious when six of them took turns on me. When I regained consciousness, I could smell the stench of rakia [home-made brandy]. I couldn't get up. I don't know what they did to me.'[6] She estimated that she had been raped by more than a hundred soldiers during several months of captivity.

Soldiers at Foča mixed humiliation and sadism with their assaults: they would rape mothers and daughters side by side, or keep women to do chores by day and sex by night. In one instance, soldiers forced teenage girls to pole-dance at gunpoint; another group were made to perform a nude version of *Swan Lake*. The local Bosnian Serb authorities even issued official permits granting the holder permission to carry out a designated number of rapes. For witness 48, the ordeal was worse than death: 'I told them to take the rifle and kill me,' she told the court. The soldiers, however, preferred to keep her alive. Their motives appeared to be a mixture of sexual desire, sadism and even boredom, since they had little to do guarding a town far behind the front line.

Another victim, also appearing anonymously, told the court that after her husband was taken away and killed, she and her 12-year-old daughter were kept at the rape camp. Age was no protection and the daughter was raped many times. Finally they were put aboard a bus with other refugees, and they hoped their ordeal was over. The bus was driven into Yugoslavia. But it was stopped at the border by police on a bridge over the Drina River. Serb soldiers boarded the bus, and they knew for whom they were looking – the witness's daughter. She was snatched from her arms and taken away. Her body has never been found, but her mother learned later that she had been sold to the soldiers by the rape camp guards for 200 German marks. In court, shown a photograph of her missing daughter and asked to confirm, for the court stenographer, the name of the person in the picture, the witness could not speak. Instead, she let out a long wail. 'It lasted half a minute, a long, deep, whining sound of somebody, a human being or an animal, so deadly wounded that it can make no other sound but a howl,' wrote novelist Salvenka Drakulić, who sat watching in the public gallery behind bullet-proof glass.[7]

Amid their ordeals, the women said that occasionally they would find acts of kindness – a reminder that individual men, not the Serb nation, were on trial. One soldier, part of a unit visiting Foča, took one of the women into an abandoned house and locked the door, not to rape her, but to protect her from his comrades. 'On one occasion, one guard tried to stop the soldiers, but the soldiers said they had been given certificates from the police chief,' said protected witness 95.[8]

Kunarac came out fighting, denying that he had committed any rapes or allowed other troops to do so. The defence came up with the bizarre claim that a teenage girl he had forced herself on him and, despite being armed with a machine gun, he had been unable to resist: 'I had sexual intercourse with her against my will,' he told the judges.[9] One defence lawyer asserted that the rapes were not serious, pointing out that in most cases no 'physical harm' had been done to the women and that therefore the ordeal was not as serious as physical wounding.[10] The judges were unimpressed and Kunarac was jailed for twenty-eight years, with the other two soldiers receiving lesser sentences. For the prosecutors, there was the satisfaction of having seen a rape case through from first investigation to arrest and conviction – and the conviction also set a legal precedent, as this was the first time that rape had been deemed a Crime Against Humanity.[11]

Such cases played on the minds of the Hague prosecutors. The Tribunal was drawing back, further than in any previous war, the veil on the motives of those who had committed war crimes. While it was true that the campaign of ethnic cleansing was coordinated by generals and presidents, it was also clear that the brutality with which the orders were carried out was perpetrated, with pleasure, by individual soldiers. 'Anyone is capable of it, I believe. Most of these guys wouldn't have done this stuff if there hadn't been a war. They would not have been killing people, they would have been going to factories, serving their time in the military or whatever – having their life,' said Frease. She was annoyed when working around Srebrenica to hear local Serbs express surprise that seven thousand Muslims had been massacred on their doorstep, claiming that they had seen nothing at the time. This seemed hard to explain, given that Srebrenica has just one main road, down which the prisoners and the bodies would need to have passed, and given that the bulldozers that dug the mass graves and ploughed in the bodies were driven by local civilians. 'Everybody knew what was going on, you couldn't not know. You had to have all of the logistics, you had to capture the people, then it was buses, requisitioning buses from all the various municipalities.'

Frease's work ended in a series of indictments against the Srebrenica commanders, starting with army commander Mladić and former president Karadžić and working on down from there. In 2002 General Radislav Krstić, the commander of the army corps that oversaw the killings, was jailed for what was at the time a record forty-six years.

Other cases went less well. Dražen Erdemović, a Croat who had given himself up as a member of a Srebrenica execution squad, saw his case returned to court. At the first hearing, he had told the court that he was guilty and was jailed for ten years. On appeal, however, court president Antonio Cassese ruled that the trial judge had been too harsh and that Erdemović should have been informed that he had the right to claim diminished responsibility, because had he not carried out the executions he would have had reason to fear that he himself would have been shot. His case was returned and he was convicted on a lesser charge, with his sentence reduced to five years.

More problems arose with Tadić. His original sentence was twenty years, but on an appeal it was increased to twenty-five. Then a defence appeal was upheld and it was restored to twenty years, after which he demanded a review which was only finally rejected in July 2002, eight years after his initial arrest. His case had raised a whole host of legal issues. The trial judges had ruled that a witness could give evidence anonymously, but then appeal judges struck this ruling down. A key witness was sent home after claiming that the Bosnian government had briefed him to exaggerate his evidence against Tadić. All this took years of court time and cost millions of dollars. As with Erdemović, this was a comparatively simple case. How much more difficult, many wondered, would it be if the Milošević case, with its mamouth charge sheet and the need to prove a long and intricate chain of command, ever came to trial?

One bizarre hiccup was the case of the so-called 'sleeping judge'. During the trial of three Muslims and a Croat for offences against Serb prisoners at the Bosnian government's Ćelebiči detention camp, the defence noticed that one of the three judges, Adolphus Karibi-Whyte, was asleep. They checked the court video and found that he had slept through about thirty hours of the case, which took place in 1998, and they used this as part of their appeal in the summer of 2000.[12]

October 2000 marked the end of Del Ponte's first year in office. The Hague Tribunal had in this period truly come of age with some outstanding trials. The problem remained, however, of how to put Milošević behind bars. But it was a problem that Milošević himself was about to solve.

After the Kosovo war, Milošević continued his gradual decline. He tried to portray the withdrawal of his forces and the arrival of NATO to garrison Kosovo as a victory, but the facts told a different story. Under Milošević, the Serbs had lost wars in Croatia, Bosnia and now Kosovo. Sanctions were in place against Yugoslavia and outsiders did not want to do business with a state headed by a war crimes suspect.

With the coming of the new millennium a bright new opposition force began to appear on the streets. Named Otpor – the Serb word for 'resistance' – this was very different from the earlier collection of opposition parties which had been famous for their squabbling. Otpor boasted of having a horizontal leadership, and although this was not strictly true, it was the case that many young Serbs joined without direction from above. Otpor had a single policy and a single slogan: 'Gotov je' – 'He's finished'. The key weapon was graffiti. On lamp-posts and bus shelters and walls across Yugoslavia's main cities the slogan began to appear, along with a stencil of the group's logo, a clenched fist, sprayed in black paint. The fist began to take off as a salute. Students would make the sign to each other, and then fans at Red Star Belgrade, once the bedrock of Milošević's support, started to make the salute during matches. The secret service probably infiltrated the leadership, but to little practical effect: their only real strategy was to protest as often as possible. By early 2000 Otpor supporters had added a new tactic, late at night painting long trails of red footprints along Belgrade's pavements. The symbolism was plain: they were a symbolic instruction to Milošević to start walking.

Milošević's leadership was not one that encouraged retirement. He micro-managed his regime using an ever-tightening circle of trusted aides. Purges had seen him ditch his army commander, General Momčilo Perišić, and his secret service chief, Jovica Stanišić, because of their less than total support at the time of the student protests in the winter of 1996–7. He was rarely seen in public, and his government, which had once prided itself on its wall-to-wall propaganda, now mounted only a half-hearted effort to court popularity. One public relations move was to invite ordinary people to email their problems to slobodan.milosevic@gov.yu. The address was gleefully swamped by Otpor students and there are no recorded cases of anyone receiving a reply.

Instead of confronting the protests, Milošević retreated into himself. He became a recluse, making no public appearances and few speeches on radio or television. The bold nationalism of previous years was a faded memory. The economy, starved of investment, continued its grim slide. By 2000 unemployment stood at 44 per cent and the few reliable opinion polls put Milošević's support at 20 per cent. His main asset lay in the divisions that ran through the opposition. There were more than twenty opposition parties, and three leading figures who detested each other at least as much as they disliked Milošević. The liberal opposition was headed by Belgrade's mayor, Zoran Djindjić, a bitter rival to the liberal-nationalist Serbian Renewal Party of the bearded writer Vuk Drašković. The most powerful single opposition group was the Radical Party of extreme nationalist and former paramilitary commander Vojislav Šešelj, blamed for the murder of 255 Croats in the Vukovar hospital massacre of 1991. Šešelj's frenetic brand of nationalism accused Milošević of not being extreme enough, blaming the country's plight on an outside world that had conspired mightily against the Serb nation. The phrase 'Only Unity Saves the Serbs' was the national slogan, but hidden within it was a warning: disunity is the Serb curse. Milošević had betrayed the Serbs of Croatia, Bosnia and Kosovo, and now the opposition parties were squabbling for position – just as the two 'royal' houses, the Karadjordjes and the Obrenovićs, had squabbled a century before. From his palace, behind bullet-proof glass and special forces guards, Milošević glared out at the country he commanded, giving no indication of where he thought he was taking the Serbs.

The one institution that still seemed to work was the secret service. It was blamed for organising an assassination attempt on Vuk Drašković in October 1999, when a truck swerved into his motorcade but hit the wrong car, killing his brother-in-law and two bodyguards. Since then Drašković had been living in Montenegro, where in 2000 the president, Milo Djukanović, declared that he wanted to separate from Yugoslavia in order to escape UN sanctions.[13]

In January 2000 Milošević's top paramilitary commander, Željko Ražnatović, better known as Arkan, was shot dead in dramatic fashion in the Hotel Intercontinental in Belgrade. He was waiting in the lobby with his bodyguards, but they were deployed to intimidate rather than to guard. The men who came to kill him were able to machine-gun the whole party, spraying 36 bullets into them in two seconds, three of which entered Arkan's head. His wife, pop star Svetlana, nicknamed Ceca, who had been shopping in the hotel's boutiques, ran to cradle her husband's body. With her sister, she managed to get him to a car, but he was dead long before he reached hospital.[14] Rumours, fuelled by lack of progress in the police investigation, suggested that Milošević had ordered the killing because Arkan had been in touch with the war crimes prosecutors, offering information on Milošević in return for immunity.[15] Arkan had a big televised funeral featuring hundreds of his former Tigers in solemn vigil.

The killing was followed by more assassinations: Yugoslavia's defence minister was gunned down in a Belgrade restaurant. Then the head of Yugoslav Airlines, Zika Petrović, an acquaintance of Milošević's since his schooldays, was shot dead. In the summer of 2000 a sniper shot and wounded Vuk Drašković, the bullet grazing his forehead. These attacks came among a steady stream of mafia killings, leaving Serbs divided as to whether the secret service was responsible or whether Milošević had simply lost control of the gangsters. Rumours swept Belgrade that he was using a group of secret service hitmen, named the 'Men in Black', to shoot anyone who could give evidence against him at The Hague.

With the warm weather Otpor organised protest rallies and rock concerts against Milošević, and opponents looked forward to July 2001, the date when he would have to stand for re-election as Yugoslav president. By mid-summer he appeared to be running out of options. In late July he played one last card, announcing that he would hold the election early, on 24 September, in the hope that the opposition would be too divided to unite around a single presidential candidate.

That summer, a new figure entered the picture. Ivan Stambolić was Milošević's former mentor, the man he had crushed politically in order to secure his own control of Serbia. After eleven years in the political wilderness, Stambolić decided to return to the fray. An old friend, former Yugoslav prime minister Ante Marković, warned him against it. So many people were being assassinated in lawless Belgrade that Stambolić would be putting his life at risk by challenging Milošević.[16] On 25 August, Stambolić went for his normal morning jog in a Belgrade park and was seen resting on a bench. A white van drove up and several men got out. The back doors were thrown open and they bundled him inside. He was never seen again until his body was discovered in 2003 and Milošević, by then no longer president, was charged with having ordered his murder.

Milošević had calculated that the opposition would fail to unite around any of the key figures in time for the elections, and he was nearly right. However, a compromise candidate emerged – a Belgrade law professor with a low political profile named Vojislav Kostunica. Djindjić gave him his backing, but Drasković ran on his own ticket, as did the ultra-nationalist Šešelj. On 25 September election monitors announced the result and Serbia was stunned. Kostunica, despite running an underfunded campaign with little access to the airwaves or time to organise, had won 52 per cent of the vote against Milošević's 35 per cent.

Milošević refused to accept the result. According to one press report, he grabbed Serbian prime minister Nikola Šainović, one of his few remaining confidants, by his bushy moustache and demanded he fix the results. Whatever the truth of this, the election commission announced later the same day that they had got their figures wrong. In fact, Milošević had 38 per cent and Kostunica 48 per cent. The difference was important, because Yugoslav election law stipulated that if no one candidate won more than half the vote, a second round of voting must be held between the two leading candidates. Kostunica could expect to win that round, but he refused to accept the adjusted figures. Perhaps he recognised Milošević's capacity for causing trouble: in the two weeks between the rounds he would have time to fix the vote, invent a scandal, or cancel the election – or, quite possibly, assassinate Kostunica. He also knew that if the subsequent result were fixed, it would be hard to argue against it if he had already accepted the first, fixed result.

Kostunica's refusal triggered protests across Serbia. Miners in the south downed tools. Shops and schools closed their doors. Workers who had once formed the backbone of Milošević's support now marched for his removal. Even the meteorological institute went on strike. The opposition set 5 October as a day of action, and Milošević ordered police units to block the main highways to Belgrade. As the day approached the army told the opposition that it would not use troops to block the protest.

On 4 October, Belgrade mayor Zoran Djindjić met with the commander of Milošević's most elite unit, Milorad Luković of the Red Berets, the Interior Ministry commandos. Luković, nicknamed Legija because he had once fought with the French Foreign Legion, was a lantern-jawed soldier who had made his name as a commander with Arkan's Tigers during the ethnic cleansing of Bosnia. He had later commanded the Red Berets in Kosovo and after the war drifted into Belgrade's informal gangster network, which was nicknamed the Zemun clan after the blue-collar suburb of that name. Now he agreed to meet Djindjić in the most secret place he could devise, the inside of one of his armoured cars. Djindjić joined the vehicle at a street corner and while it cruised the streets of Belgrade he made Legija an offer. If the Red Berets would support the opposition, or at least stay out of the way of the protests, he would ensure that Legija was never handed over to the Hague war crimes court. The commander agreed, the deal was set, and Milošević's last force was about to crumble.

On 5 October columns of protestors converged on Belgrade from across Serbia. Police in some towns tried to stop them, then melted away in the face of determined resistance. Among the columns heading into the city was a group of paratroopers disguised as civilians in jeans and tracksuit tops. They were unarmed but ready to provide the shock troops for the coming demonstrations. By early afternoon the federal parliament building, the scene of so much drama over the past thirteen years, was surrounded by protestors and guarded by a thin line of riot police.

Shortly after 3 p.m. a workman who had come to Belgrade on his bulldozer, Ljubislav Djokić, drove at the police line. The huge metal shovel crushed the concrete flower boxes in front of the parliament building. Police fired volleys of rubber bullets and canisters of tear gas but they bounced off the bulldozer. Tear gas wafted across the square. The protestors, eyes stinging, some retching, swarmed forwards, hurling the smoking canisters back at the riot police. Police reinforcements were called, but their transport became stuck in the massive crowds. Then the paratroopers, posing as ordinary demonstrators, surged forward and charged the police lines. The police melted away and thousands of protestors surged into the building. Moments later, fire broke out and part of the parliament started to burn.

Elsewhere in the city, demonstrators swarmed around the headquarters of the television station, with Milošević's staff barricaded inside. With the police refusing to obey orders, Milošević, operating from his presidential mansion on the other side of the city, ordered in his final reserve, the Red Berets. Legija had assembled his men at a base inside Belgrade and now led a column of jeeps and armoured cars along the empty highway to Belgrade's television headquarters. By now the crowd outside included policemen who had changed sides, and they tensed as they saw the heavily armed vehicles of the Red Berets approaching.

The lead jeep stopped close to the line of protestors and Legija stepped out. There was complete silence as his eyes scanned the crowd. Then he smiled, made a three-fingered salute, a Serb nationalist gesture, got back in his jeep and led the convoy back to barracks. In that moment the opposition knew it had won. Milošević realised his Greater Serbia had now shrunk to the command of a security detachment surrounding his residence.

Among the first to congratulate the new Yugoslav president Vojislav Kostunica on his appointment was the Hague's chief prosecutor Carla Del Ponte. She told him that the war crimes court was ready to take charge of Milošević 'at any time'. Kostunica curtly informed her that Milošević would not be handed over. He announced that he did intend to arrest him, but only so that he could be put on trial for corruption in Yugoslavia, not to be sent abroad. Kostunica said that, as a law professor, he was in a position to know that the war crimes court violated Yugoslav law and that to hand someone over to it would be illegal. For the moment, he said, Milošević would be allowed to remain in his presidential palace with a small guard for protection.

Del Ponte tried again in January 2001, journeying to Belgrade to remind Kostunica that as a member of the United Nations, Yugoslavia had a duty to hand over Milošević. The country could hardly pick and choose which UN rules it would observe. Kostunica was unmoved and Del Ponte stormed out of the meeting.[17] Two months later, after yet another rebuff, Del Ponte publicly denounced Kostunica as 'a man of the past', saying that for all his democratic pretensions he was acting like someone from the old Communist era. She said: 'It felt like reading those books that I've read about Communism twenty or thirty years ago.'[18]

In April the police finally came for Milošević. He had previously vowed he would never be taken alive and there was a stand-off with his bodyguards. A few shots were fired. Then Milošević abruptly surrendered and allowed police into the presidential palace to take him away. Inside, they found an anti-tank rocket launcher, thirty assault rifles and two cases of hand grenades. His daughter Marija was found to be carrying three pistols: a Beretta, a derringer and a Walther.[19] Hysterical from a cocktail of cognac and her mother's tranquillisers, she fired five shots into the air as her father was driven away.[20]

Milošević was taken to Belgrade district prison to await prosecution on corruption charges. In the weeks prior to his arrest Kostunica had released details of a wave of cash payments to cronies and the theft of huge sums from the state coffers. Little was said about war crimes in Croatia, Bosnia and Kosovo. Later, the prison governor, Dragisa Blanusa, published an account of his confinement, imaginatively titled *I Guarded Milošević*.[21] This book cost Blanusa his job but gave the world a glimpse into the mind of the secretive former president, prisoner 101980.

Blanusa reported that Milošević's time in prison was mostly spent in depression, his black moods lifted by daily visits from Mira who often brought food with her. She would arrive most days at noon and stay for an hour, the maximum time permitted. His daughter Marija came too, but Marko stayed away. He had fled Yugoslavia, apparently fearing attack by Serbs angry about his former playboy lifestyle and gangster ways. Marija seemed to be in denial, telling her father: 'When you leave prison, I will never allow you to go into politics again.'

When the Christian Orthodox Easter came in late April, Mira brought her husband painted eggs, apparently having turned her back on her former atheistic Marxist beliefs.[22] On one occasion she shouted at prison staff – later apologising for what she said was a 'surplus of female hormones'. In contrast, most of Milošević's former associates stayed away.

Opinion polls showed that while most Serbs disliked Milošević, and were happy for him to stand trial for corruption, they opposed sending him to The Hague. The reasons for this are complex. Belgrade was jammed with Serb refugees from the country's unsuccessful wars, including a quarter of a million Serbs who feared to return to their homes in Croatia. Approximately three quarters of The Hague indictees were Serbs, and the long sentences were all being handed down to Serbs. Chief prosecutor Del Ponte created more unpopularity by ruling that there was no evidence to prosecute NATO for three incidents during the Kosovo war: the bombing of a bridge as a train was crossing it; the mistaken bombing of the Chinese embassy in Belgrade; and the bombing of Serbia's national television headquarters.[23]

In The Hague, Del Ponte decided that if Yugoslavia would not hand over Milošević voluntarily, it must be compelled to do so. An international aid conference was scheduled for 1 July 2001 at which the outside world was due to pledge US$1 billion to rebuild Yugoslavia. Del Ponte wanted that money to be made conditional on Milošević being handed over to the court. She embarked on a tour of key Western capitals hoping to gain support.

America by now had a new president, George W. Bush, whose administration made no secret of its suspicion of the war crimes process, seeing the courts as a potential threat to national sovereignty. So Del Ponte began her trip in Europe. However, in meetings with British, French and German officials, diplomats refused to endorse her demand that aid be made conditional on the surrender of Milošević. They were worried that Kostunica might call their bluff and that without aid Yugoslavia would crumble, perhaps even seeing a return of the nationalists.

This was a potentially devastating blow to Del Ponte, who knew that if Yugoslavia were able to retain Milošević it would probably also refuse to hand over other suspects. Fearing the worst, she made the trip across the Atlantic to meet senators and congressmen in the new America of George W. Bush. Here she had a major surprise. She did not get to meet the president, but congressmen from both the Democrats and the Republicans offered their warm support. The Senate had already ruled that aid to Yugoslavia would require yearly certification, partly dependent upon whether the country was cooperating with war crimes investigations. One of the co-authors of the certification bill, Democrat senator Patrick Leahy, said: 'Like any country, Yugoslavia has an obligation to uphold international law. Its government needs to arrest and transfer to The Hague those responsible for the most heinous crimes in Europe since the Second World War.'

The Bush administration then delivered the single most important piece of news the court had ever heard: it would refuse all aid to Yugoslavia if Milošević were not surrendered. American money would be withheld at the 1 July donor conference and, US diplomats discreetly added, they would be expecting the Europeans and the UN itself to follow suit. 'We were surprised, yes, pleasantly surprised,' said Del Ponte's spokeswoman Florence Hartmann. 'She went at the beginning of May to Washington and explained that something is possible. She said, we just need your help, the Europeans don't believe we can get him, but it is possible. They said yes.'[24]

Whether President Kostunica would have agreed to surrender Milošević in return for money was never put to the test. Instead, US officials took advantage of the division of power between Yugoslavia and its two republics, Serbia and Montenegro, to approach the new Serbian prime minister Zoran Djindjić. He was considered more forward-looking than Kostunica, and he quickly agreed to help.

In Belgrade rumours that the West was threatening to withhold aid unless Milošević were handed over were printed in the newspapers. On 16 June four thousand of his supporters demonstrated outside Belgrade jail. Inside, he met with his wife Mira and daughter Marija. He told Mira: 'My poppet, you are very tired. Sleep a little.' Mira replied: 'I love the rain. This is my weather.' Marija said: 'We love the night, not the sun. The night is our time, we sleep in the daytime, and live at night time.'[25]

Rumours of a possible handover were swirling around Belgrade, although Kostunica insisted that he would do no such thing. 'I am completely at peace. My conscience is clear,' Milošević told the prison governor, labelling the Kostunica regime 'motherfuckers'. On 26 June the governor brought him some whisky. He told him that if he feared he was being poisoned he could choose which glass to use and he, the governor, would drink from the other one. Then he asked the question to which millions of Serbs, not to mention the world's politicians and diplomats, wanted to know the answer. The question was, why had Milošević, having risen so high, ended up like this, a prisoner in his own land? 'Why didn't you quit while you were ahead, while you were still popular? You could be lying on a beach somewhere now.'[26] Milošević made a little speech about how he had decided to keep hold of power for the sake of the Serb nation, but then his enthusiasm seemed to wane. He paused, then said: 'Yes, you're right. I did make a mistake.' The governor waited, but there was no more. The slight chink in the armour of self-belief vanished as quickly as it had appeared, and Milošević's expression of self-assurance returned.

On 28 June 2001, twelve years to the day after Milošević had addressed a rally of more than half a million adoring Serbs at Gazimestan in Kosovo, Serbia's cabinet held a special early morning session presided over by prime minister Zoran Djindjić. The Yugoslav president, Vojislav Kostunica, was not informed of the meeting. There was only one item on the agenda and agreement was reached in a matter of minutes. Orders were sent out of the room to the commanders of a police unit which had been briefed on its very special mission the night before. The prison governor was contacted, and he relayed to Milošević the news that he was going to be taken away that evening. At midday, his wife and daughter arrived at the jail and they ate a quiet lunch together, consisting of watermelon, fried courgettes, a single sardine, potato salad, cheese and fruit. To drink, they had water from plastic glasses. Milošević produced seven little cardboard boats from his pocket, telling Marija that he had made them and that she should give them to his grandson. She began to cry, and then so did his wife. Milošević cried too, and told his wife 'You have to be very strong.' At 6 p.m. he was sitting alone in his cell when the prison governor came to tell him to collect his things and prepare to leave. 'Where are you taking me?' he asked. 'To The Hague,' the governor replied.[27]

Milošević dressed slowly, picked up four of his books, apparently chosen at random, plus a toilet bag and his raincoat. Instead of a police escort, the governor himself led the former president down the corridor. After going a little way, he stopped and said: 'Warden, what's this? It's not right, this is a kidnapping.' The governor insisted they keep walking, guiding him through the prison and out into the yard where there was a police van with the back door open. Milošević got in and the governor stepped in beside him.

The transfer was conducted by the police of Serbia, with no involvement of either the Yugoslav federal police or the military which were under the control of President Kostunica. He would later claim that the operation was illegal because only the state had the power to transfer a prisoner out of the country. But Serbia's prime minister, with a billion dollar lifeline at stake, was beyond considering such niceties.

Milošević was driven through Belgrade's early evening traffic to a police base with a yard large enough for a helicopter to land. Djindjić did not want to ask for the use of an air force base. Getting out of the police van, Milošević said: 'Well done, you lot, you can take your money now.'[28]

A helicopter was waiting, with two men and one woman, all in civilian dress, standing by its side door. One of the men was a Hague investigator, the other a Dutch police officer and the woman was a translator. Asked which language he spoke, Milošević replied 'Serbian,' and his war crimes indictment was read to him, the interpreter translating from English. This took some time, and Milošević lit a cigarette while he listened. Finally the investigator said: 'I am arresting you. You are now under the jurisdiction of the Hague Tribunal.' He was helped aboard the helicopter, and someone folded his raincoat and placed it under his seat. He looked up, and called to the pilot and co-pilot: 'How are you, lads?' The pilot replied: 'All right, Mr President.'

Milošević turned to the governor and asked: 'Warden, where is my raincoat?' These turned out to be his last words on Yugoslav soil.[29]

In the evening the helicopter landed at Tuzla, a big American airbase in northern Bosnia. A Royal Air Force plane was already on the tarmac and Milošević was escorted aboard. The Hague has no international airport, so the flight was given permission to land at a Dutch air force base outside the city. From there a prison van drove Milošević to the Hague Tribunal's Scheveningen prison, arriving at 11 p.m. The twin wooden gates opened and the van drove in, passing between the two fortress-style gate towers. The Big Fish was finally in the net.

America Turns   8

This article here, this is my uncle. This one here, my late wife. This one here, my niece. This is not just paper for me.

Sierra Leone delegate to the 1998 conference preceding the establishment
of an International Criminal Court[1]

I f ever a picture could tell a story, this was it: the place was Rome, the date Friday, 17 July 1998, and history was being made. In a large, bright conference hall diplomats from almost all the world's nations, surrounded by their national flags, were sitting in rows, clapping rhythmically, all facing the front where a young Canadian lawyer, Philippe Kirsch, had just announced the result of the vote to create the first truly global war crimes tribunal. By a majority of 120 votes to seven, with 21 abstentions, they had voted for the creation of an International Criminal Court, to be based in The Hague, not far from the existing UN war crimes court.

Sitting in the middle of the crowd, not clapping or even smiling, was the American delegation. America, the country that, more than any other, had been the prime mover in the war crimes process a few years previously was one of only seven nations to vote against this new tribunal. American leaders, happy to support courts for Yugoslavia and Rwanda, were determined to prevent this turning into a permanent, worldwide process.

The origins of the International Criminal Court, or ICC, lay long before the UN created the war crimes tribunals for the former Yugoslavia and for Rwanda. When the United Nations was formed, after the Second World War, one of its first acts was to order an International Law Commission to put together plans for a world court. The model was the Nuremberg trials of Nazi war criminals in 1946, which had already established what their American chief prosecutor, Robert Jackson, called a 'beaten path' of precedent for the holding of international war crimes trials.[2] The plan was ready by 1949 but was never implemented because the necessary consensus vanished with the onset of the Cold War.[3]

When the Cold War had begun to come to an end, the idea was resurrected. The inspiration came in 1989 from Trinidad and Tobago, which asked the UN to create an international court not to deal with war crimes but to combat drug smuggling. The UN once more asked the International Law Commission to study the idea, and plans were still being made and shuttled from committee to committee when the UN Security Council created the Hague Tribunal. From then on, the Commission was able to use the former Yugoslavia and Rwanda tribunals as a living laboratory, taking note of their successes and failures.

Slowly, through the 1990s, the Commission drew up its plans. The Soviet Union collapsed and democracy came to Russia, to a clutch of new states in Central Asia, and to the former Eastern Bloc. Democracy also took hold in South Africa and across South America. China introduced economic, if not political, reforms, and economies in the region galloped ahead. The European Union harmonised laws under the Maastricht Treaty. In this climate of optimism, human rights ideas flourished. The world's states agreed, at least in principle, the Kyoto agreement on global warming and, at the instigation of Britain's Princess Diana, the Land Mines Convention. Both treaties were imperfect, but they seemed to many to be a step in the right direction.

Meanwhile new war crimes courts were created. The wars in Cambodia, East Timor and Sierra Leone all ended with internationally supervised war crimes tribunals setting to work, with varying degrees of effectiveness. Suddenly no war could end without the question of a war crimes court being raised – something unheard of just a decade before.

In July 1998, after innumerable committees and discussions, the UN was finally ready to present the idea of an International Criminal Court to the world. World leaders, if they noticed at all, saw no particular urgency in the idea and few turned up to the Rome conference where it was to be debated. But the human rights community thought differently. Groups such as Amnesty International and Human Rights Watch felt that this treaty was the potential climax of decades of work, because for the first time it would see their demands enshrined in law. More than two hundred and fifty human rights and legal organisations arrived in Rome, many of them determined to make sure that the treaty was signed. In March 1998, President Clinton, speaking to survivors of the Rwanda genocide in the capital, Kigali, gave forceful support to the idea of a global war crimes court.

The US Senate, however, viewed the idea with alarm. For the Republicans, and also some Democrats, the proposed court was a very different thing from the existing UN tribunals. These had been set up because Yugoslav and Rwandan law had broken down. The proposed International Criminal Court was, in contrast, envisaged as a justice system that would embrace healthy democracies as well as war zones. Moreoever, it would have precedence over the governments of individual member states. This seemed to many Americans – and not just on the right – to go against the principle that there should be no legislation without representation. In a democracy, the law works within a permanent feedback loop which allows the citizens to decide on the laws that govern their lives. A worldwide court would have no such mechanism and the only democratic controls would be indirect, through governments of member states. Even this would not protect a state from having laws imposed on it by an unelected body, regardless of the wishes of its voters.

Mixed in with this concern was the fear that Americans might become the target for 'political' prosecutions, with the judges of the little states 'ganging up' on America much as their diplomats sometimes did in the UN General Assembly. Human rights organisations pointed out that the checks and balances envisaged in such a court meant that political prosecutions were impossible – or at any rate would involve so many judges and prosecutors that most of the rest of the world would have to join in the conspiracy.

Human rights activists suspected that darker motives were also at work. American officials cannot have been unaware that such a court was likely to make an entire raft of subversive activities illegal. In the 1980s the CIA had been accused of mining the harbours of Nicaragua and arming a murderous paramilitary group, the Contras, as well as supporting several dictatorships from Chile to Pakistan. Whatever the motive, the Republican leader of the US Senate's Foreign Relations Committee declared, shortly before the Rome conference was due to start, that any proposal to include America within the jurisdiction of such a court, without a total veto, would be 'dead on arrival' in the Senate.[4]

The US named an eminent lawyer, David Scheffer, as its war crimes ambassador and sent him to Rome for the 1998 conference with the difficult task of trying to negotiate a compromise treaty. Scheffer, ever the optimist, told me later that he went to Rome confident that he could pull it off by inserting enough preconditions into any new court to meet with Senate approval. He had also sounded out generals in the Pentagon who voiced the same doubts as the senators. They could see little to gain, and much to lose, by having their troops, already based in more than a hundred nations around the world, subject to possible indictments from this new court.[5]

In Rome, the human rights movement lobbied hard and found two groups of states willing to give their support. The first was the European Union, most of whose members saw no problem in supporting the idea of an ICC – after all, it was hardly likely that Denmark, for example, would ever find itself in a situation to be accused of systematic war crimes. The other group of states backing the court comprised the new South American democracies. Many of their statesmen had experienced war crimes at first hand under previous military juntas. Argentina had witnessed the murder of thousands of innocent people – 'the disappeared'. Chile had endured the savage killing of socialists after General Augusto Pinochet seized power in a US-backed coup in the 1970s. For these delegates, the ICC was perceived as a form of insurance policy against the return of military dictatorship. Similar sentiments were felt among many other new democracies, from Eastern Europe to Africa, with the ICC seen as a way of 'contracting out' of their own justice systems.

For four weeks the conference crept along, with delegates voting on the more than one thousand separate issues that had been left unresolved by the UN lawyers who had drafted the treaty. The arguments exploded in the fifth and final week. Scheffer made it clear that America would require checks on the court's authority. One suggestion was that member governments be given the right to stop prosecutions – an idea rejected by most other delegates because it would mean that dictators could grant themselves immunity. A second idea was that each of the five permanent Security Council members – of which, of course, America was one – should be given a veto over prosecutions. This, too, was rejected by most other states because it would have amounted to giving the permanent five a 'get out of jail card'.

Human rights groups, meanwhile, were pushing the other way, trying to get agreement that the ICC should be able to prosecute anyone at all, not just citizens of states that had signed up to the court. The example cited was the fondness of certain dictators for shopping in the boutiques of Paris. As things stood, they could shop till they dropped with no fear of arrest if they had not signed the ICC treaty.

The Americans remained concerned that even a slimmed-down treaty would be dangerous. Scheffer asked one correspondent: 'What if the American army finds itself deployed on the territory of Iraq as part of a UN force. Now, Hussein and his nationals are not subject to this treaty because he hasn't signed on. But what if suddenly he pulls a fast one, accuses some of our men of war crimes and, as head of the territory in question, extends the court permission to go after them on a one-time basis?'[6]

Early in the fifth week of the conference, a dinner was hosted by Russia with only the other permanent Security Council members – America, Britain, China and France – invited. Human rights groups worried that they were about to agree a common front and demand that they be given a veto over ICC prosecutions. Activists worked fast, contacting the one power that they felt sure would oppose this idea – Britain. They were right. Calls to the media and to government officials meant that word got back to the Labour government's Foreign

Secretary, Robin Cook, who was publicly committed to the ICC. His reaction is not recorded, but what is certain is that no deal was agreed over the brandy and after-dinner mints.[7]

As the final week wore on, Scheffer hardened his position. He made it clear that America would not sign a treaty unless it were allowed some sort of veto over prosecutions. And if America did not sign up, then the court would have to be outside the United Nations. This was a double blow to many ICC supporters. There was a scramble to put the Americans at their ease. First, it was agreed that the ICC would only prosecute war crimes if domestic courts had tried and failed. However, this did not satisfy the Americans, who pointed out that it would be the ICC that would decide whether the domestic courts were working or not. Second, it was agreed that even if the UN would not recognise the ICC, the ICC would still recognise the UN. A rule was also inserted whereby the UN Security Council had the right to veto prosecutions, but only if all the members of the Council were in agreement. This, too, did not satisfy the Americans, who wanted a specific US veto. The result was stalemate. 'It's as if we're being forced to choose. A court crippled by American requirements with regard to state consent, or a court crippled by lack of American participation,' South Korean delegate Kak-Soo Shih told *New Yorker* journalist Lawrence Weschler.[8]

On 17 July the conference moved to a vote, bursting into sustained applause when it became clear that, even with the Americans opposed, a huge majority wanted the new court. What these nations had agreed to was a court to try war crimes, genocide and crimes against humanity in any member nation. The court was to be delayed until a minimum of sixty states had adopted the court statute into their own domestic law.[9]

Back in the United States, Scheffer met with senators who congratulated him on his fortitude, and he remains one of the few individuals in the ICC argument who is well regarded by both those opposed to and those in favour of the court.[10] He himself felt that he had failed and stated that he remains committed to the idea of the ICC, albeit with more limited powers. Later in 1998 US policy makers had another rude shock when Chile's former dictator, Augusto

Pinochet, visiting London for medical treatment, was arrested on a Spanish extradition warrant. Spanish judge Baltasar Garzón had indicted Pinochet for the murder of Spaniards in Chile, and now he applied to Britain to extradite the former general. Britain's supreme court, the House of Lords, was divided on the issue, because extradition law would allow the transfer of the suspect only if the crime he stood accused of in Spain were also a crime in Britain. Finally, the law lords ruled that he could be extradited, but only for charges related under the Torture Convention of 1986.[11] The episode ended with the Foreign Secretary, Jack Straw, intervening to send the general home on the grounds of ill health. The event was nevertheless important because a major power had ruled that the Torture Convention had the force of law. Previously most nations who had signed it, including Pinochet when he was president of Chile, had ignored its provisions.

America's hostility to the ICC deepened when George W. Bush replaced Bill Clinton in January 2001. One of Clinton's last acts as president, made in the final hours of his very last day in the White House, was to sign the ICC treaty. This was not as important an event as it might seem because more than a hundred and twenty nations had signed the treaty. Only those states incorporating ICC law into their own law could become members. The gesture appeared to be political because it obliged President Bush to 'unsign' it, earning him criticism from human rights groups.

And then came 9/11. The attack on the World Trade Center by two hijacked airliners piloted by suicide bombers suddenly threw terrorism into the world spotlight. The Bush administration, never enthusiastic about the ICC, seemed to decide that the new court was a dangerous obstruction in the new, global War on Terror.

In April 2002 the sixtieth member finally joined the ICC and on 1 July of that year the court formally became active, meaning that, for member states, war crimes committed from that date onwards came under its jurisdiction. A new headquarters was opened in The Hague, across town from the UN Tribunal, and American opposition changed from passive to active. Congress passed the American Servicemember's Protection Act, giving the US president the power to free, by military force, anyone held in an ICC jail. As the only planned jail is to be built at the ICC's Dutch headquarters, opponents quickly labelled this law the 'Hague Invasion Act'.

The rift between America and Europe over the ICC came to a head in September 2002 when the EU issued a directive to its members stating that they were unable to sign agreements with Washington giving Americans immunity from prosecution. The problem lay with a single word in a single article, Article 16, of the ICC treaty. This article allows a member to sign a deal promising not to arrest nationals of another country, but only if those individuals have been 'sent' by that country. To most lawyers, the word 'sent' implies that those individuals must be on official business. The EU therefore said that it could offer America a deal giving immunity to its troops, diplomats and anyone else on government business. America refused, insisting that all Americans should have immunity.

Afterwards, US diplomats fanned out across the globe trying to persuade other nations, both inside and outside the ICC, to sign full immunity deals. By the end of 2002 ninety states had joined the ICC and about forty had signed, or were ready to sign, US immunity deals. Some, notably Romania, had signed both, leaving only confusion because it is unclear which agreement would have precedence.

More arguments were still to come. During 2002 America announced that it would pull its peacekeeping troops out of Bosnia-Hercegovina unless that nation, an ICC member, gave them immunity from prosecution. Bosnia was unable to do this under the terms of the ICC treaty, but a last-minute deal was agreed by the UN Security Council to give American soldiers exemption on a yearly basis.[12]

On 11 March 2003 the ICC court was formally opened.[13] On the beach at nearby Scheveningen peace protesters dug a series of shallow bunkers in the sand, complete with sandbags, in symbolic defiance of America's theoretical power to send US Marines to storm the ICC jail under the 'Hague Invasion Act'.[14]

In July 2003 Congress passed a new law that allowed President Bush to deny military aid to any nation not giving Americans immunity from the ICC. Although this was not immediately invoked, its provisions caused alarm across much of the world. In Africa, states prone to famine worried that they might not receive airdrops of food that relied on planes from the US Air Force. In the Caribbean, ICC members feared that the US Navy might not come to their aid when hurricanes struck. And in Eastern Europe the Baltic states were concerned that America might deny them membership of NATO.

In the summer of 2003 a new war crimes dispute arose when several human rights groups announced that they would launch war crimes prosecutions against President Bush and Israel's president, Ariel Sharon, through courts in Belgium. This was possible because Belgium, fulfilling its obligations under the Geneva Conventions, had passed laws allowing war crimes prosecutions in its domestic courts. The prospect of a prosecution against Bush succeeding was remote, but there was still the chance that should he or his officials visit Belgium they could be arrested and held until a hearing could be arranged for the charge to be dropped. US Defense Secretary Donald Rumsfeld publicly threatened to have NATO's headquarters moved from Belgium unless the law were changed. Under this pressure, Belgian legislators rewrote the law to forbid foreigners from bringing war crimes prosecutions. A crisis was averted, but American suspicion of war crimes courts deepened.

All of this had its effect on The Hague Tribunal. America, once its key backer, turned hostile. In late 2001 the US froze its share of funding after the new war crimes ambassador, Pierre-Richard Prosper, told Congress that there had been financial 'abuses'. These did not seem very significant. The only one relating to misspent money was the practice of fee splitting, whereby a suspect hires a lawyer only when that lawyer promises to remit part of the fee, which is paid by the UN, to the suspect's family. This is a serious issue, but does not directly affect the Tribunal. In fact, one of its unsung achievements is a clean accounting record, in contrast to the abuses and corruption that have tainted so many other UN bodies over the years.

In March 2002, shortly after the trial of Milošević finally got under way, Prosper came to The Hague and met with chief prosecutor Carla Del Ponte. He declared that America was unfreezing its payments, and also that the war crimes court had agreed to American demands that it close in 2008. Although it was never formally spelled out, staff at The Hague felt a chill wind blowing from Washington. Officially, America still supported the Tribunal, but the enthusiasm of the Albright State Department was now a distant memory.

What this meant was that there was now extra pressure on the Milošević trial, which would be seen not just as the key prosecution of the Hague Tribunal but the key test of war crimes justice at large. A good, clean trial, with all charges proven, would be a mighty advertisement for war crimes trials and a boost for the ICC. Nobody expected Milošević to escape jail, but if the trial appeared muddled or confused, or ended with key charges unproven, it would provide an opportunity for the US administration to argue that global war crimes justice, while a fine idea on paper, was in reality deeply flawed.

Courtroom Number One 9

It's not going to be won by the law, it's going to be won by the lawyers.

Tom Cruise, A Few Good Men

The wall of bullet-proof glass separating Courtroom One at The Hague from the public gallery gives the onlooker a feeling similar to viewing a museum diorama where figures are posed in historic scenes. Instead of 'Lee Surrendering to Grant' or 'Nelson Dying on the *Victory*', we have 'Milošević on Trial', a diorama full of instantly recognisable characters. The judges are identified by their red robes, the prosecutor looks appropriately stern in his black cloak and white wig, the guards look bright and youthful in their crisp blue shirts, and Milošević is instantly recognisable by his trademark swept-back white hair. The effect of being disconnected from the room on the far side of the glass is enhanced by the bright lighting which ensures that there is a shadow-free environment for the four little television cameras mounted on the ceiling.[1]

On most days the viewing gallery is three-quarters empty, with half a dozen journalists, a few lawyers, and parties of bored Dutch schoolchildren. But on 12 February 2002 it was packed to overflowing. For the first time in nine years the press office had to issue tickets, and many journalists were forced to watch proceedings downstairs in the entry hall, clustered around closed-circuit television screens. Outside the building, television cables snaked across the green lawn in front of the courthouse. A row of white vans were parked nose to tail outside the main fence, their satellite dishes pointing at the sky. Security was tight. Armed Dutch police officers occupied cabins outside the walls. Inside the building the UN guards were, as always, unarmed. Their weapon is the 'lock-down', a procedure whereby the bullet-proof glass doors separating corridors and stairwells can be locked and staff passes deactivated. Anyone wanting to spring Milošević from the court would need to attack the building with a rocket launcher.

On that cold February day one problem for the television crews was finding identifying features to show that they were filming outside the international court. The white brick building is plain and drab. The only sign of activity is a single blue flag hanging limply from a tall white pole. On 12 February 2002 it became the most filmed flag in the world.

A few moments before nine that morning Milošević was led into court by two young guards. His face, with its high, broad forehead and small mouth, turned to examine the sea of faces on the far side of the glass wall and he showed amused surprise. He wore an immaculate dark suit of conservative cut, a crisp white shirt and a red, white and blue silk tie. Facing him was chief prosecutor Carla Del Ponte, her white hair cut short, her eyes scanning him from behind black-rimmed glasses. 'Good morning, your honours,' said the court registrar, one of three black-robed officials sitting at a desk below the judges' bench. 'Case number IT-02-54-T, the Prosecutor versus Slobodan Milošević.' And so it began.

The charges had already been read to Milošević at one of a series of pre-trial hearings after he arrived in The Hague in June 2001. He had refused to plead and a not-guilty plea had been entered by the judges. Now Del Ponte led off with a short speech explaining in formal terms why he was in the dock. 'Your honours, the chamber will now begin the trial of this man for the wrongs he is said to have done to the people of his own country and to his neighbours.' She paused, injecting a note of drama, and added: 'How simple that statement is to make today. How easily those words pass into the record of these proceedings.'

Del Ponte told the court that her aim was to demonstrate that the wars of Yugoslavia were not, as many supposed, the result of inter-ethnic tension but rather of cold calculation on the part of Slobodan Milošević. She read from an official report into Balkan violence which concluded: 'the true culprits are those who misled public opinion and took advantage of people's ignorance.' This report, she revealed, was written not about the horrors of the 1990s but about the two Balkan wars of 1912 and 1913. The report was the work of a Frenchman, Baron d'Estournelles de Constant, in 1914, who had no doubt that the ethnic wars that he had witnessed, far from being spontaneous and tribal, were the result of manipulation at the highest level. 'Your honours, no words could better set the scene for the matters this chamber will now try,' said Del Ponte.

Before sitting down, she introduced the man who would run her case. She had appointed one of the top criminal lawyers available, Geoffrey Nice, a hugely experienced barrister and Queen's Counsel, or QC.[2] Slim, dark-haired, middle-aged, Nice affected gravity and seriousness, aided by deep furrows running down each cheek. Before the Milošević case, he had cut his teeth with the successful prosecution of two of the bloodiest war criminals, Serb camp commander Goran Jelisić and Dario Kordić, a Bosnian Croat who masterminded the massacre at Ahmići. He told one interviewer that he had taken the Hague job in 1998 out of a sense of adventure and a wish to help the court, saying it was a 'leap in the dark'.[3] By appointing him, Del Ponte was showing that she was taking no chances. He was one of her most experienced prosecutors and was steeped in the same Anglo-Saxon legal tradition as the court's own rules and procedures.

Nice began what seemed likely to be his most famous case by reminding the court of the horrors laid at Milošević's door. He isolated a single incident during the 1992 ethnic cleansing of Bosnia, telling the story of a pregnant Muslim woman who was chased from her home in the town of Visegrad by Serbian paramilitary soldiers. She fled with her cousins and uncles into the forest around the town, where she had given birth. A few days later the group was arrested by the paramilitaries and marched back to Visegrad. There, the Serb commander told them that the Red Cross would send a bus to pick them up, and that they should wait in an empty house that had been prepared for them. Stepping inside, the woman realised something was wrong. Looking around, her cousins saw that the carpets in some rooms had been soaked in petrol. There was no time to run, as the guards slammed the door and set the petrol alight. In seconds the inside of the house was an inferno, with people running from room to room trying to find a way out. In the panic the woman found a way out through a window, landing in the garden unseen by the Serbs. She could do nothing for her relatives still trapped inside. 'They were burned alive,' said Nice. 'And the baby's screams were heard for some two hours before it too succumbed.'[4]

The first witnesses Nice called began the process of reliving the ethnic cleansing of Kosovo by Serb forces in 1999. Survivors came to tell their stories from a chair facing the judges. Some appeared anonymously, their faces hidden by ochre blinds. One Kosovo Albanian told the court that he was kept in the Serbian Dubrava prison in northern Kosovo as a guerrilla suspect during the NATO bombing campaign. In May of that year alliance aircraft, mistaking the prison for an army base, bombed it, shattering a cell block and killing some prisoners. The next day, he recalled, the guards ordered them to gather their belongings and line up outside. The prisoners, mostly ethnic Albanians, hoped they were going to be taken away. Instead, without warning, a machine gun in a watchtower opened fire, working its way methodically along the line. The prisoners scattered, some running back inside and hiding in basements and drains. The survivor told the court that the next day Serbian army units arrived and began dropping hand grenades into drains, sewers and cellars in a slaughter that left approximately fifty more men dead.[5]

BBC correspondent Jacky Rowland was shown the bodies by the Serbs shortly after the bombing, and in August 2002 she told the court that their wounds indicated that most had not in fact been killed by NATO bombs, as the Serbs had claimed. 'I have strong doubts that all those prisoners were killed as a direct result of the NATO bombing,' Rowland told Milošević. 'If you were hit by a bomb, heaven forbid, I think I'd be able to tell by looking at your body whether that was the manner of death.'[6] She said that her work was 'balanced, impartial, fair reporting'. Milošević smiled and said: 'A Serbian proverb says "one swallow does not make a spring" so please do not generalise regarding this one objective report about the reporting of the BBC in general.' Rowland later revealed that Nice referred to Milošević as 'old grumpy paws'.[7]

Other witnesses told of the slaughter by Serb forces that took place in a chain of villages shortly after the NATO bombing campaign began. One group of forty-four men was arrested at gunpoint in the village of

Suva Reka, once a stronghold of the Kosovo Liberation Army. They were ordered inside a coffee shop and then grenades were thrown in, causing terrible carnage among the tightly packed men.[8] Another witness told of surviving a similar ordeal, when one hundred and five men were herded into a single house in the village of Mala Krusa. Once they were inside, Serb soldiers had again thrown grenades in through the windows. Other survivors were burned alive when the Serbs set fire to the house.

Forensic scientists who investigated the massacre of forty-six Albanians at Račak in January 1999 – the event that led, ultimately, to the NATO war – told of finding the bodies piled together, some with their hands tied, with powder burns around their wounds indicating that they had been shot at close range. Evidence also came from the other side of the action, when prosecutors persuaded a former Yugoslav soldier, identified in court only as K-32, to testify that his unit had been ordered to use artillery to bombard ethnic Albanian villages and later to execute captured menfolk.

Through all of this, Milošević showed no sign of sadness or remorse. The first part of the trial was the prosecution case, with Milošević's defence coming later, but he was allowed to make a presentation. He showed a mixture of video and still pictures of disembowelled bodies, the result of an erroneous NATO attack which had hit a convoy of Kosovan civilians on tractors, mistaking them for Serbian army trucks. The court was quiet, the only sound being Milošević's terse 'next' after each photograph. He followed with a speech accusing the court of being part of a NATO conspiracy. British leading judge Richard May broke in at the end to tell him: 'Your views on this court are entirely irrelevant.' Milošević would not be stopped, declaring that his trial was 'a crime against the Serb people'. Looking at the judges, he added: 'It is also a crime against the truth. The whole world knows this is a political trial.'

His chance to talk came when he was allowed to cross-examine witnesses. For the first part of the hearings, when they gave their evidence he would sit, usually slumped back in his chair, scribbling notes on yellow legal pads. He displayed a repertoire of expressions – sometimes stern, sometimes angry, sometimes visibly bored, occasionally quizzical with a raised right eyebrow and a slight smile. The body language was that of a man who believed he was in a show trial. He used much of the time allotted for cross-examination to pour scorn on the Tribunal, calling it a 'NATO court',[9] and denouncing his trial as a propaganda exercise masterminded by enemies of the Serb people. He also proved a deft lawyer. His cross-examinations mixed political fury with well-constructed exposures of even tiny inconsistencies in the evidence of witnesses.

Not all of this was down to Milošević's sharp mind and law degree. Despite having no court-appointed lawyer, he had a team of legal experts based in Belgrade. At any one time, at least one of these lawyers would be in the public gallery. Because he did not recognise the court, he refused to appoint them as his official representatives. Keen to demonstrate fairness and impartiality, the judges ordered that two of these lawyers could have VIP status, being allowed to sit on the press side of the public gallery which was closer to the defendant. The lawyers also had access to him during the regular court breaks. In addition, his cell in the detention centre was equipped with fax, computer, email, television and radio, and a mobile phone, enabling contact with his Belgrade team in the evenings. A frequent visitor was his wife Mira, although the court kept secret details of whether the couple took advantage of a special room in the jail that featured a bed and was available for sexual intercourse. One court official, annoyed at being repeatedly asked what sort of things went on there, said: 'The room is for people in long-standing relationships; you can't send out for a call girl.'[10]

In the early days journalists, and presumably prosecutors, were puzzled by how Milošević always seemed to know so much about each witness, as well as about the battles and incidents mentioned in court. He knew their birthdates, the villages they came from, and details of battles in their part of Kosovo. On one occasion, he revealed that he even had access to a witness's school records. Then a Belgrade newspaper, *Nedeljni Telegraf*, solved the mystery, revealing that Milošević's former secret police chief, Rade Marković, had spirited away truckloads of documents in the three months after his boss was deposed in October

2000. Marković, said the report, had also copied the Yugoslav military archive on Kosovo onto CDs.[11] Now all this information was being combed through by Milošević's lawyers in Belgrade. Prosecutors were frustrated that they themselves could not get hold of these files because the Serbian and Yugoslav governments both refused access.[12]

Since first appearing in The Hague in the summer of 2001 for pre-trial hearings, Milošević had stuck to his line that he did not recognise the legitimacy of the court. He scored a tiny victory over the matter of translation. Defendants in other cases wore headphones, as did the lawyers and judges, because the official language of the court was English. Milošević refused to wear headphones but also said that he did not understand English – a language he in fact knew fluently from his time as a banker visiting the United States. The judges bent to his wishes and Judge May decreed that he could have a loudspeaker, mounted on a metal frame, facing him in the dock. This broadcast the nearly simultaneous Serbo-Croat translation, reportedly distracting court staff on the far side of the room who heard it as a constant buzzing.

Milošević showed himself a master of the sound bite when he clashed with the prosecution's very first witness, Kosovo Albanian politician Mahmut Bakalli. Bakalli had been the Communist government's leader in the province during the 1970s. He gave evidence about the first large-scale attack of the Kosovo war when Serb forces smashed the Prekaz farmstead, killing rebel leader Adem Jashari and sixty-eight other Kosovo Albanians in March 1998. Bakalli was called by the prosecutors to provide what was, in effect, a single brick in the wall of evidence that they were trying to construct. He had not seen the battle, but he had met witnesses to its ferocity and had gone with a delegation to tell Milošević about it in the spring of 1998. Evidence of this meeting was needed in order to show that Milošević knew about the killings perpetrated by his armed forces. Bakalli performed his assigned role, but then came the cross-examination. Milošević highlighted the fact that Bakalli, in his earlier evidence, had mixed up two dates: that of the change in the Kosovo constitution, and that of a huge rally Milošević had held in Kosovo in June 1987.

'What is going on here, Mr Bakalli?' Milošević asked. 'The 28th of March, which is in fact three months prior to the 28th of June, that was the day when the final act of proclamation of the constitution of Serbia took place. Yes or no?'[13]

'I don't know, remember, the dates exactly. I cannot pronounce my views on that.'

The cameras caught it all – Milošević bold, sure of himself, and Bakalli, nervous and unsure. The exchange was shown on Serbian television and seemed to show the prosecution witness uncertain and hesitant and Milošević roaring ahead. In fact, the day almost certainly belonged to the prosecutors. They had got the only thing they needed from Bakalli, which was uncontested evidence that Milošević knew all about the massacre at Prekaz.

The episode set the pattern for much of what was to follow, and it encapsulated one of the problems of a televised trial. The power of a trial lies in going through the evidence piece by piece, strand by strand, taking as long as necessary. It is the very opposite of the sound bite. One ethnic Albanian journalist complained to me that witnesses were being judged back home according to how well they had appeared to attack Milošević. Some returned to a hero's welcome, with at least one man carried through the streets of Mitrovica.

Prosecutor Nice produced one of the world's most respected generals, Sir Peter de la Billiere, commander of British forces in the 1991 Gulf War, to provide expert opinion on the ethnic cleansing of 1999. He told the court that his own analysis of dozens of atrocities and attacks on civilians in the spring of that year showed that Serb forces had been acting to a plan of military precision. 'It was no rogue operation,' he told the court.

A second study was produced for the prosecutors by a sociologist, Patrick Ball, who told the court that a year-long study into the times and places of the killing of 4,211 civilians revealed a systematic campaign to rid the Kosovo countryside of ethnic Albanians. He was sure that the individual atrocities could be shown to build up into a pattern that indicated that it had been planned at a high level.[14] Milošević, ever alert, struck immediately at the Achilles heel of this argument, asking Ball: 'Where is the plan?' It was a good question because it highlighted a growing problem faced by the prosecution. They could find no documents showing that Milošević ordered war crimes and no witnesses who remembered him giving such orders. 'Cases like this would be easy to prove if there was one member of the accused's inner circle who was able to give a fully accurate and acceptable testimony of everything that had happened,' Nice told the court. 'Unfortunately, life isn't like that. As regards the witnesses, the closer they are to the accused, the more difficult they are to approach and to use.'[15]

This was not necessarily fatal to the trial. The prosecutors could still hope to convict Milošević by proving the atrocities and by providing circumstantial evidence that ethnic cleansing was planned at a high level. They accused him under two separate headings. The first was rule 7.1 of the Hague statute, under which he was accused of responsibility for ordering the crimes listed. The second was more vague: under rule 7.3 he was accused of responsibility for the crimes not because he ordered them but because, as commander-in-chief of the units that carried them out, he was ultimately responsible for their conduct. Nice could prove both allegations using circumstantial evidence if the judges decided that the ethnic cleansing operation had, beyond reasonable doubt, been ordered by the man in charge – Slobodan Milošević.

One of the best witnesses was British politician and former Royal Marine, Paddy Ashdown. He arrived in The Hague in the spring of 2002 from his job as Bosnia's High Representative, the top Western official in the country. In 1998 he had decided to go on a personal mission to Kosovo, reporting back to prime minister Tony Blair and bypassing normal Foreign Office channels.

Ashdown told the trial how he had been taken to Kosovo by the British ambassador in Belgrade in September 1998 and had headed for south-eastern Kosovo where guerrilla activity was high. At the time, Milošević had publicly assured the world that his forces were not committing crimes against the local people and that they had opened the roads to allow them to travel. Ashdown told the court that, rounding a corner north of the town of Prizren, he had met Albanian villagers fleeing from Serb forces. Close to tears, he told the court: 'I found it very difficult to cope with at the time . . . they were desperately frightened and I found it a deeply terrible sight.'[16]

Later he had watched Serb artillery shelling a village in a bombardment that was 'indiscriminate, systematic and of a nature to terrorise and drive out the civilian population'. He had also filmed the event and had later journeyed to Belgrade to confront Milošević with the evidence: 'I warned you that if you took those steps and went on doing this, you would end up in court, and here you are,' he said.

Milošević replied: 'Could the witness please answer my questions rather than make speeches?' He then suggested to the court that Ashdown was not telling the full truth about why he had gone to Kosovo. 'Is it customary for the leader of a small opposition party to visit a region where there is a war on ten times a year?' Ashdown replied: 'I've heard some conspiracy theories, but that takes the biscuit.'[17]

Nice did not give interviews while the case was running, but it is safe to assume he was delighted by Ashdown's evidence. From a single witness he had the proof of a war crime, proof that Milošević was in command, and proof that he had been told about it and had failed to discipline the men involved. But the prosecution wanted more. It wanted to prove not just that Milošević was responsible for these crimes but that he had actually ordered them, either on his own or as part of a conspiracy, termed a 'joint criminal enterprise'.[18]

While Nice continued with the prosecution, Del Ponte decided to try to find the extra evidence she needed. She flew to Belgrade in the summer of 2002 to demand that Serb premier Zoran Djindjić give her access both to secret service files and to inside witnesses. In particular, she wanted the Serbs to drop a threat made to potential witnesses that they would be charged if they gave state secrets to war crimes prosecutors. Fearing that economic sanctions would follow if he refused, Djindjić agreed to her demand, though he told her that he feared a backlash from nationalists, now enjoying a revival following the failure of his government to bring prosperity during their first two years in office.

The effect of dropping the prosecution threat saw two Serbian policemen, Caslav Golubović and Zoran Stijović, appear in Courtroom One in the autumn of 2002 with details of a bizarre story of how bodies from a massacre in Kosovo had been dumped in the Danube River. It began in April 2000, when a fisherman on the river had come across a container truck in the water. The container had been dragged ashore and forced open, upon which a human arm fell out. The truck contained the bodies of eighty-six ethnic Albanians who had been murdered in Kosovo in the spring of 1999. The two police officers said that interior minister Vlajko Stojiljković had personally ordered the police to rebury the bodies at Batajnica airbase, near Belgrade. This was important evidence because Stojiljković was an official from within Milošević's inner circle and one of four suspects charged with the same crimes as him. The chain of command was inching very close to Milošević.

A few weeks later, a Serbian police captain, also giving evidence about the Danube bodies cover-up, stated that he had been told that it had been ordered by Milošević, with instructions passed on to secret police chief Rade Marković. The captain's word would not on its own be enough to convince the judges, but it focused attention on Marković. He was now in a Belgrade jail, having been convicted on corruption charges. Prosecution officers from The Hague flew to Belgrade to see whether he would give evidence at the trial of his former boss. Marković agreed, and a frisson of excitement went around The Hague when it was announced that he would be appearing as a witness. Many wondered if he would provide the 'smoking gun' – evidence definitively tying Milošević to war crimes.

Marković arrived in July 2002. He had been secret police chief after the former commander, Jovica Stanišić, was sacked in October 1998. Now, asked about atrocities in Kosovo, he replied that some had indeed been committed by Serb units, but the Interior Ministry had subsequently prosecuted two hundred officers responsible for them. The prosecutors were displeased but perhaps not surprised. Marković could not be expected to incriminate himself. They would be happy if he would simply incriminate his former president.

The first indication that something was going wrong came when Milošević began to ask Marković questions, and started calling him by his first name. 'Radomir,' he began, using a friendly tone, 'did you ever get any kind of report or have you ever heard of an order to forcibly expel Albanians from Kosovo?' Marković stared straight back and answered: 'I never got such a report.'[19] Milošević started to speak again, sounding self-assured and confident, as if he knew the answer he was going to receive. 'It is true that the opposite was said? We always insisted that civilians should be protected, that civilians should be taken care of, so that they are not hurt in the course of anti-terrorist operations? Do you remember that?'

Marković replied, 'Certainly' – and with that word the prospect of the 'smoking gun' vanished. Marković clarified his answer. 'Specifically there was this ban on which you insisted, that houses in Kosovo must not be set on fire and nothing must be stolen.' He said nothing about any secret meeting to discuss disposing of the bodies in the Danube, and all hope that Milošević could be tied to that incident faded.

In September 2002 one of the three Amići lawyers, a Dutchman, Michail Wladimiroff, had to resign after telling a newspaper that Milošević was probably going to be found guilty. He was a veteran war crimes lawyer, having defended the very first contested trial, that of Serb camp guard Duško Tadić. Why he chose to give the newspaper interview, one day before the end of the Kosovo part of the case, is a mystery. His comments, he later complained, had been misrepresented, and his original intention had been to warn Milošević that he should take the chance that the court gave him to mount a proper defence.

After the three-week summer break the hunt for inside sources grew more urgent because the trial was now moving on to deal with the Bosnia and Croatia indictments. The Kosovo case had been easier to tackle because Milošević, as Yugoslav president, was then in command of the security forces and therefore their crimes were his crimes. In contrast, he had no formal relationship to the forces in Bosnia and Croatia, and such links would need to be proven before the court. A second problem was that the Bosnia indictment charged him with genocide, which is not just the most serious charge on the Tribunal's books but also the most difficult to prove. It requires proof not just that the events took place but also that the intention of the perpetrator was genocidal.

Milošević had one more surprise in store for The Hague. Instead of denying the clearest case of genocide in Bosnia, the massacre at Srebrenica, he agreed that it might have taken place but claimed that he was not involved. Instead, he blamed renegade Serb forces paid by the French secret service. Why he blamed France for this operation was not explained, and perhaps for Milošević it did not matter. France was a NATO member, and many Serbs back home would find it plausible that some such foreign power was behind the attack. After all, they might ask, what did Serbia have to gain by killing so many people? The massacre had turned the world against the Serbs, so, in their minds, it might be reasonable to assume that their enemies had paid for it.[20] 'I want the truth to be revealed for this insane crime,' said Milošević. 'Ask Jacques Chirac about Srebrenica.'

A few days later he compared himself to the pope, complaining that the pope was praised for offering assistance to Croatian Catholics while he was condemned for helping the Serbs. 'As Serbs helped Serbia I am a criminal, but the Vatican helped the Croats to secede by violent means but the pope remains the Holy Father.'[21]

The autumn of 2002 began with Croatians giving evidence of war crimes from 1991, their stories of suffering unfolding much as had those of the Kosovo Albanians the previous spring. A new problem now began to make itself felt: Milošević's failing health. He had suffered from coughs and colds since the start of the trial, but gradually his medical problems became worse and finally he was diagnosed with high blood pressure. These illnesses were declared at short notice, generally in the morning when he woke up and complained to his jailers that he was too sick to come to court. This caused much upset among the prosecutors, disrupting carefully prepared programmes to fly in witnesses, find them hotels and fix them up with temporary Dutch visas. Every time a day was lost, witnesses had to be turned around and sent home.

The prosecution department also clashed with the media. In October a former *Washington Post* reporter, Jonathan Randal, refused a request to testify in the case of a Bosnian Serb warlord, Radoslav Brdjanin. When prosecutors insisted, Randal stuck to his guns, saying that he would rather go to jail than be forced to testify, and he won the backing of thirty-four major American news organisations. Randal's evidence was secondary to the trial, concerning only an interview that he had conducted with the warlord, but the prosecutors nonetheless appealed to the trial judges to rule on the matter. With the American press ready to savage the court, they agreed that journalists should enjoy some immunity from having to testify.[22]

Even without Milošević's constant illnesses, the case was taking longer than expected. Television stations had long since given up on a trial that, while it was transparent, was hardly accessible. Even seasoned court reporters were left scratching their heads. The proceedings were not explained to observers, and even the spellings of the names of new witnesses could only be had by contacting the press office. Adding to the friction between the media and the court, the administration had given reporters severely restricted amenities. Most of the building, including the library, the canteen and, absurdly, the press office, was closed to reporters. The only way for a journalist to summon a press officer was to ask the UN guard on duty in the main hall. The press office was supposed to provide copies of the indictments and other documents but, with money being shaved off the budget, these were often unavailable. Del Ponte issued strict instructions that her prosecution officers, even translators and clerks, were to have no contact with journalists, not even socially – while at the same time prosecutors, judges and officials, often holding privileged information not to be divulged to the other side, regularly ate and drank together.

Press reports began to question the wisdom of the Hague prosecutors in charging Milošević on three separate indictments in a trial that was stretching way beyond the original target of two years. Why not charge him just with one – such as that for Kosovo – and have done with the whole thing? The prosecutors, however, insisted that their witness list, which would finally run to over three hundred, was the minimum they needed for their complex case. Press officers complained that journalists had no idea of the pressures the court was under; with over a thousand employees the Tribunal was now a vast operation, but money was tight.

In October 2002 Carla Del Ponte went to the UN Security Council to complain that, despite her protests, Yugoslavia was not giving her investigators access to official files and was still threatening to prosecute state officials if they went to The Hague to testify. 'A very important witness in the Milošević trial has recently been threatened with actual prosecution by the federal authorities, merely for having spoken with our investigators. We are beginning to be able to present what I might call crucial insider witnesses or sensitive sources. But fresh hurdles are being erected and placed in the way of such people. They are being told that talking to my staff brings with it the risk of prosecution. Make no mistake, I have said it before, and I repeat it now, Belgrade's cooperation is at best selective. It is slow, and it is insufficient.'[23]

Tribunal president Claude Jorda used his annual report, issued the same month, to deliver a similar message. He also complained that Yugoslavia was refusing to hand over eleven top war crimes suspects. 'The Federal Republic of Yugoslavia is cooperating at best only partially, and that is a euphemism.'[24]

Offstage, Del Ponte clashed with the Croatian government which refused to hand over its former army commander, Janko Bobetko, wanted for war crimes committed during the 1993 attack on the Serb-held Medak pocket. Croatia's worries were similar to those of the Serbs. The country had elected a democratic government in January 2000 after the death of their wartime president, Franjo Tudjman. But the nationalists remained a potent force and, like Serb nationalists, were opposed to the Hague court which they saw as a means for the West to persecute innocent Croats. Del Ponte shuttled back and forth between Belgrade and Zagreb meeting only with intransigence.

It was not that there was no evidence against Milošević. There was plenty of it, but the problem was that none of it showed him giving the orders. In October a former Serbian intelligence officer, Slobodan Lazarević told the trial that Milošević was in charge of the ethnic cleansing of Croatia. He said Milošević was referred to by the security forces as 'the boss', and his secret service chief, Jovica Stanišić, was nicknamed 'daddy', which backed the prosecution claim that the ethnic cleansing was masterminded by Milošević. 'All the supplies and finances would come from Yugoslavia,' Lazarević said.[25] This was good testimony and showed that investigators were achieving success in persuading Serbian officials to talk, but Lazarević, like other witnesses, had not met Milošević and had not seen him giving the orders.

Investigators had been working hard behind the scenes in Serbia, however, and in December a high-grade witness was finally persuaded to testify. At first his name was not disclosed to the public and he appeared only as C-061. Later it became clear that he was Milan Babić, the former leader of the Croatian Serbs and a man with close contacts with Milošević. Babić appeared in court to authenticate Milošević's voice on a series of fifty-one tapes handed anonymously to the prosecutors. Some featured Milošević giving orders to Radovan Karadžić. The tapes appeared to show that Milošević had command over forces outside his own country, but nowhere did they have him ordering war crimes. Typical was this exchange:

Milošević: 'Let them go immediately, and the others as well after they have settled the issue of borders with us.'

Karadžić: 'Yes, yes . . . you see, tonight we have them shooting, they have shot at [inaudible], they have had a burst fired at his window. So that what . . . should be . . . done is to do things very quickly.'

Milošević: 'We should take radical steps, and speed up things.'[26]

Babić, giving evidence from behind a screen, told the court that Milošević had sent cash, delivered in suitcases, to support the Serbs in Croatia during the 1991 war. Then the secret popped out when Milošević used Babić's name during cross-examination. Judge May ordered the name struck out of the court records, but nonetheless word went around the building that a high-grade witness, a possible 'smoking gun', was in the court. Milošević used Babić's name a second time, and again it was struck out. Finally, thrown off balance by Milošević, May himself named Babić and had to order the stenographer to strike out his own words. Finally Babić announced that there was no point in keeping his name secret and it was made public.[27]

If Milošević's reaction was any guide, then Babić's evidence was strong. The former president was angry and agitated, launching into fierce exchanges with the man who was once his henchman. At one point he called Babić a liar. Babić insisted that he was telling the truth, and Milošević snapped back: 'I just explained it is not the way you describe!' Judge May interrupted: 'He's entitled to give his opinion.' Milošević would not be silenced, shouting: 'You are right, Mr May. The witness has the right not to know something – but he doesn't have the right to lie.'

Babić told the court that Milošević, despite being on paper president of Serbia, a republic inside Yugoslavia, in fact controlled the entire ethnic cleansing operation in Croatia in 1991 through the use of dual command lines, one running through the army, the other through the secret police. 'Milošević connected these two lines of command; everybody willingly subordinated themselves to him.'

Milošević questioned how reliable Babić could be as a witness, given that he was himself indicted for war crimes and would be hoping to win a lighter sentence by giving evidence against Milošević: 'In addition to the fact of your testifying against me are you also a suspect of this institution?' he asked. Babić replied: 'I am not testifying against you, I am testifying to the truth.'[28]

Babić was not the only high-grade witness to come forward. The new Croatian president, Stipe Mesić, had appeared in October to tell the court that Milošević had fought for a Serb-only land. 'What he was interested in was a "Greater Serbia", that would be created on the ruins of the former Yugoslavia. Milošević said he was fighting for Yugoslavia but he was doing everything to destroy it. I never saw him show any emotions. He could have desisted from the option of war, but he never took any action to stop it.'[29]

Despite these witnesses, as well as the evidence of Paddy Ashdown, 2002 ended in disappointment for the prosecutors. They had yet to find a single person, out of 129 witnesses, who could remember Milošević ordering any war crimes, with even Babić admitting that he had never heard such words from Milošević's lips. Del Ponte had the frustration of knowing that time was running out and that key witnesses were refusing to come forward. Some feared prosecution in Yugoslavia for revealing classified information. But the Serb press was also full of stories of how some potential witnesses were too frightened to testify because they were receiving threatening phone calls from anonymous Milošević sympathisers, presumably linked to the former security service.

It was clear by the end of the year that Del Ponte had taken a gamble with her bold indictments and had begun the case without having all the witnesses in place to back up the charges. She had arrived in office in October 1999 after her predecessor, Louise Arbour, had already charged Milošević with war crimes in Kosovo. Straight away she had announced that there would be two separate indictments, one for Bosnia and one for Croatia, and that they would be ready by December 2000. They were not. She then announced a second deadline of May 2001,[30] but missed that one too. Only in September 2001 did she feel confident enough to hand the Croatia indictment to the judges for confirmation. The Bosnia indictment came later still, arriving in November,[31] only three months before the trial was due to start. It appears that some of the witnesses, in particular those linking Milošević to genocide, had not been found by then.

The Hague judges agreed in December 2002 to extend the deadline for the prosecutors from April to July 2003. Del Ponte had until then to find the evidence that was lacking and to persuade key witnesses to come forward. The clock was ticking and the prosecutors needed something to change. And something did. But not in a way they could have anticipated.

The Smoking Guns   10

From now on no government may kill off a large block of its own subjects or
citizens of any country with impunity.

New York Times, *5 January 1947, commenting on UN resolution condeming genocide*

On a cold Wednesday morning in March 2003 a black armoured
BMW carrying Serbia's prime minister, Zoran Djindjić, swept
into the compound in front of his office in downtown Belgrade.

These were nervous times for Djindjić. He had recently begun to take
on two powerful groups in Yugoslavia: organised crime and former
paramilitary leaders. His economic reforms were carving into the profits
of the mafia clans who had thrived under the regime of Slobodan
Milošević. Under pressure from the West, he was poised to make new
war crimes arrests for the Hague Tribunal. Both measures, he knew, put
him in the gunsights of the country's most powerful mafia, the co-called
Zemun clan, whose members included former paramilitary soldiers
already identified by the Hague court as war criminals. Two weeks
earlier, on the way to the airport, a truck had veered across the
motorway, heading for his car. Only his driver's quick reactions had
saved his life, and police later arrested the truck driver and confirmed
that he was a member of the Zemun clan.

The weekend before, Djindjić had received another reminder of the
dangers of his course of action, albeit in a more subtle guise, when
American-built Humvee jeeps of the elite Red Berets had been cruising
the streets around his official residence in Dedinje. This unit was the
creation of Milošević, and many of its commanders were both involved
in the Zemun clan and on the list of war crimes suspects. Top of that list
was Milorad Luković, otherwise known as Legija, the man who had
agreed to defect to Djindjić after Milošević lost the presidential election
in October 2000.

That March morning, however, gave Djindjić cause to smile. While many Western leaders had shunned him because of the slow progress on war crimes issues, one who had not was Sweden's charismatic foreign minister, Anna Lindh, and she was waiting to see him in his office. The mere fact of her visiting was a powerful fillip for a man entitled to feel that he was under siege.

The car stopped by the steps leading to his office. Normally, the 50-year-old Djindjić would walk briskly up them. But at the weekend he had broken a leg playing football, and it was now in plaster. He hauled himself out of his limousine, then stood waiting while an aide reached into the car for his crutch. This did not take long, perhaps five seconds, but it was long enough. From an open window in an office block two hundred metres away, and high enough to look over the wall of the parliament compound, a sniper opened fire. Two high-velocity bullets sliced into Djindjić's body, one striking him in the stomach, the other in the back. The prime minister slumped down. As his security detail covered him, aides pulled him back into the car. The driver raced out into the traffic, not waiting for the motorcycle escort, and by the time the car arrived at Belgrade military hospital doctors were waiting in the forecourt. They were not needed. Djindjić was dead on arrival.

On the same Wednesday morning Slobodan Milošević was in the middle of cross-examining a witness in Courtroom One at The Hague. The witness was Dr Helena Ranta, a Finnish pathologist who had examined the bodies of forty-six Kosovo Albanians killed in the village of Račak in January 1999. The massacre, which led to the NATO bombing of Yugoslavia, was blamed on Milošević because of his role as commander-in-chief of the security forces. At the time of the killings, the Serbs had blamed the Kosovo Albanians for dressing dead soldiers in civilian clothes and then arranging them in a shallow ditch outside the village to make it look like a massacre. Dr Ranta had been called by the prosecutors to testify that the bodies were those of civilians.

Carefully she went through her grisly evidence, explaining how the bodies had almost certainly been killed where they were found, the proof being that chips of bone and teeth, with DNA matching that of the dead, had been recovered from the site. Bullets were also found in the ground, some with bits of flesh and clothing on them that matched with the injuries on some of the dead.

Milošević was not in agreement. Did the doctor know, he asked, that Serbian pathologists had performed separate checks on the bodies, and had used a test, the paraffin test, on the hands of the dead which had revealed that most had traces of gunpowder on their fingers, indicating that they had been handling firearms? Dr Ranta dismissed the test: 'This was the first time in my professional career that I ever came across the practice of applying the paraffin test to detect gunshot residues. It was abandoned already at the Interpol meeting in 1968. It is of no scientific value because it does not indicate the presence of any gunshot residue specifically.'

Milošević made no answer, but moved to his next question which was why, if these people had truly been killed where they lay, was there so little blood on the ground? Dr Ranta had a chilling answer: the victims had been wearing four or five layers of clothing against the winter cold, and inspection had showed that the blood leaking from their bodies had been trapped and had congealed between these layers.

Again there was no acknowledgement from Milošević. His questions were not asked in the manner of an inquiry but presented as statements of fact. None of the answers ruffled his businesslike mood of self-assurance. Having run out of forensic questions, he switched abruptly to one of geopolitics: 'But are you aware, Mrs Ranta, that this statement of yours, whether it's your personal opinion or not, was used as an alibi to conduct an aggression against a country?' His point, made earlier in the cross-examination, was that Ranta's findings had been used by NATO to provide the excuse for going to war against the Serbs.

Judge Richard May intervened: 'That is not for the witness to say. It's merely your supposition. Now, go on to something dealing with her evidence.'

But Milošević would not be stopped. 'It is for her to answer whether she's aware of it or not.'

'No, no,' insisted May. 'Because the question you put forward is merely a supposition on your part. If you're going to go on making speeches, I'm going to cut this short.'

This made Milošević stop and think. The one thing that he seemed genuinely to fear was the power of the judge to turn off the microphone in the dock. With most of his cross-examinations, Milošević tended to wander off the point, throwing political questions at witnesses and then refusing to let them answer. May would allow this to go on for a few minutes but then would cut him short, reminding him that the time for statements would come when he presented his own defence.

These confrontations had developed into a routine over the months. In the early days, they would go on until the judge would turn off his microphone, treating the press gallery to the sight of a shouting, gesticulating, but completely silent Milošević. Now, a year into the trial, he had become more practised in controlling his fury. 'You either ask this question,' said May, 'you either ask this witness proper questions or you're stopped altogether.' Milošević knew this was his final warning. He hesitated before speaking. And Dr Ranta took her chance to jump in: 'I wish to emphasise also the fact that the European Union team members were all of Finnish origin, Finnish nationals, and Finland is not a member of NATO.' 'All the worse,' growled Milošević.

Prosecutor Geoffrey Nice watched most of this as a spectator. The day's hearing was panning out in a familiar pattern. He had asked a witness along to add a particular piece of evidence, in this case to nail down any doubts the judges might have that the Račak massacre did actually happen, and that Serb forces were almost certainly responsible. It looked as if this had been accomplished today, but it must have been deeply frustrating for Nice, a man so conscious of the length of time it was all taking, to see two thirds of most court days taken up with cross-examinations dominated by political diatribes and arguments with the judge.

The case had until July to run but Milošević kept falling sick, and Nice was also still waiting for Del Ponte's investigators to come up with a key insider witness. In January 2003 it had seemed that this witness might have arrived in the shape of Captain Dragan, one of the many maverick warriors that the Balkan wars were in the habit of throwing up.

Captain Dragan, whose real name was Dragan Vasiljković, was a rich Australian of Serb descent who, when war came to Yugoslavia, had flown his private plane across the Atlantic from America. He first landed not in Serb territory but in the Croat city of Rijeka, from where, after refuelling, he was allowed to continue. Once in Croatian Serb territory he offered his services, as a former Australian soldier, to train the Croatian Serb army. He was given permission by Milošević's secret service chief, Jovica Stanišić, to set up a training centre inside the great castle above the Croatian Serb capital, Knin. However, as the months passed, he came to hear of a series of atrocities perpetrated against Croat civilians by local Serb forces. When he complained about this, Stanišić fired him and the Croatian Serb leader Milan Babić went on television to denounce Captain Dragan as a mercenary.[1]

Later, Serb leaders claimed that the soldiers under their command had fought independently, and this seems to have motivated Captain Dragan to come to The Hague to set the record straight. In January 2003 he took the stand to state that, far from being outside official control, Serb combat units, the good ones as well as the bad ones, were under full command. 'I am angry that today some people are trying to wash their hands of people who died believing they were serving,' he told the court. 'All people had to be under the command of the army or the police. No unit could have operated separately,' he said on day one of his testimony.

The Hague prosecutors hoped that this man would go on to give them insider testimony on the commands he received from Stanišić and others. Instead, on day two, Captain Dragan performed a sudden, unexplained, about-turn. The cross-examination by Milošević seemed oddly similar to that he had used against his former secret police chief, Rade Marković, the previous summer. He was polite and respectful to the captain, asking him in gently supportive tones if he would not mind clarifying his remarks of the day before.

As if waiting for this chance, Captain Dragan said that he had never meant to imply that the Serb forces committing atrocities were directed from Belgrade, only that they were directed by local commanders. In a few short minutes it was clear that Captain Dragan had rendered himself useless as a prosecution witness. Whatever else he knew, he was not saying it to this war crimes trial.

That was in January. Now, in March, there were no more potential 'smoking guns'. It was beginning to look as if the case would resemble trench warfare more than a blitzkrieg: rather than key witnesses, it might turn on Nice's ability to assemble circumstantial evidence, layer on layer, to prove his case.

At 2 p.m., a quarter of an hour later than usual, due to an overrun by Milošević, the trial broke for lunch with the judges telling Dr Ranta that there would be no afternoon session and that she was free to go. As the court staff wandered downstairs news was already coming through that prime minister Djindjić had been shot dead.

The mood in the corridors of the Tribunal turned grim that afternoon. Djindjić, it was true, had been far from compliant with the various orders and demands made by the court. However, at least with him as prime minister the door to cooperation was partially open. Now, with his death, there might be a coup or else the government might become intimidated, and the door might well slam shut.

On the streets of Belgrade that night long tallow candles, an Orthodox tradition, flickered from improvised shrines outside the prime minister's office and the hospital where Djindjić had been taken. The city was in shock. Hours after the killing Serbia's cabinet met in emergency session. Before them was a single, disturbing piece of news. The police had caught the man they believed to be the sniper, and he proved to be a former Red Berets commander. Many feared that the Red Berets were preparing a coup, although there were no reports of any troop movements and the army high command insisted that its units remained loyal to the elected authorities. Divided and quarrelsome while Djindjić was alive, the government, bound together by anger and also by fear, attained strength and unity with the prime minister's death.

The Serbian cabinet appointed Zoran Živković as the new prime minister and agreed to declare a state of emergency for the republic. Early the next morning armed police units blocked the main highway leading from the Red Berets' base at Kula to Belgrade. Air force jets made low-level passes over the base as a warning to the soldiers to stay where they were.

Meanwhile, in Belgrade police launched sudden and widespread raids targeting suspected underworld leaders, together with anyone remotely likely to back a nationalist coup. Among the first into the net were Milošević's former secret service chief, Jovica Stanišić, and his former head of special forces, Franko Simatović. Raiding parties also went out looking for Legija, the former Red Berets commander, but he was not to be found. Police units had more success with gangster leaders, of whom dozens were rounded up. By the end of the day, two hundred suspects were in jail. As the week wore on, the dragnet spread across Yugoslavia. Some of Belgrade's smartest doors were kicked in that week. In the Zemun villa of one former Red Beret officer, cells were found cemented into the basement – apparently used in Milošević's time to keep prisoners who were not registered with the police.

The police raids produced a vast haul of weapons, drugs and suitcases full of cash. Among those raided was Ceca, widow of former warlord Arkan. Her villa was built to look like a little castle, and inside police found an armoury to match, including machine guns, pistols, silencers, night sights, handcuffs and five thousand rounds of ammunition. She and two suspects found with her were taken to jail.

By the end of the week a thousand people were under arrest, and by the end of March the figure had jumped to ten thousand, filling all the cells in every police station. More than seven thousand were soon released without charge, but the government's plan had worked. The gangsters and the Red Berets who had ruled the roost in Milošević's time were too shell-shocked to mount any resistance. In late March the Red Berets were formally disbanded.

Among the discoveries made as a result of this dragnet operation was that of the body of Ivan Stambolić, Milošević's former mentor who had been kidnapped and disappeared in the summer of 2000. In April 2003 Milošević and his wife Mira were both charged as conspirators in Stambolić's murder. It was then discovered that Mira was no longer in the country. She had gone to Moscow in February to join Milošević's brother Borislav, the former ambassador to Russia, and when Djindjić was assassinated she decided to stay away. The charge had one important effect: it meant that Mira would probably never again see Milošević, since a trip to The Netherlands would most likely mean her arrest and extradition to Yugoslavia.

For the Hague prosecutors, the killing of Djindjić changed everything. Initial fears that the door to cooperation would be closed were replaced by the realisation that something much more profound was about to happen. Suddenly, high-grade witnesses started to come forward. Somewhere among the thousands of people arrested were the Milošević supporters who had been making intimidating phone calls to likely witnesses. Stanišić and Simatović were both in jail, and as soon as the court could rush through war crimes indictments the Belgrade authorities gratefully dispatched both men to The Netherlands.

By mid-April the Milošević trial had not one but two of the best witnesses it would hear from. The first would lift the lid on a secret war Milošević had waged in Bosnia. The second would provide the first and only eye-witness testimony to Milošević supervising atrocities in Croatia.

The first was neither a soldier nor a politician but a secretary. Her job was to help administer the affairs of the paramilitary commander Arkan and his Tigers. For some observers, the idea that Arkan would employ a secretary was as improbable as finding one working for Captain Hook, yet for two days, on 16 and 17 April, she gave the Tribunal some of the most powerful testimony it had ever heard. She was not named and appeared in Courtroom One amid all the usual paraphernalia of a protected witness: blinds were pulled down for her entrance, her face was scrambled for the television monitors and her voice altered for the microphones. She gave evidence under the code name C-129. Taking the stand, she explained that she had never been a hardline nationalist and had even taken part in anti-Milošević demonstrations in 1991.

However, in 1993, with the economy in tatters, she needed a job and when Arkan advertised for secretaries she applied.

Arkan was at the time fighting an election, so she joined the political wing of his Serbian Volunteer Guard, the Tigers, which was called the Party of Serb Unity. The two organisations had offices on different floors of the same building. When the election was over the party dissolved and she found herself moved over to work for the Tigers. Officially, the Tigers were simply volunteers, with no connection to the Serb state. In reality, said C-129, they were an army of the Interior Ministry and Milošević's most trusted formation. By 1993 their base had been moved out of Serbia to Erdut in Serb-controlled Croatia, so that the government could disown them if necessary. This distance led to a bizarre system of payment: wages were paid in cash, in hard currency. Sacks of German marks, millions at a time, would arrive direct from the Interior Ministry (known as the DB). They would be dumped on a big table in the main office and all the secretaries would gather round and sort the money into bundles, each man receiving 1500 marks per month. 'During the Banja Luka operation, money was delivered about ten times and there was between three and four million Deutschmarks,' she told the court. She said that Arkan would hover around the counting and when it was over he took any spare cash and put it in his personal safe. 'He would just tell me that he had brought the money from the DB and that it was up to me to organise the counting of the money.'

By 1993 the Tigers had become a professional unit. Training was to army standards and discipline was tough. Twice when the witness was visiting the Erdut base she saw men being given 100 lashes as punishment for drunkenness. By that time the ethnic cleansing of Bosnia was over and other paramilitary units had been disbanded. Arkan was under new orders. Now his unit was being used for special operations in a secret war Milošević was waging in Bosnia. Officially, Bosnia was a separate country from Yugoslavia and Milošević, ever conscious of the need to avoid UN sanctions, wanted to keep his distance.

The Tigers were also working hand in glove with the elite Red Berets. Their connections were tight. The Red Berets' commander, Legija, had previously worked with Arkan. Both units were under the command of the Interior Ministry. 'Whenever it [the DB] didn't have enough men for the front, it would take some of the members of the Serb Volunteer Guard,' said the witness. 'Arkan would always say that without orders from the DB, the state security, the Tigers were not deployed anywhere.'[2]

In Bosnia the conduct of both the Red Berets and the Tigers could be brutal. Prosecutor Nice asked her: 'What was your understanding of Arkan's phrase that he did not or they did not have prisoners?'

'I and all the rest understood this as meaning that those prisoners of war were in fact killed. He said that members of the state security had tortured most of the captured Muslims and then killed them. What has been imprinted in my memory most is that he said that on one occasion they pushed a bottle into the anus of one of the prisoners.'

In 1994 the Tigers and Red Berets went to fight alongside a renegade Muslim army, led by Fikret Abdić who had turned against the Sarajevo government and set up his own enclave around the north-western town of Velika Kladuša. The witness said that soldiers returning from the operation reported that the battle had gone well and that captured Muslim soldiers had been brutalised both by the Tigers and by Abdić's men. 'What, according to what you were told, was the treatment of the prisoners like?' asked Nice.

'Most of the prisoners succumbed to their wounds received from beatings several days later.'

'Witness 129,' Nice continued. 'In one sentence, what were you told later by Tigers about the fate of those Muslim prisoners?

'I asked them what happened to those Muslims, and afterwards I was told that I was never to ask that again, never to ask about that again, and that's what I did, or rather, didn't do.'

Despite having no official status, the Tigers led a privileged life. In Belgrade their vehicles had Tiger emblems emblazoned on their sides and the police left them alone. In case they did encounter any problems, the secretary was given a phone line direct to Franko Simatović, head of special operations at the Interior Ministry. All she had to say was the code word 'Pauk', the Serbian word for 'spider', and she would be put straight through. Once, she recalled, three men in Erdut were given ceremonial pistols to mark a Serbian holy day. They drove south into Serbia proper and were stopped by police who found the guns in their car and arrested them. They contacted the secretary and she phoned the Interior Ministry. Almost immediately they had been freed and their guns returned.

By 1993 the UN had established checkpoints on the bridges over the Drina River linking Serbia with Bosnia in order to monitor Milošević's claims that he had nothing to do with the war there. To ensure that the Tigers could nonetheless move men and weapons into Bosnia, the Interior Ministry gave Arkan a set of official number plates providing the equivalent of diplomatic protection. These would be screwed onto whatever vehicle was crossing the border and the UN guards would have to wave it through. For one operation, Belgrade was so nervous about the Tigers being discovered that they were told to remove their shoulder flashes and Arkan was forbidden from accompanying them because his face was too well known. Instead, they were placed under the charge of Legija, the witness said.

For Nice, the key part of this testimony lay in the secret war fought by these units inside Bosnia. It was the answer to a prayer. Instead of having to try to prove a long and awkward chain of command between Milošević and Bosnian Serb forces, he could show that Milošević had his own forces operating in the country.

The final flourish from this witness was her identification of the voices of Arkan and Legija discussing ethnic cleansing captured on a telephone intercept one day in the summer of 1992. On the tape, Legija complains that the regular Yugoslav army is not showing the paramilitaries proper respect and has rejected a deal that the Tigers had made with the Bosnian government to hand over seven thousand kidnapped Muslims in return for control of an arms dump.

Legija: 'These people here, this command up here, they are not registering us. They refuse to accept who we are and what we are. I don't want to quarrel any longer. They will soon arrest me.'

Arkan: 'Well, if that is how it is, what are you doing there? They really are stinkers [a term of abuse applied to anyone from the regular police or Interior Ministry].'

Legija: 'They should have released these soldiers at eight this morning, but when the convoy left the barracks, Juka's men – there's someone called Juka, some guy who is the leader of the Green Berets [a Bosnian Muslim unit] – he started shooting at them and they turned back. All of our men were afraid and decided to let them go.'

Arkan: 'Damn them.'

Legija: 'I was barely able to persuade Mladić [Ratko, commander of the Bosnian Serb army] to retain the convoy because for as long as the convoy is in your hands, their side will not attack. He then started blathering again. I haven't got the patience to quarrel with them here. They all quarrel about who will be in command, and no one wants a discussion on how to attack and launch an offensive to finally bring about the fall of Sarajevo. I have spoken to Sulc and Bajke, and I think the best solution is to return there.'

Besides revealing the confusion as the Bosnian Serbs squabbled for power in the summer of 1992, the tape also placed the Tigers, and the Yugoslav army, inside Bosnia during the war – just what the prosecution needed in order to link Milošević to Bosnian war crimes.

If Milošević were dismayed by this evidence, he showed no sign of it. In his cross-examination he tried to turn the very comprehensiveness of the witness's evidence against her. 'Did you talk to anybody to have them remind you of certain details and events? Because it seems to me rather improbable for you to be able to testify about four years when you didn't work on the basis of your recollections or on the basis of what people said in those particular years.' She replied: 'Had you worked over there, you would have remembered things your entire life, because to bury twelve young men who were fighting for the Serbian people is a very difficult thing. And that is why I wanted to say what I know, because it would appear that the war boiled down to smuggling and that those young men had died for no reason whatsoever'.[3]

The secretary's testimony was dynamite, throwing up a series of connections between Milošević and war crimes in Bosnia. A week later the second star witness, known as protected witness C-048, took the stand. He came with an extraordinary story. He was a Serb living in the northern city of Novi Sad, and his job during the war had been to manage the restaurant of a casino favoured by the warlords and gangsters of Belgrade. He had been recruited into the lower ranks of the secret police early in the war, enabling them to bug the home of a Croat Catholic priest who had been his friend. The bugging was part of an operation to terrify the Croat community into leaving the region. The witness told the court that he was giving evidence in penance for an action he now considered to have been a betrayal of a friend.

He stated that the casino was a place for these men to let their hair down and that he had the task of procuring prostitutes: 'They were used for – how shall I put it? For the satisfaction of certain needs of politicians and other persons who came there.'[4]

He recalled that on 23 March 1993 a group of high-ranking Serbs arrived for a meeting, booking the private room adjacent to the restaurant. The chairman was Slobodan Milošević. C-048 was in the restaurant, marshalling the waiters and making sure that everyone had their glasses topped up with Chivas Regal whisky. As he watched, secret service chief Stanišić told Milošević that an ethnic cleansing operation to remove Croats from territory in Croatia was complete: 'Very well, so we have completed the main part of the job,' said Milošević. 'Carry on like that – but in a subtle way.' The witness mentioned that Milošević had even managed a joke: 'Well, I'm really looking forward to how the Croats would ask for the Krajina as now the majority of the population there is Serb.'

The weakness of the manager's evidence was that most of it was, like that of Arkan's secretary, just one person's word. Milošević immediately denied knowledge of either the meeting or the manager. But the evidence was still a major boost for the prosecuting team. Later, in April 2003, a Serb helicopter pilot from an elite unit, the Scorpions, testified that he flew Red Berets in and out of Bosnia on their secret missions.

Milošević suggested in cross-examination that the men were actually going to Bosnia for vacations, though why they would holiday in a war zone, or insist on going there by helicopter, he did not explain.

Then came direct evidence of Red Beret atrocities in Bosnia. In June 2003 a former member of the unit took the stand. He explained that he was a Serb and a patriot, and had joined the Red Berets believing in the war. But what he had seen when he went to Bosnia had changed his mind.[5]

Giving evidence in the by-now familiar guise of a protected witness, the former soldier said that he arrived in Bosnia to find that torture and sadism had become routine. His unit was based near the southern city of Mostar. When one Croat civilian was taken prisoner he was dragged out of a house by the Red Berets and kicked down the street 'like a football' until he finally fell dead.

Another civilian prisoner was taken to an open manhole and pushed inside. Then a grenade was dropped in after him. Still another prisoner, an elderly Muslim, was held down by soldiers who sliced off both his ears with a knife. He was then pushed into a lake. As he floated in the water, bricks were thrown at his head, smashing his skull. Back at the Red Berets' base near Mostar, the witness stated that one house had been set aside with Muslim women apparently kept there as sex slaves. 'I don't know what happened to them,' he said. 'But I saw Red Beret members going in and out of their bungalow.'

One day, while occupying an observation post on a high building, he saw his comrades leading a long line of Muslim civilians down to the banks of the Neretva River. They were lined up on the bank. Then the soldiers began a frenzied killing spree using machine guns, pistols, and knives. 'That is the reason I am here,' he told the court. Soon afterwards, the Interior Ministry forces commander Franko Simatović flew in by helicopter to make a speech praising the Red Berets' work. 'We were lined up and he gave a patriotic speech about Serb knights – I can no longer remember – but it was some sort of patriotic trash.'

Prosecutors next heard evidence from a man on the receiving end of Red Beret brutality. The Bosnian Muslim, appearing as a protected witness, told of how he and eleven other prisoners had been driven in a truck to a deserted shed. They were ordered to walk in, two by two, and there they were executed. The man he was paired with asked the soldiers if he could buy his way out. The soldiers said that for 5000 German marks they would drive him to his house and let him go, but the man said he had only about two hundred marks. The soldiers told him that that was not enough, and both men were marched into the shed. Inside, they saw the bodies of the other prisoners. Then the Serb guards opened fire and the witness was hit in the shoulder, collapsing on top of the other bodies. He played dead while other prisoners were brought in and shot, and was then hit again, the bullet that killed one man entering his leg. Still he played dead. When all twelve prisoners had been shot, the soldiers came in and, to make sure, began shooting each body in the head. The witness was sure he was going to die, but when the bullet came it smashed his chin. He waited until the soldiers left and then escaped.[6]

Amid so much gripping eye-witness evidence, Nice also unveiled a report into the extent to which Milošević controlled the purse strings of the Bosnian and Croatian Serbs. Both their mini-states were propped up by billions of dinars that, Nice was able to show, were diverted from Serbian banks. Milošević fought back, arguing that there was nothing illegal in one state supporting another: 'It is no secret we extended assistance to the RS [Bosnian Serbs] and RSK [Croatian Serbs] and would have been the worst scoundrels if we didn't.' The hope was that by showing a financial link from Milošević to the Serbs of Bosnia and Croatia, prosecutors would also be able to show that he was complicit in their war crimes.

In May the Hague judges ruled that the prosecution case, due to come to an end in July, could instead continue until February, with a hundred more days of court time, mostly to make up for time lost due to Milošević's bouts of illness. Just as satisfying for prosecutors was the progress of other cases at The Hague. They were making headway with each of the three big areas of the Bosnian war – the camps, Sarajevo, and Srebrenica. A total of nineteen men had been indicted in relation to the camps, and trials were continuing.

That summer General Stanislav Galić, an army corps commander at Sarajevo, was jailed for twenty years for his part in the siege and the killing of civilians. And the former head of the Prijedor Crisis Staff, Milomir Stakić, was involved in a case that would end in December with his receiving the first ever life sentence for war crimes.

The record of indictments was also beginning to show that war crimes do not pay. Milošević and many of his henchmen were either in jail or on the run. Of four senior government figures charged along with Milošević for war crimes in Kosovo, three were awaiting their own trials and one had committed suicide. The two Croatian Serb leaders, Milan Babić and Milan Martić, were awaiting trial. Of the five top Bosnian Serb leaders, one – Biljana Plavšić, the woman who kissed Arkan – was in jail, and another – Momčilo Krajišnik – was awaiting trial. A third – Nikola Koljević, the Shakesperean scholar who had entertained journalist Ed Vulliamy prior to his visit to the camps – had committed suicide. The Bosnian Serb leaders – General Ratko Mladić and former president Radovan Karadžić – were still free, but both were on the run. One of Milošević's former secret police chiefs, Rade Marković, was in jail in Serbia while the other, Jovica Stanišić, was awaiting trial in The Hague. Stanišić had had two right-hand men. One, Franko Simatović, was in jail with him, and the other, Radovan Stojičić, known as 'Badža', had been assassinated during Belgrade's interminable gang wars. Of the two key paramilitary warlords, Arkan had been assassinated and Vojislav Šešelj was in The Hague. In other words, most of the high-level officials who had been involved in the project to carve out a Greater Serbia were either paying for their crimes or were about to do so.

This achievement went almost unremarked by the outside world. In February 2003 the United States, supported by coalition partners, invaded Iraq. International law, or the lack of it, was at the centre of heated debate before and after the war. Further controversy was raging over America's detention of prisoners at Guantanamo Bay in Cuba. This all meant that the US administration was battling anew with human rights groups such as Amnesty International and Human Rights Watch.

On 28 August, under US pressure, the UN Security Council passed a resolution determining the final closing date for the Hague Tribunal: it would be 2008 for trials, and 2010 for the completion of appeals. Chief prosecutor Carla Del Ponte was given until 2004 to finish her indictments. Unlike Goldstone and Arbour, she wanted to stay for a second term. This was granted, but her job was changed and she was stripped of her post as chief prosecutor for the Rwanda tribunal. The move was probably overdue, as it was difficult to have a single prosecutor for two tribunals on different continents, but the timing was unfortunate and Del Ponte complained that the move had been initiated by the Rwandan government which was worried that its own members were about to be indicted.

In September the Milošević trial resumed, and that autumn saw a succession of heavyweight witnesses. Former Yugoslav prime minister Ante Marković broke his 12-year silence to testify as to how Milošević broke the country apart in 1991. He was followed by the former Serbian member of the Yugoslav presidency, Borisav Jović, who spoke about the same events. Both men agreed that nothing moved in Yugoslavia without Milošević's knowledge.[7] Two more key witnesses testified that Milošević also controlled the Bosnian Serb war machine. On 9 October the former commander of the UN force in Sarajevo, British general Sir Rupert Smith, stated that his impression was that even the bullish Bosnian Serb army commander, General Ratko Mladić, could not issue orders against Milošević's wishes. Lord David Owen, the EU negotiator who worked with Milošević to end the Bosnian war in May 1993, said the same thing: Milošević supplied the Bosnian Serb war machine with everything it needed. Without him, the Bosnian Serb army would have had no diesel for its tanks, bullets for its guns, or cash to pay its officers.

These witnesses seemed to have provided strong evidence that Milošević had control of the Bosnian Serb war machine. Yet as autumn drew into winter the prosecutors still had one outstanding problem – to prove genocide. There was no evidence that Milošević had planned such a crime and no sign of an inside witness who could provide it. Yet for a conviction, prosecutors would need to prove that genocide took place in Bosnia and that Milošević planned it. Other Hague trials had proved the charge of genocide in only one case, that of Srebrenica. The other crimes, such as the camps, the bombardment of Sarajevo, and the 1992 ethnic cleansing, were ruled to be Crimes Against Humanity but not genocide, since their objective was not to destroy an ethnic group in its entirety but rather to kill large numbers of people.

Just one war crime out of all three wars had been judged genocidal – the killing of seven thousand Muslim men at Srebrenica. The commanding general, Radislav Krstić, had been jailed for forty-six years reduced in April 2004 to thirty-five years on appeal. If Geoffrey Nice wanted to nail Milošević for genocide, he would need to prove a connection with that massacre. On 4 September the first man ever to have been sent to jail by the Hague Tribunal returned to testify against Milošević. Dražen Erdemović was the Bosnian Croat press-ganged into machine-gunning hundreds of Muslims in Srebrenica in July 1995. Erdemović had given himself up in 1996, had been jailed for five years, and now, as part of his promise to put things right, came to court to testify. His evidence showed that Yugoslav army officers were present during the massacre. But, as a private soldier, he had had no access to the command and so had no idea who was running the operation. And, he admitted, the soldiers carrying out the killings were Bosnian Serbs, not Serbians.

The parade of witnesses provided powerful evidence showing that Milošević was involved in the Bosnian atrocities. It even showed that he was complicit in the Srebrenica massacre – because without his largesse it could not have happened. But none of the witnesses could demonstrate that Milošević was actually involved in the genocide.

Meanwhile the court was dealing with other problems. Having agreed in August to close its doors by 2010, Hague officials were privately admitting that this deadline was almost impossible given the average lengths of trials and Del Ponte's determination to issue fourteen new indictments, involving approximately thirty more suspects, during 2004. Only a massive increase in court capacity would allow the deadline to be met. There was one radical solution open to the court, which was to encourage plea-bargaining, whereby suspects would plead guilty to a crime in return for a lighter sentence. This had not been envisaged, though neither had it been excluded, in the statute establishing the Tribunal. The problem was that while the prosecutor could make a deal with a suspect, there was no way that they could make a deal in advance with the judge. They could only recommend a maximum sentence for a cooperative criminal and hope that the judge would stick to it.

At first things went well. A Bosnian Serb army officer involved in the Srebrenica massacre, Momir Nikolić, had agreed back in November 2002 not just to plead guilty to his own part but also to give evidence against two officers charged along with him. Nikolić went even further, providing a signed statement that implicated other Serb officers in the killing of more than a thousand Muslim men and boys in the Kravica warehouse, the worst single atrocity in the Srebrenica campaign. He agreed to testify against his fellow officers if prosecutors would recommend a twenty-year sentence. Twenty years was not light but it was better than the forty-six years that his commanding officer, Radislav Krstić, had received.

In May 2003, however, things went wrong. Nikolić confessed that he had lied and that he had not even been present at the massacre in the Kravica warehouse. The judges accepted this statement, which was made public when his trial was under way in late September. One of the Bosnian Serb officers charged along with him was Vidoje Blagojević. He had pleaded not guilty and had hired a seasoned Alaskan attorney, Michael Karnavas, as his defence lawyer. In court Karnavas tore into Nikolić, asking whether he had lied in his original statement simply in order to achieve a plea-bargain. Nikolić miserably denied this, saying that he had been confused and had not wanted to go to trial. Karnavas called the original statement a 'bald-faced lie', then asked why Nikolić should have claimed involvement in the most terrible of the Srebrenica crimes when in fact he had had nothing to do with it.

On 30 September a court-appointed doctor reported that Milošević was suffering from high blood pressure and needed rest. Prosecutor Geoffrey Nice called for the court to impose a defence lawyer on

Milošević in order to lessen his workload.[8] He also asked them to ban Milošević from smoking: 'It is our understanding from a source that smoking is a significant aggravating factor to the condition of this accused and that cessation of smoking might materially assist him.' The judges said no to the smoking ban, ruling that it would be an infringement of Milošević's rights.

It was a tense afternoon. Judge May told Nice that there were in any case only thirty-six days of trial time remaining, so it was probably not worth introducing special measures. Nice said that he thought the number was forty-six. May snapped back, 'Certainly thirty-six days'.[9]

Nice then asked that the prosecutors be allowed to have their own doctor examine Milošević. 'We cannot have a party second-guessing the court's doctors,' replied May. 'It's quite out of – quite out of all proportion and propriety.' 'Your Honour, I'm not sure there's any question of second-guessing, but Your Honour asks me whether I accept or reject the medical advice given,' said Nice. One of his clerks extricated him from the hole he was digging for himself, scribbling a note on a piece of paper and handing it to him. 'I'm helpfully reminded from elsewhere that in medical matters, second opinions are generally regarded as a good rather than a bad thing.'

While the judges had the power to force a lawyer on Milošević, such a move would be useless if Milošević refused to cooperate. 'The difficulty is how much further do we get by a standby counsel who is without instructions – and this accused has been adamant that he would not give instructions,' said May.

It was left to the British amicus lawyer Steven Kay to make what turned into one of the key speeches of the trial – and perhaps of any war crimes trial. He reminded the court that one of the bedrock principles was justice for the accused. 'As we know, the accused has a right to defend himself. When you choose to be represented by a lawyer, you give up that right. You put that right into the hands of someone else... In many respects, it is a very trusting right if you are an intelligent, competent person to try and devolve your rights to someone else and hope that they will do a job on your behalf with which you are satisfied... If you do give up that right, you give a power of attorney, and you are silent thereafter until you give evidence in court. You are more of an observer within the proceedings until the moment when you choose to give evidence. This accused plainly does not wish to play that more passive role that the court systems have available to those who choose to use lawyers . . . In our submission, it is perfectly understandable that a man in that position, given the allegations against him, would trust in his own judgement, his own skills, and his own knowledge.'[10]

In the end the judges refused to appoint a court lawyer. In any case, Milošević had lawyers working in the public gallery, who met him during each break in order to give him instructions. The judges ordered that the trial should be reduced to three days per week for the remainder of the prosecution time so as to ease Milošević's ordeal.

On 28 October there came a new plea-bargaining controversy. In one of the trials of former prison camp officers, a Serb guard called Predrag Banović had admitted kicking to death five Muslim inmates at the Keraterm prison camp, outside Prijedor, on a single night in the summer of 1992. The prosecutor had recommended a maximum of eight years in jail because Banović had pleaded guilty, and the judges agreed. Many Bosnians were furious. Relatives of the dead complained that the sentence, likely to mean six years in jail with good behaviour, was a travesty.[11] Certainly it was difficult to imagine a domestic court anywhere in the world that would give a multiple murderer only eight years. The suspicion grew that the judges were being influenced less by the requirements of justice than by the need to process cases more quickly. The Prijedor Victims Association issued an angry statement: 'The Hague Tribunal is losing its credibility. It will not fulfil any of its proclaimed aims in such a manner.'

Away from Courtroom One, chief prosecutor Carla Del Ponte was courting controversy. She went to Belgrade in October to deliver sealed indictments against four Serb officials charged with war crimes in Kosovo, one of whom, Sreten Lukić, was the current public security minister. In effect, Lukić was being asked to arrest himself. Prime minister Zoran Živković refused to accept the warrants, nervous about upsetting nationalist opinion ahead of elections in December, and later the details of the indictments were leaked to the Belgrade press.

On 10 October Del Ponte complained to the Security Council that Serbia was not cooperating. She said that seventeen men were on the run from war crimes charges and that more than half of them lived in Serbia. Živković blasted back that her indictments were a 'blow to reform'.

On 20 October former Bosnian president Alija Izetbegović died. Del Ponte, apparently keen to show that she was fair to all sides, promptly announced that she had been investigating him for war crimes but had not pressed charges. Many Bosnians were furious, arguing that it was unfair to make such a partial disclosure about a man now unable to defend himself.

If Del Ponte's intention had been to pacify the Serbs with her announcement about Izetbegović, it did not work. On 12 November, Goran Svilanović, the foreign minister of Serbia-Montenegro – the new name for the state of Yugoslavia – said that Hague prosecutors were doing a poor job in court and using his government as a scapegoat for their own failings: 'They shouldn't blame Belgrade if things are not going very well . . . they should look at the poor quality of their work.' Bosnian Muslims were also angry about the decision to prosecute the former commander of Bosnian government troops in the enclave of Srebrenica, Naser Orić. Orić, a charismatic war hero to many Bosnians, was indicted for torture and murder of Serb prisoners and for plundering Serb farms during the siege of Srebrenica between 1992 and 1995. The charges alleged his responsibility for the actions of his men, including pulling teeth out of Serb prisoners using pliers. The Bosnian Muslims protested that the case was political: Orić's alleged crimes were slight compared with those of dozens of former Serb commanders who had not been charged with anything. It seemed to them that Del Ponte was anxious not to appear to be indicting only Serbs.

On 2 December 2003 the roof fell in on the plea-bargaining strategy. Judges in The Hague, conscious of the barrage of criticism after the Banović hearing, defied the prosecutor and jailed former Bosnian Serb army officer Momir Nikolić for twenty-seven years. Nikolić, hearing the sentence, cried in the dock, and other defence lawyers realised that the judges could not be relied upon to go along with a plea-bargaining deal.

Geoffrey Nice continued to pile up evidence in the Milošević trial. On 5 November the former UN civil affairs chief for Bosnia, David Harland, had told the court that without Milošević's support the Bosnian Serbs would not have been able to besiege Sarajevo. It seemed likely that there was now overwhelming evidence that Milošević was guilty of Crimes Against Humanity in Bosnia. But there was still no sign of evidence showing he had committed genocide.

Just before Christmas former NATO commander General Wesley Clark came to give evidence. At the time Clark was running in the Democrat primaries for the chance to contest the 2004 American presidential election. For the first time in months, television vans appeared in numbers outside the Tribunal. Inside, special arrangements had been made for him to give evidence. Washington had authorised the general to talk only if he could give testimony in a closed session. It would be recorded on video but the tape would not be made public until it had been viewed by US officials, who would have the power to call for cuts to sensitive material.

However, the general's evidence proved a flop. His comments about his meetings with Milošević were of interest to historians but there was nothing new to link Milošević to genocide at Srebrenica. The testimony was in the end released with no cuts. Clark said that Milošević had told him in 1995 that he had known in advance about the plan to massacre civilians at Srebrenica but had been unable to stop it.

January 2004 arrived with a sense of anticlimax spreading through The Hague as the Milošević prosecution wound down. A former UN force commander, French general Philippe Morillon, gave evidence, but was unable to offer more than his own opinion on the Srebrenica genocide because his period in command had ended the year before. He did, however, tell the court that Muslim forces in Srebrenica had also committed war crimes.

Across the green open space from the Tribunal building is a place where local office workers and court staff lock up their bicycles. It forms, for the Tribunal, almost a 'parish pump' where people meet and talk. One cold January day, while locking my bike, I bumped into a prosecution official and asked about the Milošević case. He conceded that it was unlikely that they would now be able to convict him of genocide, but he thought that the other three charges had been proven. 'It's messy, but it's worked,' was his comment. It seemed to sum up the fate of this huge trial.

The Milošević prosecution was due to end on 17 February 2004. But even as things were winding down, there was one more crisis. On Sunday, 15 February, the Dutch news agency ANP ran the news that the chief judge, Richard May, was retiring for health reasons. Staff said that he was seriously ill and that they saw no chance of his being able to continue the trial.

The announcement triggered a new sense of crisis. Under court rules, a judge can be replaced only if the defendant agrees. Most defendants in most cases do not object, wishing only to hurry along their case. But Milošević was different. He made no comment at a hearing in early March, knowing that the court would have to take this as a refusal. The two remaining judges could decide to overrule him, or an appeal hearing could decide the same thing, but only if they felt that it was 'in the interests of justice'.

No ruling of this kind had ever been made in a Hague trial. While the prospect of a retrial was a nightmare for the judges, and would certainly mean that the 2010 deadline could not be met, it was equally difficult to imagine continuing the trial with a new judge against the defendant's wishes. For one thing, it had already taken evidence from nearly three hundred witnesses, covering twenty-thousand pages. A new judge would need somehow to read up on all of this information and be ready for the second part of the case, Milošević's defence due to start in June 2004. Even then, Milošević could argue that the new judge would be at a disadvantage, not having seen the 'demeanour' of the witnesses – something that is considered vital in many national courts.

Epilogue

I can recollect a certain day about three weeks after the battle of Minden, and a farm house in which some of us entered, and how the old woman and her daughters served us, trembling, and how we got drunk over the wine, and the house was in flame presently, and woe betide the wretched fellow afterwards who came home to look for his house and his children. It is well for gentlemen to talk of chivalry; but remember the starving brutes they lead, men nursed in poverty, entirely ignorant, made to take a pride in deeds of blood, men who can have no amusement but in drunkenness, debauchery and plunder.

- Barry Lyndon, *William Thackeray*

The final drama of the prosecution of Slobodan Milošević unfolded in the days of March and April 2004 in The Hague when Milošević refused to give his assent for a new judge, as yet unnamed, to stand in for the ailing chief trial judge Richard May. However, an appeal hearing decided that, 'in the interests of justice' they would rule that a new judge should be appointed, rather than agreeing to start the trial all over again from the beginning.

If Slobodan Milošević is convicted of even a fraction of the sixty-six charges facing him at the Hague Tribunal, he will spend the rest of his life in jail. While, at the time of writing, his defence had yet to start, the prosecution evidence is finished and it seems hard to imagine how he can escape conviction on a great many of the accusations. More than two years of court time and nearly 300 witnesses seem to have proven, beyond reasonable doubt, that Serb units committed war crimes and that Milošević had command. Prosecutors hope to prove not just that he is guilty because he failed to stop his units committing atrocities, but also that he organised the war crimes themselves, and the evidence produced makes both outcomes very likely.

The case is strongest for the war in Kosovo, because here Milošević had direct control of the security forces: witnesses such as Paddy Ashdown testified not only that they saw war crimes being committed, but also that they informed Milošević, who failed to do anything about it. For the Bosnia and Croatia indictments, the evidence is more complex because Serb forces in both countries were outside the formal command of Milošević. However, prosecutors have shown that Milošević supplied the weapons, money and fuel for the campaigns of ethnic cleansing by local Serb forces, and have also shone a light on the activities of the Red Berets and Tigers both of which were controlled from Belgrade.

Where the prosecutors may fail is in proving the most serious charge of all, that of genocide. Quite simply, they have not produced in public court any evidence to support this charge. Terrible as they were, the campaigns of ethnic cleansing in the Balkans are likely to be seen by the judges as projects to move, rather than destroy, the non-Serb populations. The only case of genocide that has been upheld in the Balkans is the massacre of more than 7,000 Muslim men and boys at Srebrenica by Bosnian Serb forces in July 1995. In the last weeks of 2003 and into 2004 the prosecutors produced a stream of witnesses to attest to the horror of this atrocity, but none who could decisively pin the blame on Milošević. He may yet be found guilty of conspiracy to commit genocide because, to wipe out that many people, the Bosnian Serbs appear to have used weapons and fuel provided by Milošević.

The Milošević prosecution was more dramatic than almost any case in history, although it was hardly the fault of the prosecutor – Geoffrey Nice – that he had to run a case while investigators were scrambling to find him the necessary witnesses. The confusion, and any failure to prove genocide, will be seized upon by the many Serbs who continue to support Milošević in the claim his trial is flawed.

The case is likely to run at least until the end of 2006, with Milošević probably using all means to draw the trial out as long as possible. If, in doing this, the case becomes unwieldy, or if Milošević becomes too sick for it to continue, then the gamble of the prosecutors in deciding to try him for Kosovo, Bosnia and Croatia war crimes will be seen to have failed. If he lasts the course, and is eventually found guilty, then prosecutors are likely to feel a sense of triumph in proving their central contention, which is that Milošević was responsible for the web of ethnic cleansing and war crimes in all three wars.

Yet despite its many failings, the trial seems to have been a success. Never before has the apparatus behind a series of wars been laid out so comprehensively, nor have war crimes been chronicled so meticulously. Milošević has been given every chance to refute the allegations put to him, and his right to mount his own defence was asserted in a speech by the Amicus Curae lawyer Steven Kay that deserves to be nailed to the wall of every law school across the world.

The Milošević trial will be the measure of the entire war crimes process and, if it goes well, it will become a powerful tool for those arguing that the process should be permanent.

As to whether the court has succeeded in its mission, opinion is divided. Through no fault of its own, the Tribunal was set up too late, and with too few resources, to even start a case while the Bosnian war still raged. However, the court has had an enormous impact on making the peace process work. Key warlords have been removed from the system. In Prijedor, north-west Bosnia, 25,000 Muslims, including Nusreta Sivac, who spent several months in the Omarska prison camp, have returned to live among the Serbs.

These trials will also show future generations the full horror of what happened in these wars. Historians will be shown, above all, that inter-ethnic wars are not as spontaneous as they sometimes seem, and that in the case of both Yugoslavia and Rwanda, apparently random violence was in reality tightly controlled. The success of these trials in jailing senior leaders may also deter budding warlords from committing crimes in potential wars.

The future of the war crimes process now rests on the slender shoulders of the International Criminal Court, which is installed in a gleaming steel and glass headquarters in The Hague. The ICC has 93 nations as full members, but it lacks many important players, including America, China,

India, Israel and Russia. The ICC's 2004 budget was £20 million, less than a third of the UN court's, thus severely restricting its powers. But it has a key advantage, because the idea of war crimes justice, unheard of before 1993, is now a reality. 'It's amazing how preconceptions have changed,' Rod Dixon, a Hague law expert, told me. 'Ten or fifteen years ago they would say it's impossible. And now you can point to war crimes courts in Yugoslavia, Rwanda, East Timor, Cambodia, and Sierra Leone. There is a new trend now, it's part of foreign policy; when a war ends they ask about reconstruction, peacekeepers, and then they ask about war crimes. The hardest thing is taking that first step. Now it has become so much more difficult for countries to say it applies to Yugoslavia but not to us. The significance of all these tribunals is that policy is put to the test, policy is subject to legal scrutiny.'

The future of war crimes justice depends ultimately on the United States, and for the moment the prognosis is not good. America, which once prided itself on its support for democracy and the law, is led now by a government that appears to believe in the dictum 'might is right.' The White House, frustrated by the very real failings of multi-lateralism, has embarked on an experiment to see if America can get what it wants by simply using its strength to impose its will, irrespective of international law.

America's 'War On Terror' has seen international law flouted: hundreds of terror suspects have been arrested and held without trial at the American base at Guantanamo Bay, Cuba, in apparent violation of treaties from the Geneva Conventions to Habeas Corpus. Amnesty International is among human rights groups cataloguing a series of attacks on civilians by US forces in Iraq which have not been investigated by military prosecutors. The invasion of Iraq was itself highly questionable, given that the UN Security Council did not specifically authorise it.

These policies are approved by a White House that has decided it has no time for international law, and wants to rely on military muscle alone to enforce its will. This looks to be a mistake. As any counter-terrorism expert will tell you, the fight against terrorists and guerrillas can only partly be won through military means. Much more important than military might, in the war against terrorism, is the fight for ideas. It is here, ironically, that America is at its strongest. Unlike the terrorists, America has a constitution and extensive guarantees for personal freedom. The rule of law is the most powerful weapon in the arsenal of democracy because it promises security to the weak, not just the strong. Of course the law cannot smash a terrorist network, but over time it can convince the broad mass of support that terrorists must depend on that there is another way.

For the moment it seems nothing can stop the American government fighting its war on terror in its own way, and its experiment in relying on force, rather than consensus, will continue until either opponents are cowed or the price in blood is so high that the US electorate turns back to the charms of multi-lateralism.

This is not to say that the war crimes process, or the ICC, should be given a 'blank cheque'. War crimes courts have very real structural failings, not least the lack of a truly independent body to watch over them, given that they are answerable to no electorate and their trials have no juries. But these are problems with the machine, not reasons to reject that machine. In a few short years, and in the face of extraordinary difficulties, the Hague Tribunal and its sister for Rwanda have shown that the war crimes process can work and that a world leader, in this case Slobodan Milošević, can be snatched from his country and put on trial. The process works. What is still unclear is whether the world has the political will to back it.

Notes

Chapter 2: The Camps

1. Author interview with Nusreta Sivac, Prijedor, Bosnia-Hercegovina, January 2004.

2. She does not remember the exact date.

3. Nusreta stayed in touch with Edna's mother during and after the war, helping her continuing attempts to trace her daughter. She said that for Edna's mother the worst experience of all had been the years of not knowing what had happened to her. The Serbs never gave a list of the dead, nor have they ever explained why they decided to draw up a list of people for execution.

4. Nusreta was released from Trnopolje a few weeks later and walked, with some of the other women, the 15 miles back to Prijedor. The authorities let her and her cousins leave the country and she lived for a while in Croatia. After the Bosnian war she came back to Prijedor, to find a Serb husband and wife living in her apartment. The woman gave her coffee, using Nusreta's coffee cups, and told her that her own apartment was in a sector of the country run by the Bosnian Federation and that she did not want to go back there. Finally, Nusreta obtained an order from the Prijedor police to recover her apartment. The woman promised that she would leave on the appointed day. Nusreta and her cousin went to the apartment on the day of the handover to find that the woman and her husband had left as promised, but that her furniture, clothes, crockery, windows, window frames and doors had been dismantled and taken away. She has not seen the couple since then. She later testified to the International Criminal Tribunal for the Former Yugoslavia at the trial of former Omarska camp commander Željko Meakić. She featured in a television documentary about war crimes in Bosnia called *Calling the Ghosts*.

5. Author interview with Ed Vulliamy, London, UK, January 2004.

6. On 6 August 1992 Vulliamy began a series of more than forty telephone interviews with radio and television stations around the world from his hotel room. He decided against calling the camps 'concentration' camps because, although it was an accurate description of their function, he felt that this would sound as if he were equating what he had seen with the death camps of Nazi Germany. While horrified by what he had seen, Vulliamy decided that a distinction had to be drawn between the Serb camps, where violence was widespread, and the Nazi camps which were designed as extermination centres. 'At the time I refused to call them concentration camps because of the invocation of the Nazi camps. Concentration camps were exactly what they were – places where all kinds of people from an ethnic group were concentrated in an enforced deportation, during which large numbers were killed, beaten, tortured. They were taking girls and women from the jails for rape. Then they sent them back again.'

7. Vulliamy won 'Foreign Correspondent of the Year' at the *British Press Awards* in 1993 for this and other stories. He kept a promise he had made to the Bosnian Serbs, and journeyed from Belgrade to visit detention camps run by the Bosnian Croats and the Bosnian government, reporting on conditions there for Serb prisoners. Subsequently he was appointed Washington correspondent at the *Observer*.

Chapter 3: The Great Dictator

1. Adam LeBor; *Milošević: a Biography*, (London: Bloomsbury, 2002).

2. Yugoslav census results 1948–1991 cited in Tim Judah, *The Serbs*, (London and New Haven; Yale University Press, 2000).

3. LeBor, p. 78.

4. Anne Pennington and Peter Levi, *Marko the Prince: Serbo-Croat Heroic Songs*, introduction and notes by Svetozar Koljević – (London: Duckworth 1984). p. 17.

5. Judah, *The Serbs*, p. 15.

6. Judah, *The Serbs*, p. 29.

7. Josip Broz was nicknamed Tito and was the towering figure of post-Second World War Yugoslavia. Half-Croat, half-Slovene, he had served in the First World War as a conscript with the Austro-Hungarian army, fighting briefly against Serbia, which was then an independent state. He was a Communist trade unionist and activist in the 1920s and was briefly jailed when bombs were found in his flat. He went to Moscow to receive instruction from the Communists, and in 1940 was in Yugoslavia and became Communist party leader. In July 1941 he began organising the partisans, drawn from all ethnicities but with most recruits from among the Serbs, and launched attacks against the occupying Germans. He also turned his guns on the Chetniks, a Serb nationalist movement supporting the king. The Chetniks made a pact with the Germans to fight jointly against the partisans. The main field of battle was Bosnia, which with its hills and valleys was ideal guerrilla territory. The Germans set up and armed a puppet regime in Croatia, the Ustache, which also sent troops into Bosnia to make war on the partisans. Bosnia's Muslims were attacked by the Ustache and many fought with the partisans. But some joined the Germans, who formed an SS division for Bosnian Muslims, which trained but never fought. The British adventurer, joint-founder of the SAS, and future writer and cabinet minister, Sir Fitzroy Maclean, was parachuted into Yugoslavia as Tito's liaison officer. He was once asked by Winston Churchill whom the British should support, Tito or the Chetniks. He replied, Tito, because his army was more effective, but added that Tito was committed to a Communist dictatorship. Churchill responded by asking Maclean if he planned to live in Yugoslavia after the war. When Maclean said no, Churchill replied, 'Neither do I.'

8. The *Memorandum*, which was leaked to the newspaper *Večernje novosti*, declared: 'It is not just that the last of the remnants of the Serbian nation are leaving their homes at an unabated rate, but according to all evidence, faced with a physical, moral and psychological reign of terror, they seem to be preparing for their final exodus. The physical, political, legal and cultural genocide of the Serbian population in Kosovo and Metohija [the Serbian name for the land bounded by the Serbian province of Kosovo] is a worse historical defeat than any experienced in the liberation wars waged by Serbia from the First Serbian uprising in 1804 to the uprising of 1941.' Kosta Mihailović and Vasilije Kristić, *Memorandum of the Serbian Academy of Sciences and Arts: Answers to Criticisms* (Belgrade, 1995) p.129, quoted in Tim Judah, *The Serbs*, p. 158.

9. LeBor, p. 79

10. *The Death of Yugoslavia*, produced by Norma Percy, Angus Macqueen and Paul Mitchell (London: Brook Lapping Associates for BBC, 1995), episode 1.

11. Lenard J. Cohen, *Serpent in the Bosom: The Rise and Fall of Slobodan Milosevic* (Boulder, CO: Westview Press, 2001), p. 64.

12. *The Death of Yugoslavia*, episode 1.

13. Ibid.

14. Cultural magazine *Književne novine*, quoted by Louise Branson and Duško Doder, *Milošević: Portrait of a Tyrant*, (New York: Free Press, 1999), p. 44.

15. Film footage of Eighth Session, *The Death of Yugoslavia*, episode 1.

16. LeBor p. 93

17. Borisav Jović, statement, Milošević trial, IT-02-54-T, 18 November 2003, p. 34.

18. Milovan Vitezović, quoted in LeBor, p. 108.

19. Milošević indictment, IT-01-50, p. 9. The 'Serbian Bloc' of presidency seats over which Milošević exercised control were Borisav Jović, representative of the Republic of Serbia, Branko Kostić, representative of the Republic of Montenegro, Jugoslav Kostić, representative of the Autonomous Province of Vojvodina, and Sejdo Bajramović, representative of the Autonomous Province of Kosovo and Metohia. The indictment says Milošević 'used Borisav Jović and Branko Kostić as his primary agents'.

20. Laura Silber and Allan Little, *The Death of Yugoslavia*, (Harmondsworth: Penguin, 1995), p. 77.

21. Jović statement, p. 6

22. Jovica Stanišić was head of the Republic of Serbia State Security, or Drzavna Bezbednost, referred to as DB in court transcripts, from March 1991 to October 1998. Communist Yugoslavia had a federal security service and security services for

Notes

each of the republics. During much of 1990 and 1991 the Serbian DB, under Stanišić, was working for Milošević and being spied on by the federal security service reporting to federal prime minister Ante Marković.

23. Judah, *The Serbs* p. 168.

24. Momir Bulatović, *Death of Yugoslavia*, episode 1.

25. Ante Marković, witness statement, Milošević trial, IT-02-54-T, p. 5 (no submission date listed on transcript).

26. Ibid, p. 7.

27. LeBor, p. 163.

28. Silber and Little, p. 139.

29. Marković statement.

30. Silber and Little, p. 139.

31. Milošević indictment, IT-01-50, p. 15.

32. Milošević indictment, IT-01-50, p. 16.

33. Judah, *The Serbs*, p. 183.

34. Silber and Little, p. 237.

35. Judah, *The Serbs*, p. 202.

36. *The Death of Yugoslavia*, episode 4.

37. Banja Luka Crisis Staff chief Radislav Brdjanin, trial transcript, 8 October 2003, p. 10318. After the war, protected witness Bt-77, who remains anonymous, said he returned and found the tree under which the men had been killed. The bag of shoes was still there.

38. Arkan and his men made sure to leave their mark. On a drive from Zvornik to Bijeljina in 1997, two years after the war, the highway was lined with Muslim homes which had been stripped, even of tiles and window frames, many with 'ARKAN' sprayed onto the walls.

39. Milošević indictment, IT-01-51, p.14.

40. Author interview with the woman who was raped, while she was staying at a centre for raped women and girls run by a German charity in Zenica, central Bosnia, 1993.

41. The full quotation reads: 'If foreign ministers had always followed their sovereigns to the front, history would have fewer wars to tell of. I have seen on a battlefield – and

what is far worse, in the hospital – the flower of our youth carried off by wounds and disease. From this window I look down on the Wilhelmstrasse and see many a cripple who looks up and thinks that if that man up there had not made that wicked war I should be at home, healthy and strong. With such memories and such sights I should not have a moment's peace if I had to reproach myself for making war irresponsibly, or out of ambition, of the vain seeking of fame.' H. von Petersdorff, ed., *Bismarck, Die gesammelten Werke* (Berlin 1923–33), vol. 7, pp. 186–7; translated into English in Edward Crankshaw, *Bismarck*, (London: Macmillan, 1981), p. 215.

Chapter 4: New World Disorder

1. British prime minister Margaret Thatcher mentioned this in 1990 after the Iraqi invasion of Kuwait and Saddam Hussein's seizure of Western hostages. In a September 1990 television interview she said: 'If anything happened to those hostages then sooner or later when any hostilities were over we could do what we did at Nuremberg and prosecute the requisite people for their totally uncivilised and brutal behaviour. They cannot say, we were under orders. That was the message of Nuremberg.' Interview with David Frost, *Frost On Sunday*, TV-AM, 3 September 1990. Bush called for such a court on 12 November 1990.

2. President George Bush speech to US Congress, 6 March 1991.

3. Brendan Simms, *Unfinest Hour: Britain and the Destruction of Bosnia* (London; Penguin Books, 2002), p. 68.

4. Samantha Power, *A Problem From Hell: America and the Age of Genocide* (New York: Basic Books, 2002), p. 265.

5. The Security Council appeared to be in violation of its own Charter with the arms embargo. Article 51 of the UN Charter confirms the 'inherent right of individual or collective self-defence if an armed attack occurs against a member of the United Nations, until the Security Council has taken measures necessary to maintain international peace and security'. In other words, the Security Council can either let a nation defend itself or do the job itself. It cannot block arms deliveries and then refuse to intervene. Time after time reporters would find Bosnian soldiers crying with frustration, asking the endless question about why, if the West would not come in and do the job, it was stopping Bosnian men from getting the weapons they needed to defend their homes.

6. Power, p. 285.

7. Power, p. 266.

8. Power, p. 266.

9. *Newsweek*, 17 August 1992, p. 19.

10. Maurice Weaver, 'Battle for Clinton's Ear', *Daily Telegraph,* 4 April 1993.

11. UN Security Council Resolution 771, 13 August 1992.

12. *On This Day*, BBC News website, 18 August 1992.

13. 'US Aide Resigned Over Balkan Policy', *Washington Post*, 26 August 1992, p. A1.

14. US Department of State Dispatch, Vol. 3, No. 35, 31 August 1992.

15. UN Security Council Resolution 780, 6 October 1992.

16. The team framed the law of the new court into a statute containing four articles. One article, 'Grave Breaches of the Geneva Conventions', was a close copy of the Geneva Conventions. A second, 'Violations of the Laws and Customs of War', covered two war crimes treaties, the Hague Conventions, signed in 1899 and 1907. A third article took in the Genocide Convention; and a fourth covered a host of other laws and treaties, bound together in the most far-reaching law, 'Crimes Against Humanity'. Although genocide was the most serious charge in the statute, the most ambitious was the charge of crimes against humanity, which covered crimes against civilians that were systematic in nature.

17. The MPs knew that Milošević controlled a lifeline supplying them with oil, guns and money. They calculated, however, that if he now cut that line, and the Serbs of Bosnia were swamped by their enemies, the Serbs of Yugoslavia would blame him and he would be toppled from power. Their calculation was correct – or at any rate Milošević, despite being furious and humiliated, returned to Belgrade and the flow of supplies continued.

Chapter 5: Habemus Papam

1. Viewed by author who was in Central Bosnia April–October 1993.

2. Author's account, the *Guardian*, April 1993.

3. The Peace Palace looks like the sort of place Dracula would be happy to call home, a Gothic building with turrets and dark walls. It was erected with a grant from the American philanthropist Andrew Carnegie in the 1920s, officially to house the court of the League of Nations, intended as a mechanism for avoiding catastrophes such as the First World War. The League fell apart in the 1930s and when the UN was created after the Second World War, the UN was given custody of the court. The International Court of Justice does solid work, but its powers are severely limited. It acts like a civil court, adjudicating on disputes, and does not have its own prosecutor. Hearings typically last many years and the worst punishment is a court-

imposed fine. Judgement is by a panel of eighteen judges, and in the entire history of the court no woman has ever been elected as a judge. It is hard not to feel that, in intention, the building was created more for the hard justice of the International Criminal Tribunal for the Former Yugoslavia, with its emphasis on individual accountability, rather than the soft justice of the International Court of Justice where punishment, and therefore deterrence, are almost meaningless. Nevertheless, the International Court of Justice got there first, so Cassese and his team are installed in the much less interesting former insurance building up the road. The International Court of Justice's most attractive feature, at least in 2004, is the friendliness of its staff, who treat journalists' visits particularly well.

4. International Criminal Tribunal for the Former Yugoslavia report to the UN General Assembly, 29 August 1994, Document A/49/342. S/1994/1007.

5. Gary Bass, *Stay The Hand of Vengeance: The Politics of War Crimes Tribunals*, (Princeton: Princeton University Press), p. 211.

6. 'There seemed a real possibility that the tribunal would flop and that, once again, the world community would be accused of promising much while delivering little,' Albright wrote later. 'We shared our technical expertise, while our volunteers helped interview witnesses and refugees.' Madeleine Albright, with Bill Woodward, *Madam Secretary* (New York: Miramax, 2003), p. 183.

7. Author interview with Jim O'Brien, Washington DC, USA, June 2003

8. The meeting also saw Albright persuade Cassese to back away from the idea of trials *in absentia*. He favoured a method, common in inquisitorial judicial systems such as those of Italy and France, where if suspects refuse to come to trial and cannot be caught, a trial is held anyway with an empty dock. Cassese remembers her asking him to think again. 'She said, "Look, Mr Cassese, I will tell you, I am not a lawyer, I am a diplomat, but as a politician I would tell you that if you insist on your view you are going to make a huge mistake." I said from a legal viewpoint I think I am right. She said, "Public opinion in the US would never accept the idea that an international tribunal can conduct trials without the defendant being there. So therefore you will not get the support of American public opinion. Without that support you will not get the support of the American administration. Only for this reason you should not insist." I decided, she is right; I may be right from the legal viewpoint but this would be wrong from the psychological political viewpoint,' he said. 'And now I can tell you that I would have made even a legal mistake. In Italy, France, it's OK *in absentia* but internationally it would not lead to a proper trial, it would be a travesty of justice.'

Characteristically, Cassese used the change of heart to win concessions from other judges who had opposed the *in absentia* idea. He went back and told them that he might be persuaded to change his mind if they agreed to something that was less than a trial but more than simply the issuing of an indictment. The result was Rule 61, whereby the prosecutor comes to court with evidence which is made public and, if it is convincing, the judges then add an international arrest warrant to the indictment. Albright told Cassese she supported this – in fact, it is similar to the American grand jury system. It is hard to disagree with her on this: the idea of holding a trial *in absentia* seems odd for a war crimes suspect. Skipping an indictment makes him a hunted person anyway.

There seems nothing to be gained from holding only one half of the trial: granted, the court could say the suspect was offered a chance to defend himself and declined, but the public would still be left in the dark about whether there was actually a trial of the evidence of competing parties. What Albright seemed to understand instinctively, and Cassese perhaps on reflection, was that in this case, more than with regular courts, justice must always be very publicly seen to be done.

9. Mark Huband, *Rwanda: The Genocide, Crimes of War* (New York and London: W.W. Norton, 1999), p. 312.

10. Huband, p. 312. This episode took place at the Nyarubuye Catholic Mission.

11. Cassese also told me that there was a large amount of dead wood to deal with: 'In any body, whatever the number, only one third of the people are really good, competent, highly motivated and keen to work to be good professionals.'

12. Author interview with John Jones.

13. See bibliography.

14. Clea Koff, *The Bone Woman: Among the Dead in Rwanda, Bosnia, Croatia and Kosovo*, (London: Atlantic Books, 2004), p. 306.

15. Stanislav Galić, commander of the Romanija Corps, was later jailed by The Hague for twenty years for Crimes Against Humanity after being found guilty of the charge of indiscriminate bombardment resulting in the deaths of more than three thousand named Sarajevo residents. His defence was novel – he declared that there had been no siege of Sarajevo and that his units were in fact defending themselves from the Sarajevo government.

16. Goldstone had also helped South Africa institute a legal revolution – the Truth and Reconciliation Commission. This provided a platform for victims to record all that had happened during the oppression of the apartheid years including the crimes of the resistance. The clever bit was that the Commission also granted amnesty to anyone who confessed their crimes. So in the 1990s South Africans were treated to a bizarre spectacle as bull-necked former policemen went on television to confess their crimes and demonstrate their former torture methods.

17. Author interview with Antonio Cassese, Florence, Italy, January 2003. Goldstone confirmed to me the two-year deal and its secrecy, but said he did not know the details of discussions between Cassese, the Secretary-General and Mandela.

18. Albright writes in her memoirs: 'Every time I demanded that other countries meet their international obligations, I was reminded that my country was violating its own commitments' Albright, p. 18.

19. Goldstone writes in his memoirs that the UN climbed down after he threatened to go to the press with his complaint: 'Whether or not that precipitated the solution, I do not know, but the United Nations officials quickly agreed that the rule would be waived.' Richard J. Goldstone, *For Humanity: Reflections of a War Crimes Investigator* (New Haven: Yale University Press, 2000). p. 83.

20. 'We were keen to have Mladić, Karadžić and some generals, but it was extremely useful for the Tribunal to start with minor cases,' said Cassese. 'It gave us the opportunity to pronounce on the legality of our Tribunal, on some basic principles of international law.'

21. Author interview with Richard Goldstone, London, UK, November 2003.

22. 'One day I got a phone call from the German ambassador saying, you know we have arrested Tadić,' said Cassese. 'He said, would I be prepared – I said of course! The Germans were wonderful, as good as the Americans. The Germans shared our feelings. They were saying, "Look, we did something awful in the past; it's the reason why we should be first now."'

23. 'I would never have been a party to an indictment unless there was sufficient evidence at the time,' Goldstone told me. He had to make sure that the evidence was there and would stand up in court. 'It's unprofessional to issue an indictment in the hope that other evidence is going to justify it. That's not to say one shouldn't add new counts after the evidence comes in. It's a hell of a serious thing to indict somebody as a war criminal.'

24. Her exact age is not given in the indictment, which records that she was aged thirteen to fifteen. Second Amended Indictment against Dragan Nikolić, document available at un.org/icty.

25. Nikolić relished his time as commandant, fashioning special metal 'knuckles' to allow him to beat his prisoners without hurting his own hands – an instrument Cassese would have remembered from his days as a Torture Commission inspector. Nikolić liked to play games with his prisoners. His favourite was taken straight from a movie: he would slowly slide the barrel of a pistol into a prisoner's mouth, waiting to build up the tension, then pull the trigger – to reveal that the gun was not loaded. A 70-year-old mother had her hands smashed for refusing to say where her son was hiding. In short, Nikolić was a worthy subject of the world's first-ever

war crimes indictment. Nikolić was indicted for Crimes Against Humanity in 1994, for crimes including murder, torture and rape. On the run since then, he was arrested by United States special forces in April 2000, still living in Vlasenica, a stone's throw from his old camp. His trial is ongoing in The Hague.

26. Goldstone had some discussions with The Netherlands foreign minister, Hans van Mierlo, about forming a commando team out of special forces soldiers, but the idea came to nothing. Tracking these suspects, and then arresting them in a hostile country, was next to impossible.

27. Borisav Jović statement to Milošević trial, The Hague, IT-02-54-T, 18 November 2003, p. 34.

28. LeBor, p. 215, quoting Mira's book *Night and Day* published in Serbian in Belgrade.

29. Mirjana Marković's column for the fortnightly *Duga,* reproduced by VIP Agency's English language news service, Belgrade, No. 509, 23 June 1995, p. 4.

30. Judah, p. 337. The sentence quoted is the final one of the book.

31. *The Death of Yugoslavia,* episode 6.

32. LeBor, p. 246

Chapter 6: Operation Tango

1. Author interview with Louise Arbour, Paris, France, November 2002.

2. Karadžić was not the only senior Bosnian Serb leader to laugh in the face of NATO. The former army commander, General Ratko Mladić, although no longer formally in charge of the army under the terms of the Dayton peace agreement, continued to work at the headquarters in Han Pisak, a bunker complex an hour's drive east of Pale. In the winter of 1996 he appeared skiing at the former Olympic resort of Jahorina, racing down the slope with four bodyguards following him like dutiful ducklings. NATO officers were also skiing on the same day, one remarking that the reason he did not try to arrest Mladić, indicted for genocide, was that they were having fun and thus could not be said to have come across Mladić 'in the course of their duties.'

3. Albright, p. 270.

4. In early summer 1997 I was working as one of two correspondents in Sarajevo for Agence France Presse. My French colleague, the bureau chief, was contacted by a well-placed source to tell us that American troops were going to arrest Karadžić the following day. He said that two helicopters with special forces on board were waiting minutes away from Pale. That day the Serbian Socialist Party was due to hold a

meeting on the far side of Pale in an old schoolhouse. Karadžić was expected to attend, and to make the twenty-minute journey from his villa, through Pale, by car. Then he would be vulnerable. His car was somehow to be blocked in and surrounded by the soldiers, who would grab him and fly him away. The local garrison of Italian troops would flood the area to provide area security. We both wrote the story, his in French and mine for the English service, and it caused a sensation. The following day the SPS congress took place, but Karadžić stayed in his villa and there was no sign of a NATO operation. Subsequently, NATO put out strenuous denials that it had planned any such operation, and I was contacted by British and American press officers and asked for the source. My French colleague went back and got hold of material that seemed to confirm that the raid had indeed been planned. For several weeks afterwards I was asked by NATO press officers for my source and each time I told them that they should be talking to my senior colleague. The nearest I came to confirmation of my own was when I later met a NATO intelligence officer who told me the operation had been planned, but that they were consoled for its failure by the fact that Karadžić had not attended the SPS meeting, which made it harder for him to exercise control over the party he had helped found. Later that summer the SAS launched their first raids, and Karadžić disappeared soon afterwards.

5. An odd footnote to these first arrest operations is that none of the subjects ever lived to stand trial. Drljača was killed in the operation, Dokmanović commited suicide and Kovačević died from illness while in the Hague detention centre awaiting trial.

6. France refused to make any war crimes arrests until a US television network embarrassed them with shots of French officers drinking in the same café as a group of war crimes suspects. They included Janko Janjić, wanted for the rape of Muslim women and girls during the 1992 ethnic cleansing of the town of Foča. He showed the television crew a grenade he always carried with him, and said that he knew he was indicted but would never be taken alive. French troops made their first arrest at the end of 1998, snatching the former chief of a Foča rape camp, Milorad Krnojelac, from the school classroom where he worked as a teacher. In early 1999 a second rape camp suspect, Dragan Gagović, was shot dead by French troops trying to arrest him. In October 2000 Janjić was as good as his word, blowing himself up with a hand grenade when German troops tried to arrest him near Foča.

7. The world heard news of this in an unusual way. The deal was brokered by US Balkans envoy Robert Gelbard. I was working as English service correspondent for Agence France Presse in Sarajevo when one afternoon the bureau was called and told to have a reporter at a certain place in the city centre within half an hour. I arrived to find reporters from Reuters and Associated Press also there. A big American Humvee jeep arrived and we were told to get into the wide back seat. Once inside, the machine sped off, heading for Sarajevo airport. Gelbard was in the front seat with a big smile on his face, and he told us that he had just concluded the

deal for Croatia to hand over the ten men the next day. At the time it was a sensation, more than doubling the total number of prisoners being held by The Hague court. We had just time to write the details and get a couple of comments when the Humvee arrived at the airport and he jumped out, telling us he had a plane to catch.

8. Over the border in Albania riots in 1997 had seen local people seize approximately half a million small arms from government depots. Now young Kosovo Albanian men stole across the mountain border to buy these weapons for 100 German marks or less and came back ready to fight.

9. LeBor, p. 268.

10. Robert Thomas, *Serbia Under Milošević* (London: Hurst and Co., 2000) p. 246.

11. LeBor, p. 274.

12. Miroslav Filipovic, 'Serb Officers Relive Killings', *IWPR Balkan Crisis Report*, No. 130, 4 April 2000.

13. Author's article in the *Scotsman*, June 1999.

14. John Hagan, *Justice in the Balkans: Prosecuting War Crimes in the Hague Tribunal* (Chicago and London: University of Chicago Press, 2003), p. 123.

15. Hagan, p 124.

Chapter 7: Prisoner 101980

1. Ed Vulliamy, 'Avenging Angel' *Observer*, 4 March 2001.

2. Hagan, p. 210.

3. Ed Vulliamy, 'Avenging Angel'.

4. Author interview with Stephanie Frease, Washington DC, USA, June 2003.

5. Hagan, p. 132.

6. IWPR Tribunal Update 174, 1–6 May 2000.

7. 'Foča's Everyday Rapists', Tribunal Update, 18–23 June 2001.

8. IWPR Tribunal Update 173, 24–29 April 2000.

9. Kunarac trial transcript, p. 4542. The Foča case gave a rare insight into the mind of a man in an extreme situation, although he was no oil-painting: 'He is a rather short man in his forties, with two strong vertical lines marking his deeply sunk cheeks.'

10. Foča trial transcript, ICTY website.

11. One of the claims made by human rights groups after this case was that it showed that rape was employed as a tool of ethnic cleansing, because it was used against a minority of women in order to terrorise the majority Muslim population of Foča and other towns into leaving. This seems wide of the mark. First, there is no documentation to back up the claim and, more importantly, the Foča case seems to disprove it. If the Serbs had wanted to spread terror, they would have raped and then released the women to publicise their ordeal, not kept them locked up for many months. Rape was common and widespread across Bosnia during the 1992 ethnic cleansing – in some instances, including one researched by the author, indulged in by entire combat units in an almost ritualistic fashion. Although rape undoubtedly had official sanction, and would certainly have helped terrorise women who learned about it, the real motive seems likely to have been different. My own experience reporting on these rapes in both Bosnia and Kosovo indicates that they were carried out not as a matter of policy but for the pleasure of inflicting pain and humiliation on the women. The rapes were quite properly prosecuted as Crimes Against Humanity because they were widespread and amounted to an officially sanctioned policy among Bosnian Serb forces. However, it is wrong to describe that policy as a war aim, and more accurate to say that it was invented for the pleasure of those who carried it out. Such a policy has been common in many wars: it was carried out by German soldiers invading Russia and then by Russian soldiers when they captured Berlin, as well as by American army units fighting Native Americans in the nineteenth century. These units did not carry out such acts as an instrument of war, but as an end in itself, or even a by-product of war. It seems important to acknowledge that acts that are widespread and officially condoned, even when they are not part of a war-winning strategy, are every bit as heinous as crimes that are part of such a strategy.

12. Čelebiči Appeal, IWPR Tribunal Update 179, 5–10 June, 2000. The appeal did not help: in 2002 and 2003 the three guilty men had their sentences confirmed: Hazim Delić, eighteen years, Esad Landzo, fifteen years; and Zdravko Mucić, nine years. A fourth defendant, Zejnil Delalić, was aquitted.

13. LeBor, p. 302.

14. Adam Higginbotham, 'Arkan and Me', *Observer Magazine*, 4 January 2004.

15. The Hague's deputy prosecutor, Graham Blewitt, confirmed that a lawyer claiming to represent Arkan had been in touch, but had received a terse reply: 'We told Arkan's lawyer that we will deal with you when your client is standing in front of the Tribunal.' LeBor, p. 302.

16. Marković told the Milošević trial: 'Milošević seemed dangerous enough to me, so I always had to think what was behind his talks and requests. The way Milošević

treated Stambolić showed that he would ruin even those who made him a successful politician if it did not serve his purposes.' Milošević trial statement from Ante Marković, IT-02-54-T, p.18. Marković told the trial that he had warned Stambolić of the danger but that Stambolić had wanted to serve his country.

17. IWPR Tribunal Update, 24 January 2001. 'Hague Tribunal Prosecutor Carla Del Ponte Storms Out of Meeting with President Kostunica'.

18. *CNN World*, 3 March 2001.

19. LeBor, p. 315.

20. LeBor, p. 316.

21. Dragisa Blanusa, 'The Inside Story', *Sunday Times* magazine, 1 September 2002. Blanusa's book was published in Belgrade in 2001 and because of it he was removed from his position. He went to work as an adviser in the Serbian Justice Ministry.

22. It is a feature no doubt comforting to religious leaders that so many Communists turn to religion in times of trouble Romania's former president, Nicolae Ceauşescu spent his professional life at odds with the Church, demolishing a series of religious buildings and even moving one, on rollers, in order to take it out of sight of his presidential office. But his tombstone in Bucharest features along with a red star, a Christian Orthodox cross. Stranger still, the tombstone announces that it was paid for by the Workers' Party, heirs to the old Communist party.

23. Of the three incidents, the only one to raise real questions was the bombing of the television station. No evidence was provided to indicate that it was transmitting military signals and it is doubtful if NATO could justify the attack on the grounds that the propaganda it was transmitting was of military value.

24. Author interview with Florence Hartmann, The Hague, The Netherlands, February 2002.

25. Blanusa.

26. Ibid.

27. Ibid.

28. Ibid.

29. His words seem oddly inappropriate, since Milošević is unlikely ever to need the use of a raincoat again. Assuming he remains in jail, the only time he is in the open air is during his exercise periods, and these are rarely allowed when it is raining.

Chapter 8: America Turns

1. Lawrence Weschler, 'Exceptional Cases in Rome: The United States and the Struggle for an ICC' in *The United States and the International Criminal Court*, ed. Sarah B. Sewall and Carl Kaysen (Lanham, MD: Rowman and Littlefield, 2000), p. 99. The delegate, who is not referred to by name, had lost relatives in his country's civil war. He made this comment to Weschler during the five-week conference held in Rome in 1998 with a view to establishing an International Criminal Court, in order to show his support for the idea.

2. Robert H. Jackson, *The Nuremberg Case* (New York: Cooper Square, 1971)

3. 'Prevention and Punishment of the Crime of Genocide', General Assembly Resolution 260 (III), reprinted in *United Nations Resolutions, Series I: Resolutions of the General Assembly 2*, ed. Dusan J. Djonovich (1957), p. 320.

4. Weschler, p. 91.

5. Author interview with David Scheffer, Washington DC, 2003.

6. Weschler, p. 106. A similar scenario to the one Scheffer sketched out in July 1998 almost did come about when the United States invaded Iraq in 2003. One week into the war, an Iraqi minister announced to the media that he had contacted lawyers in several countries to consider reporting US troops to the ICC. Visiting the new ICC offices in The Hague at the time, I was told by one official that she was 'watching the fax' each day, nervous that Iraq would indeed 'pull a fast one' and use provisions in the ICC treaty to request the court to investigate war crimes. The timeline for such an investigation could have been limited to cover the period of hostilities, and exclude Saddam Hussein's many human rights violations in previous decades. The ICC would have had little choice but to comply, but of course any investigation would have had to cover all war crimes committed in Iraq in the stipulated period, including those of Iraqi forces. This, or simple inertia, may be the reason why the Hussein regime never sent that fax.

7. Weschler, p. 105.

8. Weschler, p. 103.

9. The demand that a member state should ratify the ICC law is what gives this treaty its teeth. By contrast, more than forty nations are members of the Council of Europe, but the ultimate decision as to whether a member has broken the terms of the European Convention on Human Rights is made by politicians. In 2001 Council of Europe officials reported on systematic human rights violations by Russian army units in Chechnya, but a meeting of the ministers of member governments decided to take no action, overruling the Council's assembly which wanted to suspend Russia. However, once member states have incorporated ICC

law into their own law, a state would be breaking its own law by ignoring an ICC indictment. This was a clever move which may ensure that the ICC, although lacking cash and political power, nevertheless has considerable judicial power.

10. More than any other individual, Scheffer was the man in the middle of a new global dispute which was set to spread. He left his ambassador's job when the Bush administration took office in 2000, moving to work for the UN before, in 2003, accepting a post as a senior law professor at Georgetown University in Washington DC.

11. The issue is complicated but boils down to the problem of jurisdiction. British courts have limited powers to prosecute a non-British national for a crime against a British national outside Britain. The Spanish courts have greater powers, but Britain cannot extradite someone to another country unless the law under which he is indicted is also a crime in Britain. The murder charge thus failed the extradition test. The law lords decided that the Torture Convention did apply because it was an international treaty signed in 1986, whereby Britain agreed to prosecute criminals even if they were not British and even if they had committed the crime outside British territory.

12. The problem was that US troops in Bosnia were, in theory, open to prosecution by the ICC. Bosnia was able under the terms of the ICC treaty to give US troops exemption from prosecution, but America demanded a blanket law giving exemption to all US citizens, not just soldiers. This was ruled impossible within the ICC treaty. Instead, the Security Council met and decided that, in the extremely unlikely event that a US serviceman on peacekeeping duties in Bosnia would be prosecuted for war crimes by the ICC between July 2002 and July 2003, the Security Council would promise to vote together to veto the prosecution.

13. Although the ICC has no formal relationship with the UN, ICC officials were heartened when UN Secretary-General Kofi Annan chose to come to the opening ceremony in the Hall of Knights in the Dutch parliament. Annan's personal support was seen as a major shot in the arm and a sign that, whatever America might say, many in the UN are committed to the ICC.

14. Should the US president ever decide to send the Marines to free an American held in the ICC jail, it would create an interesting military problem because America also has an obligation under the terms of the NATO alliance to defend a member state from invasion. Presumably the Marines, enforcing one law, would be met on the shore by other US units enforcing a second law.

Chapter 9: Courtroom Number One

1. The description is not mine but comes from Guy Lesser, in his excellent article for *Harper's Magazine*, 'War Crime and Punishment', January 2004. Lesser's analogy perfectly captures the scene and I hope he will not mind my using it.

2. The British government appoints about two hundred QCs each year, and Nice received his title after twenty years working as a prosecutor, defence lawyer and judge in England. Del Ponte was lucky to have him because he had his own thriving practice in London and took a drop in salary to work on war crimes cases. He had made a name for himself in the 1980s by representing complex class-action lawsuits for the families of victims of a series of train disasters. Former Hague prosecutor Rod Dixon worked with Nice and told me the QC had joined the Hague Tribunal because he supported the idea of the war crimes court and 'wanted to make a difference.'

3. 'The Gentleman from the Other Side: A Sketch for the Portrait of Geoffrey Nice, Lead Prosecutor at the Milošević Trial', Sense News Agency, The Hague (www.sense-agency.com), 16 March 2004.

4. Milošević trial transcript.

5. Milošević trial, indictment IT-99-37-PT, p. 31.

6. Abigail Levene, 'Reporter Tells of Kosovo Massacre Suspicions', The *Scotsman,* 29 August 2002.

7. She said that, backstage, she had asked Nice what Milošević's cross-examination strategy would be: 'Oh, old grumpy paws will probably want to ask you a few questions.'

8. Milošević trial, indictment IT-99-37-PT, p. 28.

9. Milošević several times labelled the Tribunal a 'NATO court', presumably because three of the five members of the UN Security Council which created and supervised it were America, Britain and France, the same powers that had led the bombing of Yugoslavia in 1999.

10. Author interview with official, The Hague, The Netherlands, March 2004.

11. Tim Judah, 'Serbia Backs Milosevic in Trial by TV,' *Observer,* 3 March 2002.

12. These files did not always help Milošević with his defence. On one occasion, an Albanian villager, survivor of an attack by the Yugoslav army, was asked by Milošević if he or his family had been members of the Kosovo Liberation Army. The man denied it, upon which Milošević quoted from an official Yugoslav government file listing the names of guerrilla suspects. He mentioned the name of a

dead guerrilla whose body had been found by the army, asking if that was the name of his brother. The witness replied that it certainly was, and that his brother was dead, but that he was sure he had not been a guerrilla. Milošević, sensing triumph, asked how the witness could be so sure, and he replied that his brother had died of cancer some years before. In fact, the men supplying Milošević with information had made a mistake. As in many Albanian villages, dozens of the inhabitants had the same second name.

13. The full transcript is as follows: 'You just said a moment ago that after my speech, there were changes in the Constitution, and now I'm giving you the dates that were actually formally recorded as being the 28th of March 1989. This is three months before the date after which you claim the constitution had been changed. So what is going on here, Mr Bakalli?'

14. Milošević trial transcript, p. 22910.

15. Mirko Klarin, 'Analysis: Penetrating Milošević's Inner Circle', IWPR Tribunal Update 274, 8–13 July 2002.

16. Milošević trial transcript, p. 2368

17. On a subsequent mission, again with the British ambassador, I accompanied Ashdown, along with a BBC film crew and Tom Walker of the London *Times*. As on his first trip, we drove to the south-eastern village of Suva Reka and then headed north up the highway that runs parallel with the Albanian border. Across this road the KLA would bring in men and weapons, and it became a key battleground. Once more, the Serbs had insisted in international talks that all roads were open. Once more, this looked unlikely – our little convoy of armoured Land Rovers got through only because the ambassador and his staff insisted. We saw villages ransacked but no fighting. On the way back to Priština, Ashdown asked Tom and myself if we were close to guerrilla territory. We told him that we were about to pass a turn-off that led to the KLA lines; we had passed that way many times ourselves. Ashdown had undertaken not to try to contact the guerrillas, whom the Serbs termed bandits, as a condition of his being allowed a visa. But, he reasoned, if he was simply to come across them, that would be a different matter. He asked the ambassador, Brian Donnelly, to stop the cars at the junction, and we got out. Feeling sheepish, and with three British military attachés in tow, we wandered up the road towards the sleepy checkpoint where two villagers, in KLA fatigues, looked on with surprise. The ambassador's translator jogged ahead to tell the KLA men that we were not hostile, and soon Ashdown found himself face to face with the front line. We were allowed through and a surprised KLA sergeant ushered us all upstairs into a big room in an abandoned farmhouse. Minutes later a smart, suspicious commander arrived, and once again Donnelly's translator worked overtime to explain who Ashdown was and just how important he was. The

commander and the party sat down. We journalists were just getting comfortable when Ashdown asked that we leave, as the local commander seemed anxious that we do so. Afterwards we simply wandered back to the Land Rovers and continued on to Priština. Ashdown was one of the very few politicians ever to mean what he said about a fact-finding mission, and Donnelly was one of the few British ambassadors who had a real thirst for this kind of work.

Ashdown's evidence was followed by that of other senior figures: William Walker, the US diplomat who was head of the OSCE Kosovo Verification Mission, who testified about atrocities against Albanians by Serb forces, and NATO's military commander, German general Klaus Naumann.

18. Former prosecutor Louise Arbour had written in the original indictment: 'By using the word "committed" in this indictment, the prosecutor does not intend to suggest that any of the accused physically perpetrated any of the crimes charged, personally. "Committing" in this indictment refers to participation in a joint criminal enterprise as a co-perpetrator. The purpose of this joint criminal enterprise was, *inter alia*, the expulsion of a substantial portion of the Kosovo Albanian population from the territory of the province of Kosovo in an effort to ensure continued Serbian control over the province.' Milošević indictment, IT-99-37-PT, p. 5.

19. Milošević trial transcript, p. 8727.

20. If this sounds unreasonable, it is worth considering that some Germans still deny that the concentration camps really existed, on the grounds that such crimes are simply too terrible to be likely. When I was driving in southern Serbia in late 1992 I gave a lift to two female hitch-hikers who told me that they felt the BBC, which they listened to, was lying, because as Serbs from good families in a small rural town they could not imagine themselves, or their friends or families, doing such things to Muslims or anyone else. It can be easy for outsiders to conclude that because thousands of Serbs took an active part in ethnic cleansing, 'the Serbs' are to blame. The desire to remind the outside world that an entire nation is not to blame has been one of the laudable characteristics of the Hague prosecutors throughout the process.

21. Perhaps he was taking his cue from the best-known dictator of them all, Adolf Hitler, who is reputed to have said that if you want to lie, tell big lies. Whether even the Serbs believed that Chirac had organised Srebrenica and the pope the Croatian war is unclear. Milošević's comment also echoes the reported comment of Napoleon that 'a man who saves a nation commits no crime'.

22. The Randal ruling said that reporters would enjoy partial immunity. It would not be the full immunity that workers of the International Committee of the Red Cross enjoy, which allows them to travel to war zones without the fear of being taken for spies. But journalists are not to be used as witnesses unless and until it is clear that no other source can be found for vital evidence.

Notes

23. Chris Stephen, 'Regional Report: Yugoslavia "Threatening" Tribunal Witnesses', IWPR Tribunal Update 287, 28 October – 1 November 2002.

24. Chris Stephen, 'Courtside', IWPR Tribunal Update, 4 Novemeber 2002. Jorda went on to complain that Yugoslavia, instead of cooperating, had actually passed a law making cooperation more difficult. He told the UN that the new Yugoslav law 'explicitly violates the basic provisions of our statute and, in particular, the principle of primacy'.

25. 'Milošević Was the Boss, War Crimes Trial Told', Reuters, 29 October 2002.

26. Milošević trial transcript, p. 13322

27. Milošević was on the back foot: here was one of his former protégés giving evidence against him. But the former president could still turn a trick. He pounced on Babić's claim that code words were used in phone calls between senior officials in order to hide references to guns and battles. Babić claimed that phrases such as 'high quality goods' which cropped up in the phone taps meant weapons, and that the 'commodities manager' referred to by one official was in fact Milošević. 'What terms were used for blankets, oil, sugar, medicine and other things we sent?' asked Milošević. Babić admitted that no code words were used when discussing humanitarian aid. 'So if "flour" was used for "ammunition", what was used for "flour"?' queried Milošević. 'Flour was called flour,' said Babić.

28. Judith Armatta, 'The Case Is Almost Proved: Insider Says Milošević Was Responsible', CIJ, Milošević Trial Day 126, 27 November 2002.

29. Ian Black, 'Milošević Tried to Build Greater Serbia, Trial Told', *Guardian*, 2 October 2002.

30. Hagan, p 221.

31. Hagan, p. 223.

Chapter 10: The Smoking Guns

1. Captain Dragan then made contact with the Serb opposition. The secret police found out and he was summoned to Belgrade to meet their agents, the venue being a raft on a river. 'I had entered waters I didn't understand,' Captain Dragan told the court. 'They told me to leave Yugoslavia.'

2. Then Nice asked the key question: 'Were the Tigers subordinate to the Serbian DB?' 'Yes.' 'Milošević trial transcript, p. 19433.

3. Milošević trial transcript, p. 19513.

4. Milošević trial transcript, p. 19662.

5. Emir Suljagić, 'Milošević Trial: Ex-Red Beret Speaks of Atrocities', IWPR Tribunal Update, 12 June 2003. The Red Berets were formed, said the witness, to provide a force for use in Bosnia and Croatia. 'A political decision had to be made for the establishment of a unit of that kind, and that decision was made at the end of 1991 to set up units which would be within the framework of the security service and the purpose of which would be to act on the front, on the battleground in Croatia first and later on in Bosnia-Hercegovina.' Milošević trial transcript, pp. 19665–6.

6. The Muslim had a remarkable escape: he made his way to the main Bosnian Serb town, Banja Luka, and contacted a Serb friend. This friend, at considerable risk to himself, got the Muslim admitted to a Serb military hospital, telling the doctors that he was a prisoner who had been used to dig trenches on the front line and had been hit by crossfire. After ten days of treatment, the Serb again intervened, managing to smuggle his friend across the front lines to government-held territory.

7. Jović wrote a book about his life and times under Milošević, including the bitterness he felt at being cast off. *Last Days of the Socialist Federal Republic of Yugoslavia*, also called *Diary*, by Borisav Jović, was admitted in its entirety as a prosecution exhibit.

8. Nice said: 'We suggest that the preferred solution at this stage may be to assign counsel to work in tandem with the accused but in such a way as to reduce his daily workload.'

9. Milošević trial transcript, p. 27024.

10. Milošević trial transcript, p. 27049

11. Nerma Jelacić and Chris Stephen, 'Anger at Short Sentence for Prison Killer', IWPR Tribunal Update 331, 1 November 2003. The victim's son was Edin Ramulić, who said that his father Uzeir and three nephews were killed the same night as the five people Banović was accused of killing.

Epilogue

1. Archbold International Criminal Courts, Thomson Sweet and Maxwell, 2003. (See bibliography)

Bibliography

Albright, Madeleine, *Madam Secretary: A Memoir*. (London: Macmillan, 2003.)

Bass, Gary Johathan. *Stay The Hand Of Vengeance: The Politics of War Crimes Tribunals*. (Princeton: Princeton University Press, 2000.)

Bell, Martin. *Through Gates Of Fire: A Journey Into World Disorder*. (London: Weidenfeld and Nicolson, 2003.)

Best, Geoffrey. *War And Law Since 1945*. (Oxford: Clarendon Press, 1994.)

Brown, Michael, *The Black Douglases* (East Lothian, Scotland: Tuckwell Press, 1998.)

Cassese, Antonio, *The Hague, International International Law*. (Oxford: Oxford University Press, 2003.)

Cassese, Antonio, Paola Gaeta and John R.W.D Jones, *The Rome Statute of the International Criminal Court: A commentary*. (London: Oxford University Press, 2003.)

Chuter, David, and Lynne Rienner. *War Crimes: Confronting Atrocity in the Modern World*. (London: Boulder, 2003.)

Cohen, Ben, and George Stamkoski, eds. *With No Peace To Keep: United Nations Peacekeeping And The War In The Former Yugoslavia*. (London: Grainpress, 1995.)

Creveld, Martin Van, *The Art Of War: War And Military Thought*. (London: Cassell, 2000.)

Dixon, Rodney and Karim Khan. *Archbold International Criminal Courts: Practice, Procedure and Evidence*. (London: Sweet and Maxwell Ltd, 2003.)

Doder, Dusko, and Louise Branson. *Milosevic: Portrait of a Tyrant*. (New York: The Free Press, Simon And Schuster Inc. 1999.)

Eyffinger, Arthur. *The Hague: International Centre of Justice and Peace*. (The Hague: Jongbloed Law Booksellers, 2003.)

Federal Ministry of Foreign Affairs. *NATO Crimes In Yugoslavia: Documentary Evidence, 24 March - 24 April 1999*. (Belgrade, 1999.)

Harris, Whitney R. *Tyranny On Trial: The Trial Of The Major German War Criminals At The End Of World War II At Nuremberg, Germany, 1945-1946*. (Southern Methodist Press, Dallas. 1999.)

Holbrooke, Richard. *To End A War*. (New York, 1999.)

Glenny, Misha. *The Balkans 1804-1999: Nationalism, War and the Great Powers*. (London. 1999.)

Goldstone, Richard J, *For Humanity: Reflections Of A War Crimes Investigator*. (Yale University Press. 2000.)

Grimsley, Mark, and Clifford J Rogers, eds. *Civilians In The Path Of War*. (Nebraska: University of Nebraska Press, 2000.)

Gutman, Roy and Rieff, David, eds. *Crimes of War: What The Public Should Know*. (London: Norton and Company, 1999.)

Helsinki Committee for Human Rights in Serbia Human Rights, *In The Shadow Of Nationalism* (Belgrade: Zagora, 2002)

Hibbert, Christopher. *Agincourt*. (Gloucestershire: The Windrush Press, 1998.)

Hobbes, Nicholas. *Essential Militaria* (London: Atlantic Books, 2003.)

Jones, John R.W.D, and Steven Powles. *International Criminal Practice, Third Edition.* (Oxford: Oxford University Press, 2003.)

Judah, Tim, *Kosovo: War And Revenge.* (New Haven and London: Yale University Press, 2000.)

Judah, Tim. *The Serbs: History, Myth and the Destruction of Yugoslavia.* (New Haven and London, Yale University Press, 2000.)

Lanlais, Colonel Pierre. *Dien-Bien-Phu,* (Paris, Editions France-Empire, 1963.)

Meron, Theodor. *Henry's Wars and Shakespeare's Laws: Perspectives on the Law of War in the Later Middle Ages.* (Oxford: Clarendon Press, 1993.)

Owen, David. *Balkan Odyssey.* (San Diego: Harcourt, 1995.)

Power, Samantha. *A Problem From Hell, America And The Age Of Genocide.* (New York. Basic Books, 2002.)

Ramet, Sabrina P, Balkan Babel: *The Disintegration of Yugoslavia from the Death of Tito to the Fall of Milosevic.* (Cambridge: Westview Press, 2002.)

Ratner, Steven R and Jason S Abrams. *Accountability For Human Rights Atrocities In International Law: Beyond the Nuremberg Legacy. Second Edition.* (New York: Oxford University Press, 2001.)

Robertson, Geoffrey. *Crimes Against Humanity: The Struggle For Global Justice.* (Suffolk, England: Allen Lanes, The Penguin Press. 1999.)

Schabas, William A, *An Introduction To The International Criminal Court.* (Cambridge, New York: Cambridge University Press. 2001.)

Scharf, Michael P, and William A Shabas. *Slobodan Milosevic On Trial: A Companion.* (New York, London: Continuum, 2002.)

Sewall, Sarah B and Carl Kaysen, eds. *The United States and the International Criminal Court* (New York: Rowan and Littlefield Publishers Inc, 2000.)

Seward, Desmond. *The Hundred Years War: The English In France 1337-1453.* (Hong Kong: Constable and Co. 1996.)

Silber, Laura and Little, Allan. *The Death of Yugoslavia.* (London: Penguin 1995.)

Shawcross, William. *Deliver Us From Evil: Warlords And Peacekeepers In A World Of Endless Conflict.* (London: Bloomsbury, 2000.)

Stankovic, Milos. *Trusted Mole: A Soldier's Journey Into Bosnia's Heart Of Darkness.* (London: Harper Collins, 2000.)

Sutherland, John, and Watts, Cedric, *Henry V, War Criminal? And Other Shakespeare Puzzles.* (New York, Oxford University Inc. 2000.)

Trotsky, Leon. *The War Correspondence of Leon Trotsky: The Balkan Wars, 1912–13.* (New York: Monad 1991.)

UN. *The Path to the Hague: Selected Documents on the Origins of the ICTY.* UN ISBN: 92-1-056706-4. (The Netherlands)

Vickers, Miranda. *Between Serb and Albanian: A History of Kosovo.* (London: Hurst & Co 1998.)

Von Hippel, Karin, *Democracy By Force: US Military Intervention In The Post Cold-War World.* (Cambridge: Cambridge University Press, 2000.)

Wesselingh, Isabelle, and Arnaud Vaulerin. *Bosnie, la memoire a Vif.* (Paris: Buchet Chastel. 2003.)

West, Rebecca. *Black Lamb and Grey Falcon: The Record of a Journey through Yugoslavia in 1937, 2 vols.* (Edinburgh: Canongate, 1993.)

Index

Index

Index

Index